Sunset

VEGETABLE GARDENING

BY LANCE WALHEIM AND THE EDITORS OF SUNSET BOOKS

SUNSET PUBLISHING CORP. • MENLO PARK, CALIFORNIA

FRESH FOOD FROM YOUR GARDEN

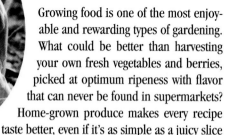

Growing food is one of the most enjoyable and rewarding types of gardening. What could be better than harvesting your own fresh vegetables and berries, picked at optimum ripeness with flavor that can never be found in supermarkets? Home-grown produce makes every recipe taste better, even if it's as simple as a juicy slice of tomato on a salad of crisp greens. And nothing matches the nutritional value of garden vegetables and berries, not to mention the peace of mind that comes with knowing where your produce has been and what's been put on it.

Whether you are a novice or an experienced gardener, you can use this book to help you plan your garden, find out about varieties of vegetables and berries, and even learn some basic gardening skills.

The first chapter offers the key elements of planning a vegetable and berry garden, showing you how to design one that fits your climate, grows the produce you like, and meets your gardening and landscape needs. Next, you'll find an encyclopedia of essential information on the wide variety of vegetables and herbs you can grow. All the aspects of berry gardening, from blackberries to strawberries, are brought together in the following chapter. And the last chapter gives you an in-depth look at the steps in preparing, planting, and maintaining a productive vegetable and berry garden.

Creating this book took a team effort. We'd like to extend special thanks to Linda Naeve, former Extension Horticulturist, Iowa State University, Ames, Iowa; Charles Mitchell, Department of Agronomy and Soils, Auburn University, Auburn, Alabama; and Vincent Lazaneo, University of California Cooperative Extension, San Diego, California. We also want to thank the consultants who contributed to previous editions of *Sunset Vegetable Gardening*: John Bracken, Nurseryman, Dallas, Texas; Gene Joyner, Urban Horticulturist, West Palm Beach, Florida; Jane Guest Pepper, Executive Director, Pennsylvania Horticultural Society, Philadelphia, Pennsylvania; and Gil Whitton, County Extension Director, Largo, Florida.

SUNSET BOOKS

VP, General Manager: Richard A. Smeby
VP, Editorial Director: Bob Doyle
Production Director: Lory Day
Art Director: Vasken Guiragossian

Staff for this book:

Managing Editor and Copy Editor: Zipporah W. Collins

Sunset Books Senior Editor, Gardening: Suzanne Normand Eyre

Indexer: Trisha Lamb Feuerstein

Photo Researcher: Tishana Peebles

Production Coordinator: Patricia S. Williams

Art Director: Alice Rogers

Computer Production: Joan Olson

Illustrators: Mimi Osborne, Jane McCreary

Cover: Photography by Noel Barnhurst. Photo styling by Mary Ann Cleary and Andrea Lucich. Border photograph by David Cavagnaro.

4 5 6 7 8 9 QPD 04 03 02 01

Please visit our website at
www.sunsetbooks.com

PHOTOGRAPHERS:

William D. Adams: 20 top; **Curtis Anderson:** 55 bottom left; **Frank Awbray/Visuals Unlimited:** 117 left; **Max Badgley:** 113 top left, top right, bottom left, bottom middle, bottom right; **Noel Barnhurst:** 68 left; **Bill Beatty/Visuals Unlimited:** 114 left, center right, 115 center; **Thomas Boyden:** 112; **R. Calentine/Visuals Unlimited:** 114 center left, right; **David Cavagnaro:** 4, 16, 19 top, 22 top, 23, 28 left, 29 top, bottom, 30 bottom, 38 middle, bottom, 39 bottom left, 41 left, 43 middle, 47 left, 49 top, 53 top right, 58 top, 60 middle, 64 top left, top right, 65 right, 71 bottom, 88 right, 98, 102 top, bottom, 120 top right, bottom right, 125 top, bottom, 126 bottom right, back cover top left, right, bottom; **Glen Christiansen:** 91 bottom right; **Peter Christiansen:** 39 bottom right, 49 bottom, 51 bottom, 60 bottom; **Crandall & Crandall:** 113; **Rosalind Creasy:** 19 bottom, 21 middle, 25, 26 bottom, 31 top, 34 bottom, 35 middle, 51 top, middle, 56 top, 61 top, 67 top, 68 right, 70, 72, 121, 122; **John D. Cunningham/Visuals Unlimited:** 116 right; **Thomas E. Eltzroth:** 44 bottom, 52 bottom, 66 bottom, 80 top, bottom, 91 top; **Derek Fell:** 87; **Luther C. Goldman/Visuals Unlimited:** 119 middle; **Saxon Holt:** 50, 106 bottom; **Sandra Ivany:** 90 top, 91 bottom left; **Michael Landis:** 21 bottom; **Charles Mann:** 9, 34 top left, 42 middle, 58 bottom, 67 bottom, 90 bottom, 106 middle, 111, 124, 125 middle; **Steve W. Marley:** 43 top, 54 bottom, 60 top, 61 bottom, 63 bottom; **Ells W. Marugg:** 18 top, 28 right, 30 middle, 32 top, 35 bottom, 37 bottom, 46 right, 59 bottom, 71 top; **Jack McDowell:** 18 bottom, 30 top, 31 middle, 42 bottom, 44 top, 47 right, 59 top; **Jerry Pavia:** 31 bottom, 32 bottom, 48 bottom, 62, 92, 106 top, 120 left; **Joanne Pavia:** 1, 27, 126 left; **Pam Peirce:** 52 top, 115 left, right, 118 right; **Norman A. Plate:** 24 top left, top right, bottom, 33, 36 top, bottom left, bottom right, 37 top, 40 left, right, 41 right, 42 top, 43 bottom, 55 top, bottom right, 56 middle, bottom, 57 top, bottom, 64 bottom, 65 left, 66 top, 88 left, 104 bottom, 109, 126 top right, 127 top; **Susan Roth:** 39 top; **Leonard Lee Rue III/Visuals Unlimited:** 119 bottom; **Science VU/Visuals Unlimited:** 118 left, center; **Milton H. Tierney Jr./Visuals Unlimited:** 117 center; **Michael S. Thompson:** 2, 20 bottom, 21 top, 26 top, 34 top right, 35 top, 48 left, 53 top left, 54 top, 69, 104 top, 112; **Visions:** 22 bottom, 38 top, 46 left, 76, 78 left, right, 79, 86; **William J. Weber/Visuals Unlimited:** 116 left, center, 117 right, 119 top; **Darrow M. Watt:** 45, 53 middle, bottom, 63 top, 127 bottom; **Tom Woodward:** 95; **Tom Wyatt:** 74, 85

Contents

Creating a garden plan 4

Garden size and variety • Soil • Deciding on a site • Climate maps • Laying out your garden • Sample plans • Chart of plant choices

Encyclopedia of vegetables 16

Amaranth to watermelon • Herbs • Details on best soil; when, how, and how much to plant; care; problems; when and how to harvest and store

Growing berries 72

Blackberries, grapes, strawberries, and more • Maps of best growing regions • Details on planting, staking, pruning, cultivating, harvesting, and storing

Vegetable garden basics 92

Preparing the soil • Planting • Watering • Mulching • Staking • Fertilizing • Weeding • Pests and diseases • Harvesting and storage • Techniques for special garden situations • Buying from mail-order nurseries

Index 128

CREATING A
GARDEN PLAN

Thoughtful planning is the first step toward creating a healthy, productive vegetable and berry garden. In this chapter, you'll find ideas for laying out your garden and sample garden plans. Climate maps and a chart of plant categories will help you choose suitable crops for your area.

DETERMINING GARDEN SIZE AND VARIETY

Deciding which vegetables and berries and how much of each you want to grow will greatly influence how large you'll make your garden. Another crucial factor is the amount of time you want to spend tending the garden.

START SMALL. If you're new to vegetable gardening, you'll have more success if you start with a fairly small plot—say 100 to 130 square feet—and a limited variety and number of plants. As you gain experience, you'll be able to expand the garden with confidence.

CHOOSE CROPS YOU LIKE. First, decide which vegetables and berries you and your family really enjoy. Then determine how much of each you'll have to grow to satisfy your needs.

Other factors to consider are how much room individual vegetables and berries will occupy, how productive they are for the amount of space they take up, and how long they will bear a crop. For a quick reference chart of crop choices, see page 15.

CONSIDERING THE SOIL

Well-drained soil is important. Generally the best well-drained garden soils are a combination of sand, clay, and silt particles plus ample organic matter. If your soil is predominantly clay ("heavy") or sand ("light") or is low in organic matter, be pre-pared to incorporate large amounts of organic amendments into it before planting (see page 96). And for the first-time garden, at least, it's a good idea to test the soil (see page 96).

DECIDING ON A SITE

If you pay attention to a few pointers about where to put your garden, you'll greatly enhance your chances for success.

Select a plot of ground that receives at least 6 hours of full sun daily.

Avoid planting the garden close to shrubs and trees, which may cast shade and compete with your vegetable crops for water and nutrients.

Choose a spot that's protected from cold winds in spring and hot, dry winds in summer.

Steer clear of "frost pockets." Cold air seeks the lowest level, so late frosts will strike harder in garden low spots.

Place the garden near a convenient water source (usually a hose bib).

Try to select a level piece of land. In a level garden, watering and care are easier. If you have only sloping land available, look for ground that slopes toward the south or southeast to take full advantage of the sun.

Yellow signet marigolds meander through cabbages and kale, creating a decorative as well as practical garden

Considering Your Climate

Your climate and length of growing season will affect your vegetable garden choices. There are two important dates that all vegetable gardeners need to know for their area: the average dates for the last frost in spring and the first frost in fall. The number of days between these dates is the length of the growing season.

The maps on pages 7–8 give general growing seasons and spring and fall frost dates for the United States and Canada. To get more precise dates, which are very useful, ask your local nursery staff or Cooperative Extension Service.

Frost dates are important for a number of reasons. Spring dates determine planting times. Fall dates tell when you will probably have to provide protection for tender vegetables at the end of the season. More important, if you live in an area where winters are cold and summers short, the number of days between the last frost of spring and the first of fall—length of the growing season or average number of frost-free days in summer—determines whether you can successfully grow certain vegetables. Every vegetable seed packet tells you the number of days from seed to harvest for that variety. If a certain watermelon variety, for example, takes 120 days from seed to harvest, and you live in an area with a growing season of only 100 days, you must either find something else to plant or use season-extending techniques (see pages 124–125). Otherwise, your watermelons will not have enough days to ripen.

Vegetables are divided into warm-season and cool-season categories, depending on the weather that's best for their growth. On page 15 are lists of warm- and cool-season vegetables; see the descriptions of individual vegetables (pages 18–71) and berries (pages 74–91) for more precise information.

WARM-SEASON VEGETABLES. The summer crops are warm-season vegetables, which need both soil warmth and long days of high temperatures (or short days and early heat) to form fruit and ripen. Warm-season plants are killed by frost, so you have to plant them after the average date of the last frost in spring or create protected environments in which to plant them earlier (see pages 124–125).

COOL-SEASON VEGETABLES. The cool-season crops grow steadily at average temperatures 10° to 15°F/6° to 8°C below those needed by warm-season crops. Most of the cool-season crops—cabbage, for instance—will even endure frost if it is not long and severe.

Generally you plant these vegetables in very early spring, so the crop will mature before the summer heat. If planted too late, most will bolt—bloom and set seed instead of producing an edible crop—or will become bitter tasting. Most cool-season vegetables can also be planted in late summer to produce a mature crop in fall. In areas with growing seasons of fewer than 100 days or where summers are cool and foggy, such as in coastal areas of the Northwest, cool-season vegetables can be grown all summer long.

MILD-WINTER AREAS. Beneath the white line on the maps are the mild-winter areas, where frosts are light, snow is uncommon, and the ground does not freeze in winter. If you live in an area designated mild-winter, you may be able to grow vegetables year-round by raising cool-season crops during the winter months.

You can plant in late summer and early autumn while days are still warm enough for good plant growth but nights are lengthening.

GARDEN MICROCLIMATES

Microclimates within a garden are influenced by hills and hollows, points of the compass, and structures. Cold air moves downslope to the lowest point and "puddles" in basins. It will collect in other spots as well, if flow is impeded by fences, walls, or structures.

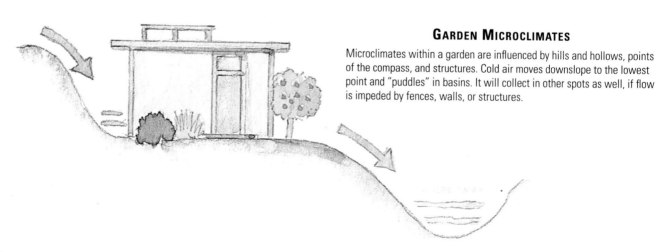

CLIMATE MAPS FOR VEGETABLES

Using state boundaries and major cities as reference points, the maps that follow divide the United States and Canada according to climate. The dates are averages based on United States and Canadian weather reports. In cold-winter areas, to have your own fresh-from-the-garden vegetables in the middle of winter, you'll have to use coldframes or greenhouses (see pages 124–125).

The divisions on these maps are not rigid. You cannot draw a line on the ground and say that on this side the last frost will be March 31 and on the other side April 30. Be sure to consider local conditions—especially elevation and nearby bodies of water—as well as seasonal fluctuations, as you plant each year.

AVERAGE GROWING SEASON LENGTH

- ▬ −60 days
- ▬ 60–120 days
- ▬ 120–180 days
- ▬ 180–240 days
- ▬ 240+ days
- ▬ Cold-Winter/Mild-Winter Boundary

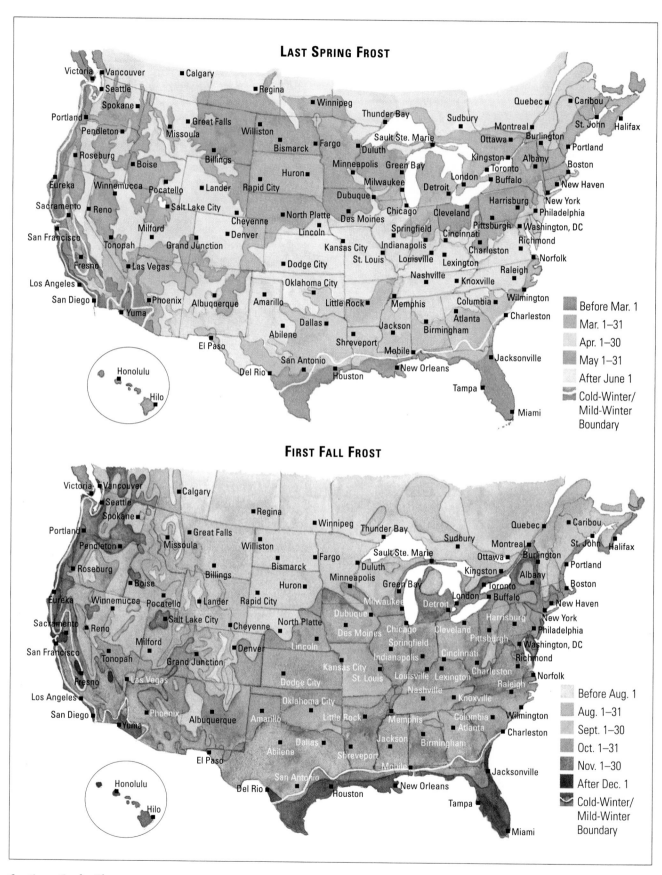

LAST SPRING FROST

Legend:
- Before Mar. 1
- Mar. 1–31
- Apr. 1–30
- May 1–31
- After June 1
- Cold-Winter/ Mild-Winter Boundary

FIRST FALL FROST

Legend:
- Before Aug. 1
- Aug. 1–31
- Sept. 1–30
- Oct. 1–31
- Nov. 1–30
- After Dec. 1
- Cold-Winter/ Mild-Winter Boundary

LAYING OUT YOUR GARDEN

The best garden starts with a plan you draw on paper and then lay out on the ground using a tape measure and string. Whether your garden is large or small, a thoughtful plan can ensure that you won't waste space and that the vegetables and berries you select will have enough room to grow successfully to maturity.

To help you visualize how your garden might be laid out, take a look at the sample plans on the next few pages. These plans show a variety of efficient, highly productive gardens that take the greatest advantage of available spaces and growing periods.

Draw your own intended garden to scale on graph paper (our examples use one square to represent 1 square foot). On the grid, indicate rows or blocks of plants. As you plan, be sure to allow for the spacing between plants suggested in the listings of individual vegetables (pages 18–71) and berries (pages 74–91).

On level ground, plan to run rows north to south; that way the plants get the maximum amount of sunlight as the sun travels in its east-to-west path. If you'll be planting on a slope, run the rows along the contour of the hill. Be sure to place tall crops, such as corn and pole beans, on the north side of the garden so that as they mature they won't shade the lower-growing plants.

Put perennial plants, such as asparagus and berries, in their own section of the garden. This way you won't disturb their roots each year (or season) when you prepare the soil for other crops.

Consider how you intend to supply water—by overhead sprinkler, by flood irrigation, or by drip irrigation (see pages 104–105). You won't want, for example, irrigation rows that run downhill or tall or large-leafed plants blocking sprinklers.

Finally, plan how you'll gain access to the plants. Be sure to allow yourself enough room to get in easily when you want to harvest the crops.

Garden plan allows room for climbing plants and successive plantings for long harvests

CONTINUOUS-HARVEST PLAN

You can lay out a garden that will produce a continuous supply of crops from spring through autumn and even winter. The plan below shows one way to push a single garden's productive season to the maximum and increase the number and variety of crops you can grow.

This basic 22-by-16-foot garden plot is divided into halves, separated by 4 feet of space to allow access for cultivation. In early spring, plant the left half of the plot with cool-season vegetables—carrots, lettuce, cabbage, peas—that will mature before the heat of summer (see the plan below, left half). One end of the plot is reserved for cane berries, such as raspberries.

In later spring, after all danger of frost is past, plant the right half of the plot with warm-season vegetables such as corn, squash, and tomatoes, which will mature in the late summer and autumn (see the plan below, right half).

In mid- to late summer, when most of the left plot is harvested or "played out," you can rework the soil and replant that plot as shown on the next page, rotating placement of crops such as cabbage to avoid fostering soilborne diseases. At this time, you can add new cool-season vegetables, such as broccoli and cauliflower, for harvest in late summer and autumn.

With this continuous-harvest plan, you can use three special techniques—succession planting, double-cropping, and intercropping—to further increase the amount and variety of your garden's output.

SUCCESSION PLANTING. For vegetables that come to maturity all at once, or within a short period of time, you can stretch the harvest period by staggering plantings of seeds or young plants at roughly 2-week intervals. These successive plantings

SPRING PLANTING

1 square = 1 square foot

Left side: plant in early spring

Right side: plant in late spring

will produce a continuous supply of a given vegetable. In the plan shown, for example, the carrots are planted in two side-by-side plots, one planted 2 weeks after the other. (The plantings of bush beans in the right half of the plot could also be divided into halves for successive sowing.)

In addition, replanting the entire left half of the plot in mid- to late summer enables you to harvest two cool-season crops from the left half while the crops in the right half, planted later, mature through the longer warm season.

DOUBLE-CROPPING. Some vegetables—radishes, lettuce, and green onions (scallions) are classic examples—grow so quickly that you can raise a second crop in the same spot within the same season after the first crop has been completely harvested. The space for carrots on the left side of the plot shown, for example, could be replanted for a second harvest within the spring growing season if your climate permits.

INTERCROPPING. Two vegetables can occupy the same allotted space if one matures quickly before the one that grows more slowly crowds it out. In the left side of the plot shown, the green onions will mature and be pulled before the cabbage plants fill the entire space. Similarly, fast-growing spinach occupies the fringe of the berry area before the berries completely take over.

Spinach, lettuce, green onions, and radishes are good intercrop choices for cool-season gardens. You also can grow them in summer gardens (between tomato plants, for example) and harvest them before the weather heats up.

SUMMER PLANTING

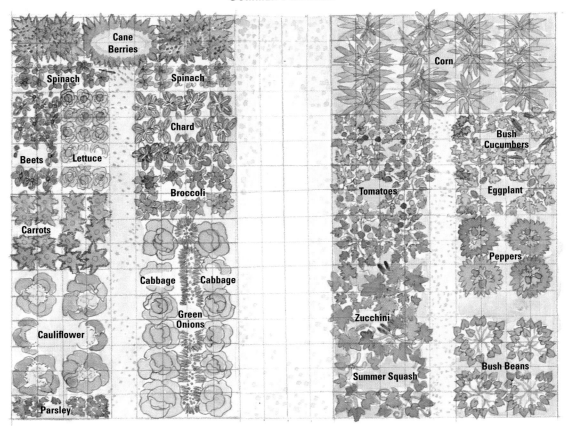

Left side: replant mid- to late summer

Right side: crops planted in late spring mature

SPACE-SAVER GARDEN PLANS

Although some gardeners might consider small space a handicap, the small produce garden offers an exciting challenge: how to reap a diverse and bountiful harvest from a limited plot. The examples here show you ways to organize two small plots—one rectangular, the other square—for maximum productivity and variety. The keys to a good harvest are thorough preparation and careful plant selection and placement.

SOIL AND WATER. In a small-space garden, you need to spend extra time on soil preparation. Add soil amendments liberally (see page 96). You might even consider double digging the ground (page 97) or planting the whole garden as a raised bed (page 98).

In addition, you may want to install a drip irrigation system (see pages 104–105). A drip system entails a minimal outlay of time and money to ensure that the entire plot is watered evenly and without waste.

WHAT TO PLANT. The small-space garden rules out crops that take a lot of room to produce low yields per square foot, such as corn, melons, and some squashes. For maximum yields, seek out varieties that are especially productive. Plant ideas can be found in the chart on page 15, in the descriptions of individual vegetables (pages 18–71) and berries (pages 74–91), and in seed catalogs.

You can also maximize your small-space productivity by planting both early- and late-maturing varieties of the same vegetable.

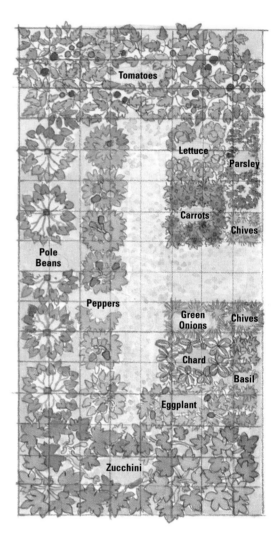

1 square = 1 square foot

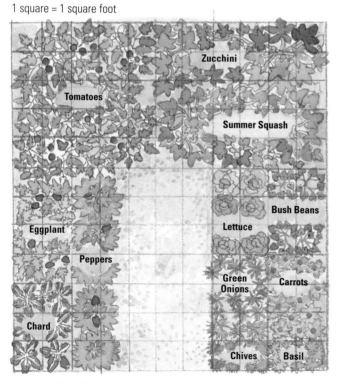

GARDEN LAYOUT. Several techniques make the most of available space. Whenever possible, use vertical supports such as stakes, frames, and trellises (see page 107) to extend your garden up rather than across. Try the various modes of continuous-harvest planting (pages 10–11). Use any chance to interplant fast-growing crops among slower-growing ones. Spinach, lettuce, green onions (scallions), and radishes are fine intercroppers. Whenever season and climate allow, practice double-cropping as soon as the first crop is harvested. In the plans on this page, lettuce, green onions, carrots, and bush beans might be double-cropped.

Note that the plans show blocks rather than rows of lettuce, carrots, and green onions. These (and other vegetables not shown) could also be planted thickly in French intensive bed fashion (see pages 14 and 123–124), with the thinnings being the first to reach your kitchen.

VEGETABLE AND ORNAMENTAL LANDSCAPE PLANS

If you hesitate to set aside space for a purely utilitarian food garden, or if your front yard is the only sunny spot for the lettuce or strawberries you want to grow, try mixing crop plants with your ornamental plantings. Many vegetables, berries, and herbs display a diverse array of showy "fruits" as well as foliage textures and colors. And a diverse mixture of plants is also more attractive to beneficial insects, those garden "good guys" that prey on plant pests. So such a garden may actually have fewer problems.

The plan below shows how vegetables can be worked into a landscape, mixed with flowering plants in a gracefully shaped bed that would look good anywhere.

CONSIDER HOW VEGETABLES LOOK. The secret to incorporating crop plants into the landscape is to look at them with a fresh eye. The foliage, shape, and color of many vegetable and berry plants are very attractive. Picture crops as part of your overall garden scheme, rather than in farm-style rows.

Some, such as lettuces and greens, can be grouped into clumps of several-to-many plants and incorporated into beds of annuals or perennials. Some plants with low or appealing foliage, such as leaf lettuce and green onions, can edge a bed of ornamentals or line a pathway. Bold-foliaged vegetables, such as rhubarb, Swiss chard, and artichokes, can be used as accent plants. Vining vegetables and berries can be used as backdrops

or as featured vertical emphasis points. And don't forget that many vegetables are also very attractive in containers and can add color and texture to sunny patios, decks, and entryways.

CONSIDER THE QUANTITY. When you're planting vegetables or berries as landscape components, it's important to estimate correctly the quantity that your planting will produce. Zucchini plants, for example, have handsome, bold-textured foliage. But if you use them as a low hedge along a driveway or property boundary, you'll have more than enough squashes to saturate the neighborhood. On the other hand, one large clump of corn, featured as a tall and grassy accent, may not be enough to satisfy your own needs.

Consider how you'll harvest. Remember that some vegetables are a one-shot proposition—you harvest the entire plant. If you use carrots to create a fernlike border or edging, you'll totally remove the effect when you harvest. Parsley used in the same situation for the same effect will last all season, because you harvest sprigs, not whole plants.

At planting time, make sure you plan access to the crops for harvest. You don't want to trample ornamentals to pick your vegetables.

Read cautions on the labels of any fertilizers or pesticides you're considering; the products used on some ornamentals could contaminate nearby edibles.

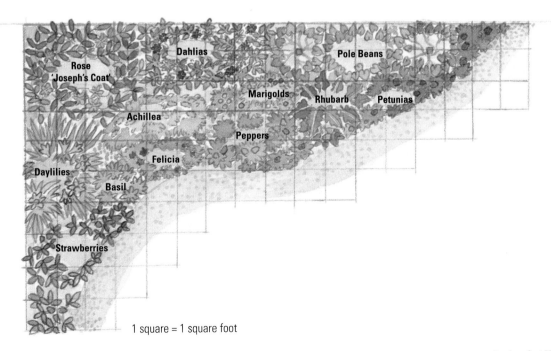

1 square = 1 square foot

FRENCH INTENSIVE GARDEN PLAN

French intensive gardening relies on close planting in wide, mounded beds to conserve soil moisture and thereby promote steady, abundant growth. To avoid crowding, you thin the plants frequently as they grow (the thinnings go to your kitchen). French intensive gardening starts with very thorough soil preparation followed by specific seeding and planting methods (see pages 123–124). Not all vegetables and berries lend themselves to this treatment; choose plants that will produce all season and tolerate regular thinning (see the chart on the next page).

The plan illustrated below shows two ways to plant the same 14-by-5-foot plot. The upper drawing is a cool-season planting; the lower drawing is a warm-season planting (or an all-season planting in mild-winter climates). Each includes vegetable and herb crops that give generous yields in small spaces, and the cool-season version incorporates a strawberry plot. Note that the beds are narrow enough for easy reach from the borders for thinning the crops as they grow; the length can vary according to your available space.

COOL-SEASON PLANTING

1 square = 1 square foot

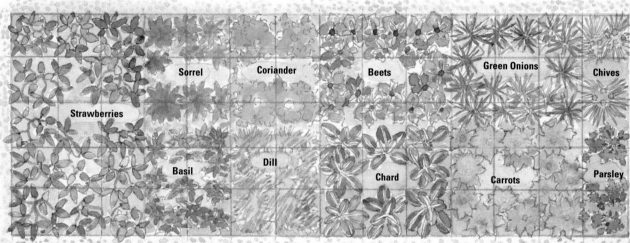

WARM-SEASON PLANTING

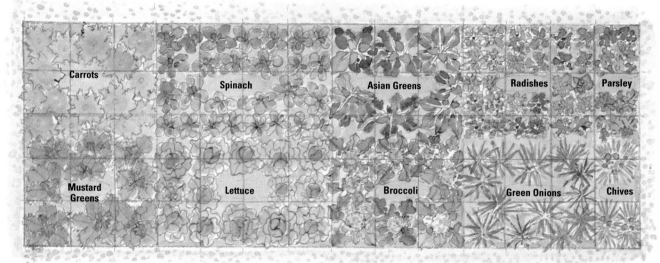

PLANT CHOICES

Everyone has favorites among the vegetables and berries, and the natural desire is to grow them in quantity. But before you plant at all, be sure that the crops' requirements match the conditions of your region and your garden. Some vegetables are fairly foolproof in nearly all regions—tomatoes, for example. At the other extreme, the raspberry aficionado had better live in a raspberry climate or get berries from the market.

The chart below lists vegetables and berries in the categories that are useful to the broadest range of growers.

CATEGORY	PLANTS
Cool-Season Crops	Artichokes; Asian greens; Asparagus; Beets; Broccoli; Brussels sprouts; Cabbage; Carrots; Cauliflower; Celery and celeriac; Collards; Cress; Endive; Garlic; Kale; Kohlrabi; Leeks; Lettuce; Mustard greens; Onions; Parsnips; Peas; Potatoes; Radishes; Rhubarb; Roquette; Rutabagas; Salsify; Shallots; Spinach; Swiss chard; Turnips
Warm-Season Crops	Amaranth; Asian melons; Beans; Chayote; Chicory; Collards; Corn; Cucumbers; Eggplant; Herbs (most); Jerusalem artichokes; Jicama; Melons; Okra; Peanuts; Peppers; Pumpkins; Southern peas; Spinach, New Zealand and Malabar; Squash; Sunflowers; Sweet potatoes; Tomatillos; Tomatoes; Watermelons
Winter Harvests in Frost-Free Zones	Asian greens; Beets; Broccoli; Brussels sprouts; Cabbage; Carrots; Cauliflower; Celery and celeriac; Cress; Lettuce and celtuce; Peas, green and edible pod; Spinach; Swiss chard; Radishes; Turnips
Fast-Maturing Crops	Amaranth; Asian greens; Cress; Herbs (most); Lettuce; Mustard greens; Onions, green (scallions); Radishes; Roquette; Spinach; Sprouts; Turnips
Prolific Producers	Asian greens; Beans; Brussels sprouts; Cucumbers; Herbs; Jerusalem artichokes; Mustard greens; Peas; Radishes; Spinach, New Zealand; Sprouts; Squash (some); Sunflowers; Tomatoes
Container Candidates	Amaranth; Asian greens; Beans; Beets; Broccoli; Cabbage (some); Carrots; Collards; Cress; Cucumbers; Eggplant; Herbs; Kale (some); Lettuce; Mustard greens; Onions, green (scallions); Peas; Peppers; Radishes; Roquette; Shallots; Sorrel; Spinach, New Zealand; Swiss chard; Tomatoes
French Intensive Garden Choices	Asian greens; Beans, bush; Beets; Carrots; Chicory; Collards; Cress; Endive; Garlic; Kale; Leeks; Lettuce; Mustard greens; Onions; Peas, dwarf; Radishes; Roquette; Rutabagas; Shallots; Sorrel; Spinach; Swiss chard; Turnips
Vines and Sprawlers	Asian melons; Beans (some); Blackberries; Chayote; Cucumbers; Gourds; Grapes; Jicama; Melons; Peas (some); Pumpkins; Raspberries; Southern peas (some); Spinach, Malabar; Squash (most); Strawberries; Sweet potatoes; Tomatillos; Tomatoes; Watermelons
Decorative Garden Plants	Artichokes; Asian greens; Asparagus; Cabbage (some); Carrots; Cardoon; Chicory; Eggplant; Herbs (most); Jerusalem artichokes; Kale (some); Lettuce (some); Mustard greens (some); Peppers; Rhubarb; Sunflowers; Swiss chard
Colorful for Cooking	Beans; Beets; Cabbage; Carrots; Cauliflower (some); Corn; Eggplant; Kohlrabi; Lettuce; Melons; Onions (some); Peppers; Potatoes (some); Pumpkins; Radishes; Rhubarb; Squash; Sweet potatoes; Swiss chard; Tomatoes; Watermelons
Roots That Store in Ground	Horseradish; Jerusalem artichokes; Parsnips; Rutabagas; Salsify; Turnips
More Than One Edible Part	Beets; Chayote; Chicory; Kohlrabi; Onions; Pumpkins; Roquette; Rutabagas; Turnips

ENCYCLOPEDIA OF
VEGETABLES

From delicately flavored heirloom varieties grown by your ancestors to the latest trendy vegetables cooked in the fanciest restaurants to exotic greens from faraway lands, there is truly a wonderful world of vegetables for you to explore. Here you'll find it all at your fingertips—the most familiar and favorite vegetables, some lesser-known ones that deserve wider appreciation, and the most useful culinary herbs.

Each description includes a sidebar list that tells you at a glance whether the crop is annual or perennial, whether an annual is cool or warm season, and what parts of the plant are edible. Summarizing care, the list tells the crop's soil preference, when and how to plant the vegetable, what care it requires during growth, what yield you can expect of the crop, and common pests and diseases you might have to combat. For ideas on how to control vegetable pests and diseases, see pages 112–119. Finally, the sidebar indicates when and how to harvest the produce and how to store properly for the longest possible enjoyment.

Use the sidebar lists as guides when choosing vegetables to grow, as well as quick reference sources for cultivation facts. But when you're selecting crops be sure to keep in mind specific conditions in your situation, from food preferences to weather. For example, although the sidebars suggest the planting season for each crop in most areas of the country, the planting season for some crops may be different where you live. Consult your Cooperative Extension Service for precise information about when to plant and harvest vegetables in your area.

TRYING VARIETIES

A number of the descriptions name some varieties, but many more exist than are mentioned. Some varieties do well in most parts of the country; others do well only in small areas. If you like to experiment, try different varieties to find the ones that do best in your garden. For more certain results, consult local gardeners, nursery personnel, and your Cooperative Extension Service.

MAKING VEGETABLE CHOICES

Still bewildered by the range of choices? Then consider these suggestions: first, grow the kinds of vegetables (and berries) that your family likes to eat. Second, select crops that will fit in the space you have, that will require no more time and energy than you can give, and that will produce amounts you can use. Finally, even though sweet corn may be as precious to you as gold, don't try to grow it—or any other crop—in a climate unsuited to its cultivation.

COMMUNITY GARDENS

Are you eager to plant more than you could possibly squeeze into your available space? If you haven't got enough room for a vegetable garden, consider joining a community garden. Community gardens offer a small plot of ground to anyone who wants to garden. Most larger cities have several, in either open land or public parks. For the location of a community garden in your area, or information on how to start one, contact the American Community Garden Association, 100 North 20th Street, 5th Floor, Philadelphia, PA 19103, or phone (215) 988-8800. Your city or county parks department may also help you locate a community garden near you.

A kaleidoscope of colors, these homegrown heirloom beans and tomatoes offer flavorful treats you can't buy at a supermarket

TYPE OF VEGETABLE. Annual; warm season.

EDIBLE PARTS. Leaves; stems.

BEST SOIL. Fertile, well drained.

WHEN TO PLANT. For summer crop, sow seeds in spring (3–4 weeks after last frost date).

HOW TO PLANT. Sow seeds ¼" deep, ½" apart, in rows spaced 2' apart; thin seedlings to 2"–24" apart, depending on variety.

CARE. Keep soil moist. Weed regularly.

PESTS AND DISEASES. Mites.

WHEN TO HARVEST. 40–56 days after sowing seeds, when plants are 6"–8" tall.

HOW TO HARVEST. Cut whole plants when they are young and small; use both stems and leaves. Cut off 4"–5" tips of leaves when plants grow large.

AMARANTH

Not many Americans are yet acquainted with this nutritious hot-weather spinach substitute. But elsewhere in the world, it has been cultivated for centuries. In China, amaranth, or *hin choy*, is popular as a leafy addition to soups and stir-fries. In the Western Hemisphere, the Aztecs relied on native kinds of amaranth as a staple, grinding its high-protein seeds into meal. In parts of Mexico, amaranth is still a market crop prized for both its seeds and its spinachlike leaves.

You'll find the kinds of amaranth that are grown for their edible leaves listed in catalogs under names such as "Tampala," "Chinese Spinach," "Hin Choy," and "Edible Amaranth." 'Mirah' is a particularly attractive variety: Its crinkled green leaves have purple veins, and it produces many edible shoots even on older plants. Other varieties with colorful new growth, such as 'Illumination' and 'Flaming Fountain', can be eaten but are usually grown as ornamentals.

Plant the edible-leaf amaranths in spring, when the weather is warm. Unlike spinach, they won't go to seed when temperatures get hot. Harvest the plants before they bloom, or remove the flowers before amaranth can reseed and become weedy.

Serve the leaves steamed or add them raw to salad. Cook the stems as you would asparagus.

TYPE OF VEGETABLE. Perennial, hardy to 30°F/–1°C; cool season.

EDIBLE PARTS. Flower buds: soft part at base of leaf (bract) and heart (base of bud).

BEST SOIL. Rich, well drained, pH 6.0.

WHEN TO PLANT. MILD-WINTER CLIMATES: Set out bud root divisions or plants in winter or spring. COLD-WINTER CLIMATES: Sow seeds in flats or pots 8–12 weeks before the last frost. Plant seedlings after danger of frost.

HOW TO PLANT. Set out root divisions or plants 4'–6' apart in rows spaced 6'–8' apart. Sow seeds ½" deep, 1"–2" apart; thin to 6"–8" apart. In hot-summer climates, plant in partial shade.

YIELD. 12 or more buds per plant.

CARE. Water weekly. Mulch heavily. Fertilize once a year.

PESTS AND DISEASES. Slugs, snails.

WHEN TO HARVEST. While buds are tight.

Continues next page >

ARTICHOKES

The prickly artichoke exterior hides a tender and delicious heart, the base of the bud. And despite its rugged appearance, the artichoke plant is fussy about climate. It needs mild winters and cool summers for best quality (it won't grow in Florida).

In areas where artichokes are well adapted, particularly coastal California, they are perennials grown from root divisions. In other areas they can be treated as annuals and planted from seed. 'Northern Star' is a hardy variety that has survived subzero temperatures. 'Imperial Star' is also hardy and produces a crop quickly from seed (90 to 100 days from transplanting). 'Green Globe' is the most widely available variety and produces some buds the first year from seed.

Water artichokes weekly during the growing season, and apply mulch heavily, especially in hot-summer climates, to hold the moisture. Fertilize the plants in spring or autumn. At the end of the growing season, cut old stalks down to the ground. In cold-winter climates, apply thick mulch, or dig and divide the roots, and store them in a cool, dark place over winter. You can begin harvesting in the spring of the first year after planting. In the following years, you'll harvest from autumn to spring.

A massive, beautiful plant, the artichoke develops into a silvery green fountain that can spread to 6 feet wide. Buds that escape harvest reveal the artichoke's family ties: They blossom into purple thistles that can be dried for arrangements.

Here are two little-known facts about artichokes. First, the name comes from an Arabic word, *al-khurshūf*, and doesn't have anything to do with the English word "choke." Second, the bud contains a chemical that makes food eaten after it taste sweet. Eventually it may become a noncaloric sweetener.

How to harvest. Cut stems 1"–1½" below buds.

How to store. Refrigerate unwashed; use as soon as possible. To preserve, freeze whole; can, freeze, or dry hearts.

Asian Vegetables

Though the flavor may be exotic, Asian vegetables—greens, broccoli, melons, squash, and radishes—are as easy to grow as their Western relatives. Growing information for most is given in these pages. For directions on growing snow peas, see "Peas," page 53; for sprouting mung beans, see "Sprouts," page 63; for Chinese parsley (coriander or cilantro) and chives (Chinese leeks), see "Herbs," page 39.

ASIAN GREENS. The mainstays of most stir-fried dishes are greens. By themselves, with other vegetables, or with meat, chicken, or seafood, thin slices of real Asian greens will make your Far Eastern recipes authentic.

Leafy Asian greens are all quick-maturing, cool-season annual vegetables. As long as the weather is cool, you can continue to sow seeds or set out plants for successive crops in spring or autumn.

Greens related to broccoli have a longer growing season than other Asian greens. Like Western broccoli, they do best in cool weather. Care is the same as for broccoli (see page 26).

Sow seeds ¼ to ½ inch deep, 2 to 4 inches apart, directly in the ground or in containers for transplanting. When seedlings are 2 to 3 inches tall, transplant or thin as indicated for each vegetable. Water and fertilize amply, and keep the soil loose and free of weeds for fast, tender growth.

Sample the leaves and flowers at various stages of growth to use your crop fully and to discover which stage you like best. Even Asian gardeners debate whether peak flavor and tenderness are reached when the first flower buds open or slightly before.

To harvest, pull up the whole plant, trim off the root end, and discard any tough stalks and leaves. Cut the tender portion in slices or chunks for stir-frying, steaming, or adding to soups.

Asian greens

Broadleaf mustard (*dai gai choy*) has large green leaves with a pungent, somewhat bitter, mustard flavor that gets stronger as the plant matures. Hot weather or lack of adequate water also makes it more pungent. It's best diluted in soup.

Thin or transplant seedlings to 10 inches apart. Harvest the plants when they are loosely headed and 10 to 14 inches tall, about 65 days after sowing seeds.

The mild member of the mustard family is *gai choy*, **Chinese mustard greens.** These are excellent in soups or stir-fried with other vegetables.

Thin or transplant seedlings to 10 inches apart. Harvest the first greens when the plants are 2 inches tall; continue harvesting until the greens are tough or bitter. It takes about 45 days after sowing seeds for plants to reach 6 to 8 inches.

'Early Jade Pagoda' Chinese cabbage

Listing continues >

'Osaka Purple-leaved' mustard greens

GROWING MELONS ON A TRELLIS

The vining habit of the melon makes it perfect for growing on a trellis. It takes a little extra work and a very sturdy trellis, but using this device you can grow quite a few melons in small space. An A-frame trellis constructed of 2-by-2 lumber and concrete-reinforcing wire (instead of twine) works well. When the melons reach about 2 inches in diameter, support them in slings made of old nylon stockings. Slip the melon inside a short section of the stocking leg, and knot the bottom end. Tie the other end to the wire trellis. The stocking will expand as the melon gets bigger. Be sure to check the melons often so you don't miss picking them at their peak.

Chinese white cabbage *(bok choy)* is one of the more familiar Asian greens. It's a tender-crisp, sweet, very mild vegetable that's good alone, with meat, in soup, and in stir-fried dishes.

Thin or transplant seedlings to 6 to 12 inches apart. Harvest Chinese cabbage approximately 50 days after sowing seeds, when it's loosely headed and 10 to 12 inches tall.

Flowering cabbage, called *yao choy, choy sum,* or *ching soy sum,* is a tender, delicate, broccoli-type vegetable, tasty when served alone or in recipes that require greens.

Thin or transplant seedlings to about 6 inches apart. Harvest when the plants are 8 to 12 inches tall. Flowering cabbage takes about 60 days to reach maturity after seeds are sown.

Chinese broccoli *(gai lohn)* is similar in flavor and texture to Western broccoli but with a slight pungency like mustard and less cabbage flavor. Its flower heads are much smaller than those of Western broccoli. It is good served by itself or in recipes that call for an assertive green.

Thin or transplant seedlings to 10 inches apart. Harvest the central stalk and side shoots when the plant is 8 to 10 inches tall or when flower buds just begin to form. Chinese broccoli needs about 70 days after seeds are sown to reach maturity.

ASIAN MELONS. Asian melons are like squash in the way they taste and the way you use them, but their growing requirements are similar to those of their cousins, Western melons and winter squash.

Members of the cucurbit (melon-squash) family, they love a long, sunny, warm growing season and rich, well-drained soil supplied with abundant water. Like most melons and trailing squash, they have rambling vines and need space to grow. It's a good idea to train them up a trellis to keep the vines from taking over the yard and to help the fruits stay clean and dry.

When the soil temperature has warmed to 70° to 75°F/21° to 24°C, sow seeds 1 inch deep, 2 inches apart in rows 4 feet apart; thin to 12 to 24 inches apart. Or plant in hills (five seeds per hill) spaced 2 feet apart; thin seedlings to three per hill. To get an early start, you can sow seeds in peat pots 2 to 3 weeks before you intend to set out plants. Plant the whole pot, so you disturb the roots as little as possible. Space the pots about 2 feet apart.

Chinese fuzzy melon

Winter melon *(doong gwah)* looks like watermelon but has white, firm flesh. It is the base for the famous winter melon soup. Its name comes from the fact that you can store and use it through the winter (or for as long as a year).

If you trellis the vines, use slings to support the heavy melons. For immediate use, harvest melons when they reach pumpkin size (about 120 days from seed). For long storage, wait until the stem of the fruit is hard and dry; keep the melon in a cool, dry place. To use, peel the melon, and cube the flesh to cook in any broth soup. For classic winter melon soup, the hollowed-out melon is used as the bowl for steaming and serving the soup.

Fuzzy melon *(moh gwah)* is a faster-maturing version of winter melon. Immature fuzzy melons, about the size of zucchini, are delicious peeled, sliced, and quickly cooked tender-firm in a little butter (or oil) and water; or stuff and bake them as you would zucchini. When melons mature to around 1 foot in diameter, use them as you would winter melon.

Chinese
bitter melon

Bitter melon (*foo gwah*) is definitely an acquired taste. You may want to grow it just for its unusual lobed leaves (which can be cooked like spinach) and bright green, lumpy, long fruit.

Harvest bitter melons when they are 4 to 8 inches long, about 75 days after sowing seeds. Plumper ridges and warts indicate milder flavor. To eat, cut in half lengthwise, scrape out and discard the seedy pulp, then immerse the halves in boiling water one or more times, discarding the water each time to reduce bitterness. Chop the melon into chunks to simmer in soup or into slices for stir-fried dishes.

If you leave the fruit on the vine, it will turn golden yellow and split up the sides to reveal showy red seeds. In India, mature bitter melon is sliced and used for curries. The red seed coat is edible, but the seed itself acts as a purgative.

Sponge gourd (*see gwah*) is also known as Chinese okra or luffa. You can use the dried gourd as a bathing sponge, or eat the immature gourd as you would cucumber or summer squash. The vines are very vigorous.

To eat, harvest before the seeds develop (about 90 days), when gourds are between 6 and 12 inches long. Peel off the ridges. Cut into slices to use raw in salads or to stir-fry with meat and vegetables. Cut into chunks to simmer in soup or deep-fry for tempura.

To harvest for sponges, leave the gourds on the vine until they're completely brown, and then pick and dry them completely. Crush the skin lightly, and soak the gourd in boiling water until the skin is soft enough to peel off easily. Remove the seeds, and soak the sponge in bleach if its fiber is discolored.

Pink and white Japanese radishes

JAPANESE RADISH. Japanese radish (*daikon*) is a large—sometimes gargantuan—version of the common radish. Asian chefs use *daikon* cooked, in soup, pickled, and as a condiment—grated or sliced raw, sometimes mixed with vinegar and hot mustard.

The very largest, the 'Sakurajima' radish, is the size of a pumpkin and takes up to 150 days to mature. Medium-size varieties, such as 'Miyashige', take only 50 days to produce roots. The smaller varieties, still gigantic in comparison with Western radishes, take 45 to 60 days to mature.

Soil preparation is crucial; there should be no hard lumps or debris in the rich, well-drained soil. Dig the soil, and mix it with amendments as deep as the roots grow, or the big roots will be distorted. Be sure to give these large radishes plenty of water. The less water they receive, the stronger their flavor.

Asparagus beans

ASPARAGUS BEAN. Asparagus bean or yard-long bean (*dow gauk*) is actually a variety of cowpea or field pea. (For growing instructions, see "Southern Peas," page 61.) The bean pods grow 25 to 30 inches long and are stringless. They can be cut and cooked like other kinds of snap beans. Grow these beans on a trellis. They are ready for harvest about 65 days after sowing seeds.

BLANCHING ASPARAGUS

Blanching turns any green variety of asparagus into a tender white delicacy. In early spring, before spears emerge, mound soil or sawdust 8 inches high over the row or hill. When tips appear from the top of the mound, push a long knife into the base of the mound to cut each spear well below the surface. Pull the cut shoots out by their tips. Level the mounds after the harvest season.

ASPARAGUS

After a winter of slush, wet boots, and sniffles, the first tender harvest of asparagus—lightly steamed and drizzled with butter—can renew your springtime determination to plant a veritable Eden of vegetables.

Asparagus is a perennial. Its bright green spear-fingers reach up to the spring sun year after year—possibly for decades—so you'll want to plan a permanent location for your patch.

Because growing asparagus takes 3 years from seed to harvest, most people choose to buy 1-year-old crowns—rhizomes (food storage stems) with scraggly dry roots growing downward and nubbly growth buds sticking up. Varieties that produce mostly male spears are most productive (they don't waste energy producing seed). 'Jersey Giant' and 'Jersey Knight' are preferred where winters are cold; they resist rust and fusarium wilt. 'Larac' is also productive in short-season areas. 'UC 157' is recommended for mild-winter areas but also performs well elsewhere.

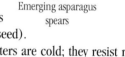

Emerging asparagus spears

Give the roots a soft, rich bed, and they'll reward you with years of plentiful spears. In well-drained soil, dig a trench 8 to 12 inches deep and 12 inches wide. (Where drainage is very bad, plant in raised beds.) If you're planting more than one row, space trenches 3 to 6 feet apart. Pile the soil to one side, waiting to cover the crowns as they grow. Into the trench put a 2- to 3-inch layer of well-rotted manure. Sprinkle in a complete fertilizer—2 pounds of 5-10-10 per 25-foot row works well. If the pH of your soil is below 6.0, add lime. Mix manure and fertilizer with the loose soil that is in the bottom of the trench, and bank it up about 6 inches.

Atop the length of the bank, space the crowns 12 to 18 inches apart and spread each crown's roots down over the sides of the ridge. Partially fill the trench with loose soil to cover the crowns 2 inches deep. (In raised beds, cover the crowns 6 inches deep.) As the shoots grow, fill in soil around them, but be careful not to cover the tips of the shoots. The crowns should eventually be covered with 6 inches of soil. Keep the bed well watered.

The first year let all the spears shoot up and leaf out; the feathery foliage nourishes the growing roots, which in turn supply the rhizome with nutrients to feed the plant

White asparagus

through the winter and give the next season's spears strength for growth. The second spring you can harvest the first few spears. When spears begin to look spindly (about ¼ inch in diameter), let them grow up and leaf out. By the third spring, the asparagus will produce spears in full force over a long season (8 to 12 weeks).

In late spring or early summer, when emerging spears are less than ¼ inch wide, stop harvesting, and let those spears develop ferny foliage, which will build food reserves for next year's crop. Remove the ferny growth when it turns brown in autumn or at the end of the year in mild-winter areas. In cold-winter climates, some gardeners leave the dried growth over winter, so it can catch insulating snow, and then they remove the foliage early in spring.

BEANS

What takes the most effort in growing beans? Some people think it's deciding which kind to grow. For instance, there are snap beans (also called green or string beans), beans for shelling when the seeds are mature but still green, beans to dry for long storage, lima beans, soybeans, and fava beans. Once you've selected the kinds you want to grow, you have to choose among the many varieties of each. Poring over seed catalogs can become an all-winter occupation when you start investigating beans.

After that, you can relax. Beans tolerate drier soil than many vegetables, although you need to keep the soil moist when the plants begin to flower and while they are forming pods. And don't bother to hoe or cultivate the soil deeply, because beans have shallow roots.

SNAP BEANS. The whopping number of varieties of snap beans attests to this vegetable's continuing popularity with home gardeners. You can buy seeds for either bush or pole varieties, each with a choice of color—green, yellow (wax), or, for novelty, purple or striped.

Bush beans are compact plants, 1 to 2 feet tall, depending on variety and growing conditions. Pole (climbing) beans grow 8 feet or more and need firm support. Bush beans bear 10 days to 2 weeks earlier than pole beans, but the crop is not as prolific.

Purple pole beans

Snap beans can be grown easily from seeds, but wait until the soil warms, or the seeds will just sit and sulk or rot. The best soil temperature for germination is 60° to 85°F/16° to 29°C. Either check with a soil thermometer or wait until late-leafing trees—oaks, hickories, pecans—uncurl new spring foliage.

To prevent the soil surface from crusting and impeding germination of the seeds, prepare the soil, water the bed, let the soil crust, and then break it up and sow the seeds. Don't water again until the seedlings sprout.

Plant seeds of bush varieties 1 to 1½ inches deep and 2 inches apart in rows spaced 2 to 3 feet apart, or sow them in wide bands with seeds spaced about 6 inches from each other. Since some bush beans require only 7 weeks to mature in warm weather, they can be grown successfully in areas with fairly short summers.

Pole bean plants are much larger and need 3 feet between rows and 6 to 12 inches between plants. Plant the seeds 1 to 1½ inches deep. Provide poles 6 to 8 feet tall and 6 to 12 inches apart or a trellis or a tepee of three or four poles (see page 24).

Romano beans, also known as Italian green beans, are another delicious type of snap bean, with a flat, wide pod that is tender and meaty. You cook the pods as you would snap beans. Pole and bush Romano beans are available. Planting and growing requirements are the same as for other bush or pole snap beans.

There are more than 50 varieties of snap beans. Your local Cooperative Extension Service can recommend specific varieties for your area. For green bush beans, a few of the reliable varieties are 'Tenderpod', 'Tenderpick', 'Tendergreen', 'Slenderette', and the 'Bush Blue Lake' types. For yellow (wax) bush beans, consider 'Kinghorn', 'Eastern Butterwax', 'Roc d'Or', or 'Gold Crop'. For novelty, there's 'Royal Burgundy', a purple-podded snap bean that turns green when cooked.

Listing continues >

TYPE OF VEGETABLE. Annual; warm-season (except for fava bean, which is cool-season).

EDIBLE PARTS. Harvested seed pods or seeds.

BEST SOIL. Fertile, well drained, pH 6.0–6.8.

WHEN TO PLANT. Sow seeds in spring (when soil has warmed and danger of frost has passed). To increase productivity and reduce need for nitrogen fertilizing, buy inoculated seeds, or dust seeds or soil with legume inoculant as label directs. Plant lima beans 2 weeks later than other varieties. Plant fava beans in early spring or autumn. Make successive plantings of bush beans.

HOW TO PLANT. Sow seeds 1"–1½" deep. (For spacing between seeds and between rows, see descriptions of specific beans.) Set up supports for pole beans at planting time. Thin seedlings to 6" apart.

YIELD. 3–10 pounds per 10' row, depending on variety.

CARE. Keep soil moist once plants flower. Don't hoe deeply; roots are shallow. Use low-nitrogen fertilizer.

PESTS AND DISEASES. Aphids, cucumber beetles, leafhoppers, Mexican bean beetles, mites; damping off, downy mildew. To prevent spread of leaf diseases, avoid working among beans when leaves are wet.

WHEN TO HARVEST. 50–100 days after sowing seeds, depending on variety.

HOW TO HARVEST. Carefully pull ripe pods from plants.

HOW TO STORE. Refrigerate green beans unwashed in plastic bag or tight container for up to 4 days. To preserve, freeze. Store dried beans in airtight container.

'Blue Lake' beans

A SIMPLE BEAN TEPEE

Building a bean tepee is a great way to involve kids in the garden. Arrange eight 6- to 8-foot narrow poles (such as bamboo) in a circle about 5 to 6 feet wide, with the poles evenly spaced about 2 feet apart. Push the bottoms of the poles into the ground a few inches, and tie the tops together with twine. Plant two seeds of a climbing bean variety at the base of each pole.

For a denser cover of bean foliage, run a circle of string around the base of the tepee, looping it around each pole. Leave an opening between two of the poles, for a "door." Then run more string vertically between the poles from the base string to the top of the tepee.

'Anasazi' beans

Pole bean varieties include the famous 'Kentucky Wonder', 'Kentucky Blue', 'Dade', and 'Blue Lake' varieties. 'Kentucky Wonder Wax' is a yellow pole-type snap bean.

For asparagus beans (yard-long beans), see page 21 of "Asian Vegetables."

Because all beans are legumes, capable of getting their nitrogen from air, if you start with inoculated seeds, you should use a low nitrogen fertilizer, such as 5-10-10. High-nitrogen fertilization can promote growth of leaves at the expense of bean pods.

Harvesting snap beans takes a certain amount of diligence to keep up with the ready crop, but not much skill. Pick bean pods when they are at least 3 inches long and before they begin to get tough and stringy. At the ideal point, beans have not started to bulge the sides of the pods. The more faithful you are about frequent picking, the longer the plants will yield.

BEANS FOR SHELLING OR DRYING. Everyone knows about snap beans and dry beans—but beans for green-shelling? Sometimes called shellies or shuckies in the South, and often called horticultural beans in the seed catalogs, beans for green-shelling are grown until their seeds are full-size but not dry.

Some beans are particularly delicious harvested at the green-shelling stage. These include the flageolet bean, a popular variety in the south of France, and the 'French Horticultural Bean', also known as the 'October Bean'. 'Vermont Cranberry Bean' is yet another tasty, succulent shelling bean, and the 'Great Northern White' bean, though mainly known as a dry bean, is delicious harvested early as a shellie. All of these green-shelling favorites grow on bush-type plants and require the same plant spacing and care as bush snap beans. You'll have to wait an average of 65 days to harvest mature green pods.

Cook fresh shellies 5 to 20 minutes until tender (time varies with size of bean and maturity). Serve them simply with butter, salt, and pepper, or add them to hearty soups or casseroles, or marinate them for salads. Left to dry, the shellies, especially the creamy-textured flageolet, are delicious cooked alone or in casseroles.

Beans cultivated especially for their flavor when they are cooked after drying include the familiar navy bean, pinto bean, and red and white kidney beans, as well as rare varieties known only to the home gardener who loves to scan seed catalogs—'Jacob's Cattle Bean', 'Dalmatian Bean', 'Soldier Bean', 'Midnight Black Turtle', and 'Red Peanut Bean'. Heirloom beans, such as 'Aztec Dwarf White', 'Mitla Black', and 'New Mexico Appaloosa', were used by Native Americans of the Southwest and are very well adapted to its hot-summer climates.

The culture for these beans is the same as for the bush type of snap bean. The main difference is that you let the beans remain on the bush until the pods turn dry or begin to shatter. Shell the ripe beans from their hulls and dry them well before storing.

LIMA BEANS. Lima beans come in frozen blocks, right? Well, give fresh-from-the-vine limas a chance, and you'll rediscover a tasty vegetable. The lima bean is a different plant species from other common beans, but its cultural requirements are nearly the same as those for snap beans.

Limas come in either bush or pole form. Bush lima beans develop more slowly than snap beans, requiring 65 to 75 days to mature; pole limas take 78 to 95 days. Limas do not produce as reliably as snap beans in extremely dry, hot weather.

Among the bush limas are 'Improved Bush', 'Henderson Bush', 'Fordhook 242', 'Jackson Wonder', and 'Dixie White Butterpea'; the last two are especially useful in hot-summer areas. 'Prizetaker' and 'King of the Garden' are good large-seeded pole limas. 'Small White Lima' or 'Sieva' is usually grown for drying, but it yields an abundance of green-shelled beans, too. 'Betty' is a good variety where summers are short. In northern, short-season areas, plant "baby" limas, which mature earlier than large-seeded varieties.

SOYBEANS. Soybeans are newcomers to home gardens. Their seeds, shelled from the short, plump, fuzzy pods, are delicious when cooked as you would cook green-shelling or lima beans. The protein content of soybeans is outstanding. These beans grow best in the warm, humid climates of the South and Midwest and do poorly in most dry climates.

The soybean bush is about the same size as the lima bean bush. Plant seeds 1 inch deep, 4 to 6 inches apart in rows spaced 2½ feet apart. Harvest soybeans when the seeds have reached full size but the pods are still green. Pour boiling water over the pods to soften them before shelling.

FAVA BEANS. The fava bean, like the flageolet and 'Great Northern' beans, is delicious used either when the seeds are still green or when the seeds are dry. The fava, also called broad bean or horse bean, is the only bean to come from the Mediterranean area; all the other well-known beans are New World plants. Unlike other beans, this is a cool-season vegetable (actually a giant vetch). It grows 2 to 4½ feet tall and produces prodigious amounts of oversize pods, up to 18 inches long.

In cold-winter areas you can plant fava beans in early spring as soon as the soil can be worked. In mild-winter climates, plant in autumn for late winter or early spring crops. Plant seeds in rows spaced 1½ to 2½ feet apart; sow seeds 1 inch deep, 4 to 5 inches apart along the row. Beans mature in 120 to 150 days, depending on the temperature. You can harvest pods for shellie beans before that, though.

A cautionary note: Most people can eat fava beans with safety; a very few (principally of Mediterranean ancestry) have a genetic enzyme deficiency that can cause severe—even fatal—reactions to the beans and the pollen.

BEETS

Beet tops (greens) as well as roots are delicious. You can add the small, tender leaves of beet thinnings to salads and prepare the larger leaves as you would spinach.

You may be surprised to find that beets come in colors and shapes other than red and round. White and yellow varieties (such as 'Burpee's Golden', pictured above) are sweeter than red beets, and their tops are milder. Long red beets seem milder and more tender than most ordinary red kinds. Some varieties, such as 'Chioggia', even have red-and-white circular stripes inside. Look for seeds of these varieties in mail-order catalogs.

Because the beet root is a storage unit that expands to accommodate food sent down from the green top, the faster the food is produced, the greater the root growth. The best conditions for food production are warm, bright days and cool nights.

Beets like fertile soil without lumps or rocks. Both lumpy soil and heavy clay soil produce misshapen roots. For a summer crop, sow seeds in spring, 2 to 4 weeks before the last frost date (or as soon as the soil can be worked in mild-winter climates). Cover the beet seeds with a ¼-inch layer of sand, vermiculite, or screened compost to improve germination. Keep the soil moist; the seeds take 14 to 21 days to germinate, so you might want to mark the seed rows by sowing a few fast-sprouting radish seeds. They'll keep your interest while you water the bed and wait for the beets to sprout. Make repeated sowings every 3 weeks until hot weather (80°F/27°C) begins. After the beets sprout, consistent watering keeps the roots tender as they grow. If you let the plants dry out, they'll become hard and woody. You can sow seeds for an autumn crop in late summer and autumn until 6 to 8 weeks before the first frost date.

Harvest the first beets when they are 1 inch wide, and continue as the roots grow 2 to 3 inches wide. Larger ones are less tender. Harvest all beets before hard frosts occur.

Harvest the first greens as you thin the seedlings. Continue until the greens are too large or tough.

BEETS

TYPE OF VEGETABLE. Annual; cool season.

EDIBLE PARTS. Roots; leaves (greens).

BEST SOIL. Fertile, well drained, even textured, pH 6.0–6.8.

WHEN TO PLANT. For summer crop, sow seeds in spring. For autumn crop, sow seeds in late summer to autumn.

HOW TO PLANT. Sow seeds ½" deep, 1" apart, in rows spaced 1½'–2' apart; or broadcast seeds in wide beds; thin seedlings to 2"–3" apart when they are 3" tall.

YIELD. 8–10 pounds per 10' row.

CARE. Keep soil moist. Remove weeds while they're small.

PESTS AND DISEASES. Flea beetles, leafhoppers, leaf miners, nematodes, wireworms; damping off.

WHEN TO HARVEST. 45–65 days after sowing seeds.

HOW TO HARVEST. Pick outer leaves of tops sparingly before harvesting whole plant. Pull up roots carefully. Before harvesting entire crop, pull up one or two beets to see how wide they are.

HOW TO STORE. *BEETS:* Keep cool and damp for 3–10 weeks. To preserve, can, freeze, or dry. *BEET GREENS:* Refrigerate unwashed; use as soon as possible. To preserve, freeze.

Type of vegetable. Annual; cool season.

Edible parts. Flower buds; stems; leaves (broccoli raab).

Best soil. Fertile, pH 6.0–6.8.

When to plant. Cold-winter climates: For summer crop, set out young plants in spring. For autumn crop, set out plants or sow seeds in mid- and late summer. Mild-winter climates: For summer crop, set out young plants in late winter or early spring. For winter and spring crops, sow seeds or set out plants in late summer and autumn.

How to plant. Set plants 15"–24" apart in rows spaced 2'–3' apart. Sow seeds ¼"–½" deep, 1" apart, in rows spaced as above. Thin seedlings to 15"–24" apart.

Yield. 4–6 pounds per 10' row.

Care. Keep soil moist. Fertilize with high-nitrogen fertilizer. Weed regularly.

Pests and diseases. *See* Cabbage, page 27.

When to harvest. 50–100 days (most popular varieties mature in about 60 days) after setting out plants, before buds open.

How to harvest. Cut main stem 6"–8" below head; when side branches grow, harvest them too.

How to store. Refrigerate unwashed; use as soon as possible. To preserve, freeze or dry.

Broccoli

Broccoli is one of the easier-to-grow members of the cole family (which includes cabbage, cauliflower, and brussels sprouts). If you meet its basic requirements, it will grow without giving you grief and will bear over a long season.

Broccoli shares the cole family preference for a cool growing season. If the temperature goes too high, it will bolt—not out of your garden, but into premature flower stalks that bloom and go to seed before you can pick them.

In cool weather, broccoli first sends up a central stalk that bears a cluster of green or purple flower buds. This unopened central bouquet, along with 6 to 8 inches of stem, is what you harvest. The central cluster may reach 6 inches in diameter—but don't wait too long or the buds will open into yellow flowers, and you'll have broccoli of inferior quality. After you cut the main broccoli stem, side branches will lengthen and produce smaller but good-tasting clusters for you to harvest throughout the growing season.

Popular varieties of broccoli include 'Packman', 'Green Comet', 'Bonanza', and 'Premium Crop'. You might also check out 'Superblend', a mixture of hybrid varieties that provides the longest possible harvest season.

Broccoli raab is an Italian relative of broccoli with a slightly stronger flavor. It is harvested when the florets are just button size. Cut a long piece of the stalk, and cook it, small leaves and all. It is delicious sautéed in olive oil with fresh herbs.

'Romanesco' broccoli is an unusual plant that produces beautiful light green heads that resemble sea coral and have the flavor and texture of cauliflower.

Sprouting broccoli differs from regular heading broccoli in that it produces many small florets instead of one tight head. There are both purple and green types. (The purple turns green when cooked.)

Chinese broccoli *(gai lohn)* is discussed with other Asian vegetables on page 20.

'Purple Sprouting' broccoli

Type of vegetable. Annual; cool season.

Edible parts. Sprouts (swollen buds).

Best soil. Fertile, pH 5.5–6.8.

When to plant. Cold-winter climates: Set out plants or sow seeds in midsummer. Mild-winter climates: Set out plants or sow seeds in late summer and autumn.

How to plant. Set out plants 15"–24" apart in rows spaced 2'–3' apart. Sow seeds ¼"–½" deep, 1" apart, in rows spaced as above. Thin seedlings to 15"–24" apart.

Yield. 3–5 pounds per 10' row.

Care. Keep soil moist. Weed regularly.

Continues next page >

Brussels sprouts

Brussels sprouts are peculiar-looking plants that would be worth growing just for the novelty even if they weren't such good food. They look like miniature palm trees with lumps growing on their trunks. The lumps—sprouts—have the flavor of sweet tiny cabbages. Unlike most true palm trees, brussels sprouts prefer to grow during cool weather—their flavor is improved by light frosts, and they are often planted as an autumn crop.

Like the rest of the cole family, brussels sprouts are happiest growing in fertile, well-drained soil. Harvest begins when the big bottom leaves start to turn yellow. Each plant should produce 50 to 100 sprouts clustered closely around the main stalk. You harvest the sprouts from the bottom of the stem to

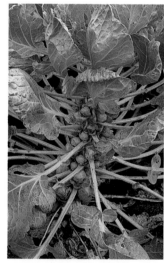

'Prince Marvel' brussels sprouts

the top, snapping off firm green sprouts that are slightly smaller than a golf ball. Remove any side leaves growing below the harvested sprouts. Continue harvesting upward along the stem as the sprouts mature, as long as the plants are productive.

'Jade Cross' and 'Valiant' are two excellent varieties of brussels sprouts.

CABBAGE

"Cole," the Old English word for cabbage, is also the general name for a family of vegetables that share a common ancestry, a preference for cool weather, and a susceptibility to certain pests and diseases. Cabbage's garden relatives include broccoli, brussels sprouts, cauliflower, collards, and kohlrabi.

The diverse appearance of cole family members comes from a remarkable family trait—the ability to thicken various plant parts. Kohlrabi has a thickened stem, broccoli has thickened immature flowering branches, and cabbage heads are rosettes of thickened leaves on a short stem.

Red cabbage

You'll find variety not only in shapes of cabbage heads—round, pointy, and flat—but also in colors and leaf textures. In addition to green cabbages, you can choose several red varieties, Savoy varieties with crinkly leaves, and Chinese white cabbage (discussed on page 20). There are miniature cabbages, such as 'Dwarf Morden' and 'Dynamo'; varieties that develop early to midseason, such as 'Early Jersey Wakefield', 'Earliana', 'Emerald Cross', 'Harvester Queen', 'Grenadier', 'King Cole', 'Salad Green' (for cole slaw), and 'Stonehead' (a firm head that develops well in hot weather); and late-maturing varieties ('Premium Flat Dutch' and 'Penn State Ballhead'). You can choose varieties that are good for storage, such as 'Danish Roundhead' and 'Winterkeeper', and varieties that are good for kraut, such as 'Surehead', 'Ultra Green', and 'Superslaw'.

For red cabbage, you can select such varieties as 'Red Head' (good winter variety) and 'Ruby Ball' (heat resistant).

Spectacular Savoy cabbage is not for the small-space garden (unless you want just one or two for show); the mature plant can be 2 feet in diameter. Full-grown, 8-inch-wide Savoy heads can weigh 4 to 4½ pounds. Savoy leaves are sweet, juicy, and somewhat milder than those of other cabbages, and form looser heads. A newcomer to many home gardens, Savoy developed in ancient times in southern Europe; today's more common solid-headed varieties were developed during the Middle Ages in northern Europe. For a late-maturing Savoy type, try 'Savoy Chieftain'. Other Savoy types include 'Savoy Ace' (develops early) and 'Savoy King'. Your Cooperative Extension Service can tell you which varieties do best in your area.

Ornamental flowering cabbage is another decorative—but edible—cabbage. The leafy 10-inch-wide heads look like giant peonies of deep blue green, marbled and edged with white, cream, rose, or purple. Flowering cabbage requires the same soil, care, and timing as conventional cabbage. The "flower" color is most dazzling after the first frost touches the plants. Plant them 15 to 18 inches apart in garden beds, or pot them singly or together. You can eat the loose-leafed heads cooked or raw, just like ordinary cabbage.

Listing continues >

PESTS AND DISEASES. *See* Cabbage, below.

WHEN TO HARVEST. 80–100 days after setting out plants.

HOW TO HARVEST. Snap sprouts from stem.

HOW TO STORE. Keep cool and damp for 3–4 weeks; to preserve, freeze or dry.

CABBAGE

TYPE OF VEGETABLE. Annual; cool season.

EDIBLE PARTS. Leafy heads.

BEST SOIL. Fertile, well drained, pH 6.0–6.8.

WHEN TO PLANT. COLD-WINTER CLIMATES: For summer crop, set out plants in spring (4–6 weeks before last frost date). For autumn crop, set out plants or sow seeds directly in garden in summer. MILD-WINTER CLIMATES: For spring and summer crops, set out plants in late winter and early spring. For winter and spring crops, set out plants or sow seeds in late summer and autumn.

HOW TO PLANT. Set out plants 15"–24" apart in rows spaced 2'–4' apart. Sow seeds ¼"–½" deep, 1" apart, in rows spaced as above. Thin seedlings to 15"–24" apart.

YIELD. 10–25 pounds per 10' row.

CARE. Keep soil moist. Fertilize. Weed and cultivate carefully.

PESTS AND DISEASES. Aphids, cabbage loopers, cabbage root maggots, cabbageworms, flea beetles, harlequin bugs; clubroot, damping off, downy mildew, fusarium wilt.

WHEN TO HARVEST. 50–100 days after setting out plants, before heads split or crack.

HOW TO HARVEST. Cut off heads.

HOW TO STORE. Keep cool and damp for 12–16 weeks. To preserve, freeze or dry.

'Sultan' cabbage

Cabbages of all varieties mature best during cool weather. You can grow spring and autumn crops where summers are hot. Sow seeds in flats 4 to 6 weeks before you intend to set out plants in garden; seeds take 7 to 14 days to germinate. Plant early-maturing varieties or hybrids in the spring; these mature from transplants in 7 to 8 weeks. Later-maturing varieties, such as the king-size kraut cabbage, need up to 12 weeks to mature from seeds and should be planted after midsummer for autumn harvest.

Cabbages need moist soil and at least one side dressing of high-nitrogen fertilizer as they grow. Weed carefully, and don't cultivate deeply; they have shallow roots.

A planting precaution: Cabbages and members of the cabbage family are susceptible to a wide variety of soilborne diseases. Rotate these crops. Don't plant any cole crop in the spot where a cole has been planted in the last 4 years.

TYPE OF VEGETABLE. Frost-sensitive perennial; warm season; dies in cold-winter climates.

EDIBLE PARTS. Leaf stalks.

BEST SOIL. Rich, well drained, pH 6.0.

WHEN TO PLANT. COLD-WINTER CLIMATES: Set out plants in spring. MILD-WINTER CLIMATES: Sow seeds in garden in spring.

HOW TO PLANT. Sow seeds ¼" deep in peat pots. Set out 3"-tall seedlings 20" apart in rows spaced 3' apart. Or sow three to five seeds in clusters ¼" deep, 20" apart, in rows spaced as above. Thin 3" seedlings to one per cluster.

YIELD. 1–2 pounds per plant.

CARE. Keep soil moist. Weed. Blanch.

PESTS AND DISEASES. Aphids.

WHEN TO HARVEST. 180 days after sowing.

HOW TO HARVEST. Cut leafy midribs into 3"–4" lengths.

HOW TO STORE. Refrigerate unwashed. To preserve, freeze.

CARDOON

Though by the time it reaches the kitchen, tender and blanched, it will remind you of celery, cardoon is actually a close cousin of the artichoke, which it resembles in leaf and flower form. Both are native perennials of southern Europe.

We eat the flower buds of artichoke plants; cardoon, though, is grown for its thick, fleshy leaf stalk. Cut in chunks and then steamed like asparagus, these stalks make an unusual and tasty delicacy. They can also be parboiled or fried.

Frost sensitive and slow to mature, cardoon needs a long, mild growing season. Where winters are cold and the summer growing season is short, start seeds indoors in spring; set out plants when the danger of frost is past. Where the frost-free growing season is 180 days or more, sow seeds directly in the garden in spring.

Give cardoon plants plenty of elbow room: they may reach 4 feet tall and 6 feet wide. In mild-winter climates, they can become weeds.

To ensure mild flavor, 4 or 5 weeks before the expected harvest date you should wrap the leaf stalks to blanch them. Tie the stalks together with string. Then encase them with either heavy paper or a sheath of straw bound with string. Avoid covering the leaf tips.

CARROTS

Growing carrots can be child's play—and turn carrot-hating children into carrot lovers—once the ground is thoroughly prepared. Plan to spend time refining the soil, unless your garden is blessed with fine, sandy loam without lumps, rocks, rusty nails, skate keys, or other archaeological treasures. You see, carrots are very sensitive; they grow straight until they hit the least obstruction, then they make a sharp turn, or fork, or otherwise grow misshapen. They also grow crooked if you put fresh manure in the soil. Time invested in breaking up clods and removing debris will increase your yield of perfectly formed carrots.

There are several ways to grow carrots in spite of problem soil. One way is to select a short variety of carrot; they tend to be sweeter, anyway. You can find baby-size carrots in heart, finger, and even golf ball shapes.

Another way around difficult soil is to soften it by soaking it. Then, when the soil has dried enough to work, dig a V-shaped planting trench 2 to 3 inches wide at the top and 6 to 8 inches deep for each row. Fill the trench with fine planting soil, ideally a combination of your best garden soil sifted with well-rotted (fine-textured) compost. The trench lets the roots expand without twisting or forking.

Yet another way to bypass poor soil is to grow carrots in containers, where you have complete control over soil quality. A good mix for container-grown carrots is two parts sand, two parts well-rotted (fine-textured) compost, and one part garden soil—lump-free, of course. Or use commercial potting soil.

Because carrots take 7 to 21 days to germinate, some soils crust over before the tiny seedlings can emerge. One trick to prevent this is to mix carrot seeds with radish seeds when planting. The quick-germinating radishes pop up and mark your planting, break up the soil crust, and help the carrots to come along later. Enjoy fresh radishes until the carrots are large enough to pull.

Once you've sown the tiny seeds as thinly as possible and covered them with ¼ to ½ inch of fine soil, keep them moist for the 2- to 3-week germination period. During hot weather, covering your bed of carrots with moist burlap or a floating row cover will help keep seeds moist until they sprout. Remove the burlap or cover once seedlings emerge. If you live in a very cool climate, try growing carrots in a heat-absorbing metal or wooden container.

You can use one watering trick to encourage long, slender carrots. Sow the seeds in fine, rich soil, and keep the seeds evenly moist while they germinate. When the little plants reach about 1 inch tall, withhold water until they start to wilt. This forces the roots to grow deeper. Then resume normal watering. You perform this trick only once. After that, consistent watering is important throughout the growing season. If carrots dry out while growing, their flesh hardens; then, when water is restored, their roots tend to split.

Harvesting actually starts with thinning. Finger-long carrots thinned from the garden taste wonderful. Try chopping them up, tops and all, to add to tossed salads for a fresh surprise. Keep thinning until the remaining carrots are about 2 inches apart; then wait until they reach your favorite eating size. Before harvesting the entire crop, pull up one or two roots to see how large they are.

In very cold winter climates, harvest all your carrots before hard frosts occur; if they are left in the ground, they'll become hard and woody. Where winters are not severely cold, you *can* leave carrots in the ground for storage; after the first hard frost, cover carrots, tops and all, with 6 to 8 inches of shredded leaves. Where summers are hot, harvest spring-planted carrots before the hottest weather arrives.

There are well over 80 varieties of carrots. Many are hybrid variations on such carrot standards as 'Chantenay', 'Danvers', 'Nantes', 'Imperator', and 'Spartan'.

For long-rooted carrots (up to 8 inches), try 'Gold Pak', 'King Midas', 'Caroline', or 'Imperator'. Medium-rooted ones (6 to 7 inches) include 'Nantes Coreless', 'Danvers Half-long', and 'Spartan Bonus'. Among the short-rooted carrots (5 inches or less) are 'Imperial Chantenay', 'Red Core Chantenay', 'Short 'n' Sweet', 'Tiny Sweet', 'Little Finger', 'Thumbelina', and golf-ball-shaped 'Gold Nugget' and 'Planet'. 'Belgium White' is a mild-flavored, white-rooted heirloom variety for using in stews.

TYPE OF VEGETABLE. Annual; cool season.

EDIBLE PARTS. Roots.

BEST SOIL. Fertile, sandy loam (no fresh manure), pH 5.5–6.8.

WHEN TO PLANT. COLD-WINTER CLIMATES: For summer crop, sow seeds in early spring. For autumn crop, sow seeds in late summer. MILD-WINTER CLIMATES: For summer crop, sow seeds in spring. For autumn, winter, and spring crops, sow seeds 30–80 days before you intend to harvest.

HOW TO PLANT. Sow seeds ¼"–½" deep, ½" apart, in rows spaced 1'–2½' apart; or broadcast seeds in wide beds. Thin 1" seedlings to 2" apart in rows or to about 4" apart in wide beds.

YIELD. 7–10 pounds per 10' row.

CARE. Keep soil moist. Remove weeds while small.

PESTS AND DISEASES. Aphids, leafhoppers, nematodes; damping off.

WHEN TO HARVEST. For baby carrots, 30–40 days after sowing seeds; for mature carrots, 50–80 days after sowing seeds.

HOW TO HARVEST. Carefully pull up or dig with a garden fork.

HOW TO STORE. Keep cool and damp for 16–20 weeks. To preserve, can, freeze, or dry.

ABOVE: 'Dragon Purple' carrots
TOP RIGHT: 'Orange Rocket' carrots

TYPE OF VEGETABLE. Annual; cool season.

EDIBLE PARTS. Heads (flower buds).

BEST SOIL. Fertile, well drained, pH 6.0–6.8.

WHEN TO PLANT. COLD-WINTER CLIMATES: Set out plants or sow seeds in early spring or mid-summer. MILD-WINTER CLIMATES: Set out plants or sow seeds in late summer or late winter to early spring. Sow seeds in flats 4–6 weeks before you intend to set out plants.

HOW TO PLANT. Set out plants 15"–24" apart in rows spaced 2'–3' apart. Sow seeds ½" deep, 1" apart, in rows spaced as above. Thin seedlings to 15"–24" apart.

YIELD. 8–10 pounds per 10' row.

CARE. Keep soil moist. Weed. Blanch.

PESTS AND DISEASES. See Cabbage, page 27.

WHEN TO HARVEST. 55–100 days after setting out plants, before buds open.

HOW TO HARVEST. Cut off heads.

HOW TO STORE. Keep cool and damp for 2–3 weeks. To preserve, freeze or dry.

CAULIFLOWER

According to Mark Twain, a cauliflower is just a cabbage that has gone to college. A pure white, solid head of cauliflower, such as you see in the produce section of the market, has been "educated" in ideal cole-family conditions: cool, humid growing season and fertile, well-drained soil that's watered often to keep it moist. If you live where summers are hot and dry, set out transplants early enough so that you can harvest well before or well after the midsummer heat. Or plant in late summer or fall, so heads mature in cool weather.

Snowy white, solid, high-quality cauliflower has also gone through a process called blanching. You tie the large outer leaves over the head when it's about 2 inches wide. Clothespins or elastic bands are good for this purpose. Blanching keeps the sun from damaging the tender head, causing discoloration and an "off" flavor.

Check the heads every 3 to 4 days; during hot weather they mature quickly.

If blanching sounds like too much trouble, you might try growing varieties that are self-blanching. On these, the outer leaves naturally grow up and over the heads and cover them. Self-blanching varieties include 'Snowball Self Blanching', 'Self Blanche', 'Montano', 'Purple Head', and 'Violet Queen'. 'Purple Head' and 'Violet Queen', as the names indicate, are a deep purple, which fades to green when cooked; these varieties taste somewhat like broccoli, as does 'Chartreuse', a green variety.

'Snow King' and 'Snow Crown' are good standard varieties of cauliflower.

TYPE OF VEGETABLE. Annual; cool season.

EDIBLE PARTS. Stalks (celery); roots (celeriac).

BEST SOIL. Rich, well-drained, sandy loam, pH 6.0–6.8.

WHEN TO PLANT. COLD-WINTER CLIMATES: Set out plants in spring. MILD-WINTER CLIMATES: Set out plants in autumn, winter, and early spring.

HOW TO PLANT. Set out plants 6"–10" apart in rows spaced 2' apart.

YIELD. 12–20 plants per 10' row.

CARE. Keep soil moist. Apply fertilizer monthly. Blanch celery stalks.

PESTS AND DISEASES. Aphids, cabbage loopers, leafhoppers, nematodes; damping off.

WHEN TO HARVEST. CELERY: 100–130 days after planting. CELERIAC: 120 days after planting.

HOW TO HARVEST. CELERY: Use sharp knife to cut stalks or entire plant. CELERIAC: Dig up roots.

HOW TO STORE. Keep cool and damp for 8–16 weeks. To preserve, can, freeze, or dry.

Celery

CELERY AND CELERIAC

Gardeners living where summers stay cool can grow celery and celeriac to perfection. These two relatives need a long (4-month), cool growing season.

Celery requires human help to turn into mild-tasting, crunchy, pale green stalks. But you don't have to fuss with celeriac's stalks—it's grown for its delicious knobby root.

To grow mild-tasting celery, you must use a blanching technique. For example, 3 to 4 weeks before you're going to harvest celery, tie the tops of the stalks together and mound garden soil along the stalks to shut out sunlight. When you're ready to harvest, pull away the soil and cut off the entire celery plant just below the base, where all the stalks come together. Or cut individual stems where they meet the base of the plant.

Or you can place 3-pound coffee cans with both ends removed over the seedlings when you plant them, or make tarpaper cylinders, or sleeves, to slip over the plants. The stalks will grow up inside the can or sleeve in a tight clump.

There are some self-blanching varieties of celery, such as 'Lathom Blanching' and 'Golden Self-blanching', but most people prefer regular varieties, such as 'Greensleeves', 'Tendercrisp', 'Ventura', or 'Tall Utah'.

Harvest celeriac by digging up the roots when they are at least 2 inches wide. Peel and eat cooked or raw.

Celeriac

CHAYOTE

Chayote, also called mirliton, vegetable pear, or mango squash, looks like a puckered pear. It has a single flat seed and tastes like a mild squash. A Central American native, chayote prefers long, warm, sunny days and bears fruit in the autumn. Popular in Louisiana and Florida, it can grow well—even rampantly—in the mild-winter regions along the Gulf Coast and in California.

Since even a single vine climbs to 50 feet with clinging tendrils, the lush plant needs sturdy supports. In early autumn and through winter, in very mild regions, it will overwhelm you with 50 to 150 fruits, which you can bake, boil, or sauté, seed and all. You can also eat the tubers, which form in the second year. They have a crisp, refreshing texture in salads.

To produce a vine, you plant the entire fruit, fat end down, at a slant with the narrow end of the fruit slightly above ground. Plant two to ensure pollination. Frost kills the plant to the ground, but where there are only occasional light frosts, chayote is a perennial.

TYPE OF VEGETABLE. Frost-sensitive perennial; warm season.

EDIBLE PARTS. Fruits; seeds; tubers.

BEST SOIL. Rich, well drained.

WHEN TO PLANT. In spring when danger of frost has passed.

HOW TO PLANT. Set whole fruit in ground. If seed has sprouted, cut sprout back to 2". Set up sturdy trellis at planting time.

YIELD. 50–150 fruits per vine.

CARE. Keep soil moist. Apply enough fertilizer to keep growth vigorous.

PESTS AND DISEASES. *See* Squash, page 64.

WHEN TO HARVEST. In autumn, 25–30 days after flowers are pollinated.

HOW TO HARVEST. Cut ripe fruits from vine. Dig tubers from 2-year-old plants.

HOW TO STORE. Keep in cool (50°F/10°C), dark, airy place for 4 weeks; or refrigerate in plastic bag for 1 week.

CHICORY AND RADICCHIO

Different chicories are grown by gardeners for three purposes: for salad greens (small-rooted varieties), for roots to make a coffee substitute (large-rooted varieties), and for Belgian or French endive ('Witloof').

To create the headlike clusters of leaves called Belgian or French endive, 'Witloof' chicory is grown from seed sown in spring or early summer to mature by autumn. In the following winter, after the greens have been trimmed to an inch of stem, the roots are dug up, buried diagonally in moist sand, and set in a dark, cool room. There, new growth is forced, its leaves pale and butter-tender.

Radicchio is the name given to a number of red-leafed chicories grown for salads. 'Red Verona' and 'Rossana' are

Salad green chicory

good varieties. They form lettuce-like heads that develop a deep rosy red as the weather grows cold in autumn or winter. Their bitterness lessens somewhat as the color develops. Radicchio is best planted in summer to mature in autumn, but some varieties, such as 'Giulio', are more heat-resistant and can be planted in spring.

Sow the seeds of salad varieties in a sunny site. The immature greens, like those of lettuce or endive, taste delicious. To harvest, carefully cut off the outer leaves.

To grow roots for the coffee substitute, sow seeds as for salad greens. Harvest roots by digging them up when they're 5 to 7 inches long and 1 to 1¾ inches wide at the top.

Radicchio

TYPE OF VEGETABLE. Perennial; cool season.

EDIBLE PARTS. Leaves (salad and endive varieties); roots (coffee-substitute varieties).

BEST SOIL. Fertile, well drained, pH 5.0–6.8.

WHEN TO PLANT. Sow seeds in spring (6–8 weeks after last frost date) or early summer.

HOW TO PLANT. Sow seeds ¼"–½" deep, 2"–3" apart, in rows spaced 18" apart; thin seedlings to 6"–12" apart.

CARE. Keep soil moist. Weed regularly.

PESTS AND DISEASES. Aphids.

WHEN TO HARVEST. For leaves, 65 days after sowing seeds. For roots, about 110 days after sowing.

HOW TO HARVEST. Cut off outer leaves. Dig up roots. Force 'Witloof' roots.

HOW TO STORE. *SALAD GREENS AND 'WITLOOF':* Refrigerate, wrapped in dry paper towel placed in plastic bag, for 2–3 days. *ROOTS:* Keep cool and damp for 16–20 weeks.

COLLARDS

Grown throughout the country for their succulent green leaves, lanky, open-growing collards are headless cabbage relatives. They are most popular in the South, where they're planted in the summer for autumn and winter harvest. (The mature plants are frost hardy and yield sweeter leaves after light frosts.)

Collards also tolerate hot weather and are among the few greens that do well in gardens all summer long. Set out transplants in early spring for a spring-into-summer crop.

Collards are thirsty, hungry vegetables. Keep the stems and leaves tender and green by watering and fertilizing the plants frequently. A well-nourished plant can grow to 3 feet tall and yield many juicy, delicious leaves.

You can eat the thinnings—the young plants that you pull up to allow others more room to grow. Later, you can harvest the lower leaves from plants as they become large enough to eat.

CORN

Even if your garden space is limited, you may be tempted to plant corn—at the sacrifice of a square of lawn or a flower garden—when you read about all the wonderful varieties of sweet corn available to home gardeners.

It's neither pride nor your imagination that makes your homegrown corn taste better than store-bought ears. Corn plucked from the stalk at its prime and hustled into a pot of boiling water is indeed sweeter than corn bought at the store. The reason? The sugar within the kernels has not yet turned into starch.

THE BASIC VARIETIES

Corn varieties are so numerous that you can find at least one to fit the requirements of your garden wherever you live.

If you're in a long-growing-season area, you can plant early, midseason, and late-maturing crops for a whole summer of sweet corn. Give a late crop time to ripen before the first frost date in autumn. In Florida, in the mildest areas, you can also sow in autumn and winter. In short-growing-season areas, you'll need early-maturing or extra-early kinds—though there is still ample choice.

Here are some tried-and-true varieties. *Early-maturing:* 'Early Sunglow' (grows well in cool weather; plants only 4½ feet tall), 'Golden Beauty' (plants grow to 5½ feet), 'Morning Sun', 'Polar Vee', and 'Seneca 60'. *Midseason-maturing:* 'Butter and Sugar' (bicolored), 'FM Cross', 'Golden Cross Bantam', 'Golden Jubilee', and 'Honey and Cream' (bicolored). *Late-maturing:* 'Country Gentleman' (shoe-peg white kernels; good for canning and freezing), 'Iochief' (large ears; wind-resistant stalks), 'Silver Queen' (white kernels), and 'Stylepak' (good for canning and freezing).

As a rule, early varieties produce smaller and tougher ears, and later varieties have larger, longer ears with better flavor. Check with your Cooperative Extension Service for varieties adapted especially for your area.

'Seneca Horizon' corn

You can wax nostalgic and grow an old-time (19th-century) favorite such as 'Country Gentleman', a white corn with an irregular pattern of shoe-peg kernels.

Traditional, too, is multicolored Indian corn. Those handsome dried ears of bronze and red Indian corn that decorate your front door and table at Thanksgiving can be grown in your backyard garden.

Another possibility to consider is popcorn—either the common, yellow-kerneled type or dark red, small-eared 'Strawberry Popcorn' (low yield, but decorative).

HIGH-SUGAR CORN

The latest developments in hybrid corn are the high-sugar varieties. Not only are they remarkably higher in sugar content than regular corn, but they also hold their sweetness longer—with these varieties you can stroll rather than run from corn patch to pot of boiling water.

You'll find three kinds of high-sugar corn: the supersweets (including 'Early Xtra-Sweet', 'Illini Xtra-Sweet', 'Honey 'N Pearl', 'How Sweet It Is', and 'Florida Stay-Sweet'), which are twice as sweet as standard corn and are often designated by (Sh$_2$) after the variety name; the sugar-enhanced hybrids, which are up to 25 percent sweeter than standard corn (look for 'Sugarloaf', 'Breeder's Choice', and 'Honeycomb') and usually identified by (se) after the variety name; and Everlasting Heritage hybrids (designated "EH" in seed catalogs).

Not only do the Everlasting Heritage hybrids have a high sugar content that stays sweeter longer, but also these varieties are not open to cross-pollination. You can plant them near other kinds of sweet corn without fear of harvesting an ear with sweet kernels, Indian corn kernels, and popcorn kernels within biting distance of each other. You should space blocks of other high-sugar corn varieties at least 250 feet apart, or you need to time your planting so maturity dates are at least 10 days apart, to prevent cross-pollination. You'll see Everlasting Heritage hybrids 'Mainliner EH', 'Kandy Korn EH' (its husks are marked with burgundy red), and 'Golden Sweet EH' listed in many seed catalogs.

THE ESSENTIALS FOR GROWING CORN

Whichever kind of corn you choose, you'll have the most success if you satisfy corn's three main requirements—ample space, warm weather, and generous amounts of fertilizer and water.

ADEQUATE SPACE. Unless you are growing just a few token stalks, you'll need a large area to plant enough corn to feed your hungry hordes—those high-as-an-elephant's-eye stalks produce only one or two ears each, maybe three if you're lucky. Some midget varieties are promoted as space savers and novelties, but they don't produce as heavily as full-size varieties.

The space you select for growing corn has to be in a block; you can't string a row of corn along the fence and expect the ears to develop. Since corn pollen from the tassels of one stalk is carried by the wind to the silks of a neighboring stalk, the pollen from a single row of corn probably would not pollinate the ears completely. Corn planted in adjacent rows has the best chance of being pollinated, so be sure to plant at least three or four rows.

Here are three other factors to keep in mind when choosing a site for corn. First, corn needs at least 8 hours of direct sunlight a day. Second, corn is tall and will cast shade over other plants, so it's best to plant it in the northern end of your garden plot. Third, if you want to grow more than one variety, you must make sure they can't cross-pollinate. You can do this by planting different varieties far enough apart so the wind will

'Fiesta' Indian corn

TYPE OF VEGETABLE. Annual; warm season.

EDIBLE PARTS. Seeds on ears.

BEST SOIL. Rich, well drained, pH 5.8–6.8.

WHEN TO PLANT. In spring, when danger of frost has passed and soil temperature is at least 50°F/10°C. Make successive sowings.

HOW TO PLANT. Sow seeds 1"–2" deep, 4"–6" apart, in rows spaced 2½'–3' apart; thin seedlings to 12"–18" apart. Sow at least three rows. Or plant in hills (clusters of seeds) spaced 3' apart; sow seeds 1"–2" deep, five or six seeds per hill; thin seedlings to three plants per hill.

YIELD. Ten to twelve ears per 10' row.

CARE. Keep soil moist. Apply high-nitrogen fertilizer when plants are 12"–15" tall and again when they are 30" tall.

PESTS AND DISEASES. Aphids, armyworms, corn borers, corn earworms, flea beetles; damping off.

WHEN TO HARVEST. 60–100 days after sowing seeds, depending on variety, usually about 20 days after silks appear.

HOW TO HARVEST. Twist ripe ears off stalks.

HOW TO STORE. Refrigerate unwashed; use as soon as possible. To preserve, can, freeze, or dry.

GIVE CORN ELBOW ROOM

Corn takes more room to grow than most vegetables. Common mistakes made by many gardeners are to cram too many plants into a small area and not to thin the seedlings properly. Unfortunately, overcrowding often results in fewer and poorer quality ears. Give the plants the room they need, even if you end up with fewer plants. Thin seedlings to 12 to 18 inches apart. And remember to plant at least three rows (more if possible) to encourage pollination.

not carry pollen from one kind to another, or by planting varieties that mature at different times, or by planting in succession so the different kinds don't mature at the same time. If your garden is small, you can avoid unwanted cross-pollination by planting only one variety.

TEMPERATURE. The proper soil and air temperature are important. Soil temperature should warm to at least 50°F/10°C before you sow seeds. Planting early in cold soil won't give you a head start. In fact, you'll probably lose some seeds to decay and possibly some seedlings to frost. The warmer the weather, the faster corn grows: corn seeds planted a week apart in May may produce ripe ears on the same day in August. (In hot areas of the Southwest, though, plant corn as early as possible to harvest by June.)

ABOVE: 'Striped Quadricolor' ornamental corn
TOP LEFT: Rows of 'Walters' and 'Cosmos' corn

WATER. Corn needs ample water; it won't produce if it's thirsty. Before you plant, make sure the ground is thoroughly moist but not so wet that you can squeeze water out of it. If the soil is moist enough when you plant seeds, you shouldn't have to water until they have sprouted and grown several inches. Seeds tend to rot if the soil is too wet. But once they are up, don't let the seedlings wilt.

In dry-summer climates, it's best to plan ahead for heavy watering by building irrigation ditches at planting time. Start by using strings to line up straight rows, about 2½ to 3 feet apart. In moist spaded or tilled soil, scoop out trenches, and pile the excavated soil along the rim of each trench. Plant the seeds 1 to 2 inches deep and 4 to 6 inches apart in this shoulder of excavated soil.

Where summers are rainy or cool, you may have to water only once or twice during the season, if at all. In such climates you can water by sprinkling.

Don't let the soil dry out once the ears start to form silks. When silks turn brown, pull back the outer husk on an ear or two. Ripe kernels will squirt milky-white juice when pinched. If possible, harvest just before you are ready to cook.

'Silver Bullet' corn

FERTILIZER. Corn needs a considerable amount of fertilizer. Mixing in compost, manure, or fertilizer before planting may be enough, but generally you should fertilize corn twice during the growing season. Apply a high-nitrogen fertilizer when plants are 12 to 15 inches tall and again when they are about 24 to 30 inches tall.

For vigorous growth, don't pull off the suckers (short side shoots) that grow from the main stalk.

Harvesting at the right time can make the difference between sweet, tender corn and tough, starchy corn. Read the directions on when to harvest in the sidebar list. Unless you've planted a variety that is extra sweet, you'll get the best flavor from ripe corn if you can begin cooking it within 1 to 2 minutes after harvesting.

CRESS

Watercress and garden cress have two things in common: a spicy, tingling flavor and their last names. Otherwise, these two salad garnishes are very different.

Watercress, a perennial, needs soaking wet soil. The best place to grow it is along the bank of an unpolluted stream. Practically speaking, you can grow watercress in a pot of sandy soil set in a basin of water. (Change the water weekly to keep it fresh.) Some gardeners also grow watercress in a coldframe or trench that's kept wet under a dripping hose or spigot.

Watercress

Garden cress

Start watercress from seeds. Sow the tiny seeds thickly, then thin out and transplant the seedlings when they are a few inches tall. You can also root sprigs of watercress in a glass of water.

Annual garden cress—also called curly cress and pepper grass—is a sprinter. You can sow its seeds indoors and harvest a crop in 10 to 14 days, or make repeated sowings outdoors to harvest every 2 to 3 weeks.

TYPE OF VEGETABLE. Perennial (watercress); annual (garden cress); cool season.

EDIBLE PARTS. Leaves; stems.

BEST SOIL. Rich, sandy loam pH 6.0–6.8.

WHEN TO PLANT. In spring.

HOW TO PLANT. *WATERCRESS:* Broadcast seeds in wide bands, and cover with ¼" of soil; thin seedlings to 2"–4" apart. *GARDEN CRESS:* Sow seeds ¼" deep, 1"–2" apart, in rows spaced 1½' apart; thin seedlings to 6"–8" apart.

CARE. Keep soil moist. Weed regularly.

PESTS AND DISEASES. Cabbage maggots, flea beetles, harlequin bugs, snails.

WHEN TO HARVEST. *WATERCRESS:* 50 days after sowing seeds. *GARDEN CRESS:* 10–14 days after sowing seeds.

HOW TO HARVEST. Cut leaves as needed.

HOW TO STORE. Stand stems in container of cold water and cover tops with plastic bag; use as soon as possible.

CUCUMBERS

Cucumbers are rich in variety. There are cukes for slicing and cukes for pickling; short, warty cukes and long, smooth cukes; dark green cukes and yellow cukes; and these are just some examples.

All cucumbers love warm weather. The seeds need warm soil to sprout (for information about using hotcaps or other devices for an early start, see pages 124–125). Warm weather also helps pollinating insects. (But temperatures above 100°F/38°C can cause bitterness or stop cucumber production.)

Cucumbers are extremely thirsty. They need long, deep drinks of water to grow fruit that is not bitter. Furrow or drip irrigation works best (see pages 104–105); sprinkling is not recommended, because it encourages mildew.

The vines of most varieties will spread more than 6 feet before the plants stop bearing. You can curb their rambling nature by training vines up trellises or confining them in containers. Or plant dwarf and compact varieties that take less space.

Cucumbers can be divided into three categories: the 8- to 15-inch slicers, the 2- to 6-inch picklers, and a mixed group of novel cucumbers. All types will produce prolifically given rich soil, warm weather, sunshine, plenty of water—and enough room to grow. Greenhouse varieties, however, must be grown in greenhouses.

Lemon cucumbers

Listing continues >

TWO COMMON MISTAKES WITH CUCUMBERS

Letting plants dry out and not picking often enough are two of the most common mistakes gardeners make when growing cucumbers.

When plants dry out, the fruits become bitter. Be sure to water regularly, mulch heavily, and examine the top few inches of soil often with your fingers to check moisture levels.

If cucumbers go unpicked, they become seedy, and the plant stops producing new fruit. For a consistent harvest of quality cucumbers, pick every few days, even if you have to give the harvest to your neighbors.

TYPE OF VEGETABLE. Annual; warm season.

EDIBLE PARTS. Fruits.

BEST SOIL. Rich, well drained, pH 5.5–6.8.

WHEN TO PLANT. For summer crop, sow seeds in spring, after last frost date, when soil temperature has warmed to at least 60°F/16°C.

HOW TO PLANT. Sow groups of four to six seeds 1" deep, 4'–6' apart in every direction; thin seedlings to two to three per hill. Or sow two to three seeds 1" deep, in clusters 8"–12" apart, in rows spaced 3'–6' apart; thin seedlings to one per cluster.

YIELD. 8–10 pounds per 10' row.

CARE. Keep soil moist; avoid overhead watering. Weed regularly. Tie vines on trellis to save space.

PESTS AND DISEASES. Aphids, cucumber beetles, flea beetles, mites, squash bugs, squash vine borers; bacterial wilt, downy mildew, powdery mildew.

WHEN TO HARVEST. 50–100 days after planting. Slicing cucumbers should be 6"–8" long (except for extra-long varieties). Pickling cucumbers should be useful size, generally more than 2" long. Harvest three or four times a week to allow new fruit to set.

HOW TO HARVEST. Cut from vine when fruits are usable size.

HOW TO STORE. Refrigerate in plastic bag for 1–2 weeks. To preserve, can.

STANDARD AND HYBRID TYPES. Among slicers and picklers, you'll find hybrid and standard varieties. Hybrids result from cross-pollinating flowers by hand. Hybrids are usually more robust and disease-resistant than older, naturally pollinated standard varieties.

Standards and many hybrids bear male and female flowers on the same vine. Vines first produce male flowers; female ones appear a little later. They are identifiable by a swollen ovary, like a miniature cucumber, just behind the flower. In the garden, insects are the main carriers of pollen from male to female flowers. Fruits won't set without pollination, so avoid insecticides that harm bees.

Some hybrids bear mostly female flowers and are called "gynoecious hybrids." Since every flower on a gynoecious hybrid vine has the potential to become a cucumber, the vine is far more productive. A few seeds (often color coded) of a variety that produces male flowers for pollination are included in seed packages of gynoecious varieties, but most of the seeds produce gynoecious plants.

'Bush Baby' pickling cucumber

SLICING CUCUMBERS. Slicing cucumbers, the kinds used for cool summer salads, are usually long, dark green, and fairly tough skinned. The tough skin makes mature slicing cucumbers undesirable for pickling, but you can pickle young slicing cukes. Harvest your slicing cucumbers before they start to turn yellow. The longer you leave them on the plant, the bigger the seeds will be. Keep the fruit picked to encourage more cucumbers to form. Excellent slicers include the hybrids 'Fanfare', 'Market More 76', 'Sweet Success', and 'Straight Eight'.

PICKLING CUCUMBERS. Pickling varieties bear short, blocky fruits with tender skin. For making sweet pickles, harvest the cucumbers when they are 2 to 3 inches long; for dills, harvest when they are 5 to 6 inches long. The pickling varieties tend to be more prolific plants than the slicing kinds—pick often so the vines will continue producing. Good choices among pickling cucumbers include 'Calypso', 'Saladin', and 'Pioneer'.

NOVELTY CUCUMBERS. The lemon cucumber leads the novelty cucumbers in popularity. Its tennis-ball-size fruit turns bright yellow and mild flavored when ripe.

The Armenian cucumber—really a long, skinny melon—is another exotic variety. Once Armenian cukes reach 18 to 20 inches, the sooner you harvest them the better they taste; left alone, the fruit will eventually grow to 30 inches.

Asian cucumbers have bumpy skins and are excellent slicers, reaching up to 2 feet long.

Greenhouse owners can take advantage of a special group of cucumbers bred just for greenhouse growing. Self-pollinating, they must be grown indoors to avoid being pollinated by stray pollen from other cucumber varieties.

Bush cucumbers are excellent choices for limited space or container gardens. Plants generally grow 3 to 4 feet wide (some are larger) and are very productive. Varieties include picklers 'Bush Baby' and 'Bush Pickle' and slicers 'Bush Champion', 'Fanfare', and 'Salad Bush'.

Dual-purpose cucumbers make picklers when small, slicers when large. Try 'Home Pickles' or 'Burpee Pickler'.

For people who have trouble digesting cucumbers, burpless varieties are worth trying: 'Sweet Success', 'Green Knight', and 'Orient Express'.

'Salad Bush' cucumber

'Bush Champion' cucumber

EGGPLANT

Purple, plump, and polished to an inky sheen, eggplants are as beautiful to behold in the garden as to taste in a cheese-rich moussaka.

Like its cousins, tomato and pepper, eggplant is an annual fruit commonly called a vegetable. Though the large, oval, purple variety is most familiar, yellow, green, and white varieties are available, as well as varieties with small fruits in rounded or cylindrical shapes.

Eggplant requires a growing season of 60 to 95 warm days and nights (with minimum night temperatures of 65°F/18°C) to produce its crop. Set out young plants in a sunny location in rich, well-drained soil. Where summers are short, choose fast-maturing varieties such as 'Dusky' and 'Mini Finger', and plant them in a warm, sheltered spot.

Various sizes, shapes, and colors of eggplant

On large varieties, thin the fruits to one per each main branch—three to six per plant. With small-fruited kinds, thinning isn't necessary. Harvest when the fruits are glossy, fully colored, firm, and about two-thirds their maximum size; as the fruits mature, they lose their sheen, grow soft and bitter, and develop larger and coarser seeds. Use clippers or a knife to pick eggplants individually as they ripen.

TYPE OF VEGETABLE. Annual; warm season.

EDIBLE PARTS. Fruits.

BEST SOIL. Fertile, pH 5.5–6.8.

WHEN TO PLANT. Set out plants in spring when day temperatures reach 70°F/21°C. Start seeds in flats 6–8 weeks before you set out plants.

HOW TO PLANT. Sow seeds ¼"–½" deep in flats. Set out plants 2'–2½' apart in rows 3' apart.

YIELD. 10–20 pounds per 10' row.

CARE. Keep soil moist. Apply complete fertilizer regularly. Weed regularly.

PESTS AND DISEASES. Aphids, Colorado potato beetles, flea beetles, whiteflies; verticillium wilt.

WHEN TO HARVEST. 60–95 days after setting out plants.

HOW TO HARVEST. Clip or cut from stems.

HOW TO STORE. Refrigerate unwashed; use as soon as possible. To preserve, freeze or dry.

ENDIVE

Endive is a leafy vegetable with lacy or ruffled foliage. Batavian endive, or escarole, is a broad-leafed version with a creamy white center. Expensive and elegant Belgian or French endive is really a blanched heart of chicory—see "Chicory," page 31. Whatever you call them, both Batavian endive and curly-leafed endive are worthy salad greens.

Sow the tiny endive seeds in a sunny spot from spring into summer, until temperatures reach 75°F/24°C in cold-winter climates. In mild-winter climates, you can sow whenever temperatures are at least 45°F/7°C. Start cutting off outer leaves to eat while the plants are still young.

Though endive tolerates higher temperatures than lettuce does, hot weather tends to make it bitter in taste. To tone down the strong flavor, it's a common practice to blanch the inner leaves. Draw up the outer leaves, and tie them together loosely to shield the interior of the plant. Water carefully to avoid wetting the leaves, or the insides may rot. The blanching process should be complete in 2 to 3 weeks.

TYPE OF VEGETABLE. Annual; cool season.

EDIBLE PARTS. Leaves.

BEST SOIL. Rich, pH 5.0–6.8.

WHEN TO PLANT. COLD-WINTER CLIMATES: Sow seeds in spring (3–4 weeks before last frost date). MILD-WINTER CLIMATES: Sow seeds year-round.

HOW TO PLANT. Sow seeds ¼" deep, 1"–2" apart, in rows 2'–3' apart; thin seedlings to 6"–12" apart.

YIELD. 3–6 pounds per 10' row.

PESTS AND DISEASES. Aphids, armyworms, flea beetles, leafhoppers, slugs, snails; downy mildew.

WHEN TO HARVEST. 85–100 days after sowing.

HOW TO HARVEST. Cut outer leaves from young plants. Pull up entire plants when mature.

HOW TO STORE. Refrigerate unwashed; use as soon as possible. Do not preserve.

Garlic bulbs and cloves

GARLIC

If you glory in garlic, why not grow it? It's practically foolproof when you start with pest-free bulbs from a nursery (some gardeners have luck with those from a grocery store).

Garlic needs a sunny spot with rich, well-drained soil. Select only the biggest cloves, ones with pieces of root attached, for planting. Keep the soil moist, weed regularly, and pinch off any blossoms. When the leaf tips start to turn yellowish brown, stop watering, and press the foliage flat to the ground. This prevents flowering and hastens maturation of the bulb.

Harvest bulbs when leaves are mostly brown. Be sure to lift out the bulbs with a garden fork—pulling by hand may crack the bulbs and decrease storage life. Dry the bulbs by hanging them in bundles in a dry, well-ventilated area until their skins are papery (about 3 weeks). Remove dirt, and cut off most of the roots, then store the garlic (braided or loose) in a cool, well-ventilated place away from direct sunlight.

Garlic plants

Unusual varieties of garlic are available, with differences in color, size, and flavor. Elephant garlic produces huge heads (up to a pound) of mild-flavored cloves. Rocambole garlic has a purplish head prized for its rich flavor. Its flower stalks produce small bulblets, which can be planted the following season. 'Inchelium Red' was discovered on an American Indian reservation. It's adapted to many climates and has an excellent sweet flavor.

Type of vegetable. Perennial; cool season.

Edible parts. Cloves (sections of bulbs).

Best soil. Rich, pH 5.5–6.8.

When to plant. Cold-winter climates: Set out cloves in early spring. Mild-winter climates: Set out cloves in autumn.

How to plant. Plant cloves with pointed ends up and tops 1" deep, 4"–8" apart, in rows spaced 1¼' apart. Space cloves of elephant garlic 8"–12" apart.

Yield. 10–30 bulbs per 10' row.

Care. Keep soil moist. Remove weeds.

Pests and diseases. Aphids, thrips.

When to harvest. 6–10 months after planting.

How to harvest. Uproot bulbs carefully with spading fork or spade.

How to store. Keep cool and dry for 24–32 weeks.

GOURDS

Mugs, jugs, masks, pipes, bowls, maracas, ladles, sponges—not to mention table decorations—all come from gourds, hard-shelled and usually inedible cousins of squash. Fast-growing white- or yellow-flowered vines, gourds bear fruits that come in a wide array of shapes, colors, and markings—round or cylindrical, solid or striped, smooth-surfaced or warty—in sizes from 3 inches to 3 feet.

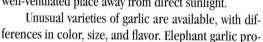

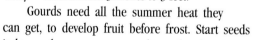

Mixed decorative gourds

Gourds need all the summer heat they can get, to develop fruit before frost. Start seeds indoors where summers are short; elsewhere, sow seeds outdoors in full sun and well-drained soil. Set up a trellis at planting time to keep individual gourds off the ground. Vines grow 10 to 15 feet long.

Let the fruits ripen on the vine. When the foliage withers, harvest the gourds, leaving a little stem on each. Be sure to harvest before frost occurs.

Wash the fruits with nonbleaching disinfectant (such as borax), dry them, and hang them up by their stems in a cool, dry, well-ventilated place away from sunlight (such as an attic), for 2 to 4 weeks. Preserve them with a coating of paste wax, lacquer, or shellac.

Type of vegetable. Annual; warm season.

Edible parts. Inedible; ornamental.

Best soil. Fertile, pH 5.5 to 6.8.

When to plant. Cold-winter climates: Sow seeds or set out plants in late spring. Mild-winter climates: Set out plants or sow seeds directly in garden in spring. For early start, sow seeds indoors in pots.

How to plant. Set out plants 2'–4' apart (vines need room) in rows spaced 4' apart. Sow seeds 2" deep, 1' apart, in rows spaced as above; thin seedlings to 2'–4' apart.

Yield. Six to twelve gourds per vine.

Care. Keep soil moist. Support vines on trellis.

Pests and diseases. Cucumber beetles, mites, squash bugs; powdery mildew.

When to harvest. 85–100 days after planting.

How to harvest. Cut stems 1"–3" from gourds.

How to store. Wash, dry, and wax or lacquer.

HERBS

Fresh herbs enrich even a simple dish immeasurably. And long before they get to the kitchen, herbs add fragrance and delicate color to the garden. Most herbs are very easy to grow: they thrive with little care in well-drained soil that is not too rich. Spring is the usual time to plant herbs, whether they are annuals or perennials, in most areas.

Harvest herb leaves for drying just as the first flower buds begin to open. Cut herbs early in the morning, after the dew has dried. Hang the plants to dry in small bundles, or strip their leaves and spread these in mesh-bottomed drying trays, placed out of direct sunlight. Stir the leaves in trays every few days until they crumble easily. The leaves of the hanging plants are ready for use when they have dried completely.

Some herbs are grown for their seeds. Harvest seed heads or pods when they turn brown. Dry them in paper bags until you can shake the seeds loose.

Store thoroughly dried leaves and seeds in airtight containers.

Dill

BASIL. The rich, pungent flavor of freshly harvested basil leaves can be yours. Sow seeds ¼ to ½ inch deep, 1¼ to 2 feet apart, or set out nursery plants directly in the garden from mid- to late spring. Available in either green or bronze purple ('Dark Opal' and 'Purple Ruffles') foliage and dwarf or small-leafed ('Fino Verde Compacto' and 'Minette'), basil can be decorative when grown in containers. Some types, such as 'Cinnamon' and 'Anise', are also scented. 'Napoletano' is an Italian variety with especially rich flavor.

Give this tender, bushy, annual herb full sun, moderate moisture, and well-drained, light soil. Pinch off tips and flowers to keep leaves coming; use the leaves fresh or dried.

CHERVIL. Chervil looks like tall (1 to 2 feet high) parsley and tastes like mild anise. The French include this annual herb in their collection of *fines herbes,* along with basil, marjoram, thyme, rosemary, and tarragon.

Sow seeds ¼ inch deep and 9 to 12 inches apart in average, well-drained soil in partial shade; keep moist.

CHIVES. Onion-flavored chives are a perennial, so you can enjoy clipping the long, pointed leaves for several years.

Grow chives from seeds planted ⅛ to ¼ inch deep or from nursery plants. Space seeds or plants 12 to 18 inches apart. Give them fairly rich, moist soil in full sun, and fertilize regularly. Container-grown chives do well indoors when placed near a sunny window. The plants also look beautiful mixed in ornamental beds.

Garlic chives, also known as Chinese chives *(gow choy)* or Chinese leeks, are similar to regular chives but their leaves have a mild garlicky flavor.

CORIANDER (CILANTRO). The seeds of this annual herb are called coriander, but its fresh leaves are most often called cilantro or Chinese parsley. The sharp, distinctive flavor of the fresh leaves is essential in many Mexican, Mediterranean, and Asian dishes. The mature seeds have a mellower flavor that's good in bean dishes, stews, curries, and sausage.

Listing continues >

LEFT: Chives flowering in the garden and harvested for cooking

A sun lover, coriander prefers moderately rich soil that drains well. Sow seeds ¼ inch deep in the garden in early spring, or in containers. Thin seedlings to 3 to 4 inches apart. Picking outer leaves will encourage more leaves to grow. Harvest seeds as soon as they're ripe.

DILL. You can use either the fresh or dried leaves or the seeds of this versatile annual herb to season many foods.

After danger of frost has passed, broadcast seeds in well-drained soil in full sun, and cover them with a thin layer of soil, or rake the ground lightly. Thin seedlings to 12 inches apart when 2 to 3 inches high.

Pinch off leaves to use after the plants are large enough to spare the foliage. Tie small paper bags over the seed heads at maturity. When the first seeds begin to drop, brush the remaining seeds into the bag, and store.

MINT. Peppermint, bergamot (orange) mint, pennyroyal, apple mint, chocolate mint, and spearmint are just a few of the refreshing mints that can thrive in your garden—or take it over if you don't restrain their roots in containers.

They thrive in full sun, partial shade, or full shade and light, moderately rich, moist soil. You can grow mint from seedlings, cuttings, or divisions. Space plants 12 to 24 inches apart. For bushy growth, keep flowers pinched back.

OREGANO. This zesty perennial herb thrives in well-drained soil in full sun. Given routine watering, seeds or cuttings will grow into bushy plants 2 to 2½ feet high. Sow seeds ¼ inch deep. Space plants 18 to 24 inches apart. Oregano makes a good container plant, but it becomes woody in about 3 years. Keep the flowers cut back to encourage bushiness.

There are many types of oregano. Cretan has woolly leaves. Greek is considered one of the best for flavor.

PARSLEY. Curly-leafed French parsley is popular because it is decorative both in the garden and on the dinner plate. Flat-leafed Italian parsley is favored by many cooks because it has a little more flavor. Either looks great mixed with flowers or vegetables.

The 6- to 12-inch plants are biennial—flowering the second year—but most gardeners treat them as annuals, starting anew from seeds or plants each year. Parsley likes partial shade and moderately rich, somewhat moist soil. To speed seed germination, soak seeds in warm water for 24 hours before sowing. Sow seeds ¼ inch deep; thin plants to 6 to 8 inches apart.

ROSEMARY. Some varieties of rosemary grow as ground covers; others are upright, and you can clip them like hedges. The dark, glossy green leaves look like short pine needles; the flowers are usually delicate blue but can also be pink or white.

Rosemary prefers full sun and will thrive in dry, poor soil as long as it is well drained. Buy nursery plants or take stem cuttings. Space upright types at least 2 feet apart and spreading types at least 3 feet apart. Rosemary does well in containers and indoors. Where temperatures seldom fall below 10°F/−12°C, it will survive winters outdoors. 'Arp' is a hardy variety that has survived temperatures as low as −15°F/−26°C.

SAGE. Sage is not always grayish green leaves on a shrubby, 2-foot-tall plant. There are many other varieties. The golden, purple, and tricolored ones are particularly attractive garden plants.

ABOVE: Cascade of mints (top to bottom)—basil, ginger, curly, chocolate, pineapple, and apple mint
RIGHT: Pot of curly mint (top right), peppermint (front), and spearmint (top left)

Sage likes poor but well-drained soil and full sun. Overwatering—especially from above—may cause mildew. You can grow all varieties from seeds or nursery plants; garden sage can be propagated from stem cuttings. Sow seeds ¼ inch deep, and space them at least 2 feet apart. Cut back stems after blooming. Though the plants are perennials, you may need to renew them every 3 to 4 years.

SUMMER SAVORY. Summer savory adds a delicate peppery flavor to soups, salad dressings, meat, fish, eggs, and beans. This annual is a loose, open plant that grows about 18 inches tall. The leaves appear in pairs along the stems, and the tiny flowers are pinkish white to rose.

Summer savory thrives in light, rich soil in full sun; it makes an excellent container plant. Sow seeds ¼ inch deep, and thin seedlings to about 18 inches apart. Water regularly.

Harvest of fresh culinary herbs

SWEET MARJORAM. Marjoram leaves, fresh or dried, taste rather like a refined, sweet relative of oregano.

In cold-winter climates, this tender perennial can be grown outdoors as an annual or indoors in containers. It's a bushy little plant about 2 feet high with soft foliage and white flowers in knotted clusters.

You can propagate marjoram from seeds, cuttings, or root divisions. Sow seeds ¼ inch deep, and space plants 6 to 9 inches apart in full sun. Keep the soil fairly moist. Cut off blossoms to encourage bushiness; trim the plant regularly to prevent woody growth.

TARRAGON. Its name comes from the French word for little dragon—referring, perhaps, to tarragon's aggressive, spreading root system. Be sure you're getting French tarragon, not the tasteless Russian tarragon. (Bruise a leaf to test for a strong anise fragrance.)

A hardy perennial, French tarragon dies to the ground in winter but returns the following spring. The attractive 2-foot-tall bush with slender dark green leaves thrives in full sun in poor but well-drained soil. French tarragon can be grown only from cuttings or divisions, spaced 24 inches apart.

THYME. There is a wealth of versatile and attractive thyme plants, all perennials and easy to grow. Some grow 8 to 12 inches high; others form a mat that you can walk on; still others have scented or variegated foliage.

Grow thyme from seeds, sown ¼ inch deep, or tip cuttings taken in spring, spaced 12 to 18 inches apart. Plant in full sun, in light sandy soil that is moderately dry. Prune after flowering. Replant when sparse, every few years.

WINTER SAVORY. Winter savory, a perennial, has a more pungent peppery flavor than summer savory and a lower, more spreading growth, which makes it a good edging for an herb or ornamental garden. Bees love its white-to-lilac blossoms.

Winter savory prefers sandy, well-drained soil and average moisture. Seeds are very slow to germinate; buy seedlings or propagate from cuttings or divisions, and space plants 6 to 12 inches apart. Harvest stems when the plants start to flower.

TOP LEFT: Kirghistan oregano
TOP RIGHT: Cretan oregano
BOTTOM LEFT: Greek oregano
BOTTOM RIGHT: Sweet marjoram oregano

TYPE OF VEGETABLE. Hardy perennial.

EDIBLE PARTS. Roots.

BEST SOIL. Rich, well-drained loam, pH 5.5–6.8.

WHEN TO PLANT. For autumn crop, set out roots in spring.

HOW TO PLANT. Set out 8"- to 14"-long root cuttings at a slant, 12"–24" apart, in 3"- to 4"-deep furrows, 2½'–3' apart. Cover with 2" of soil.

YIELD. 1 plant should give enough horseradish for a family of four.

CARE. Keep soil moist. Weed regularly.

PESTS AND DISEASES. Flea beetles, grasshoppers, leafhoppers.

WHEN TO HARVEST. From late autumn into winter.

HOW TO HARVEST. Dig up roots with spading fork.

HOW TO STORE. Use fresh or dried. Store grated 3 months in refrigerator.

TYPE OF VEGETABLE. Frost-hardy perennial.

EDIBLE PARTS. Tubers.

BEST SOIL. Fertile, well-drained, sandy loam.

WHEN TO PLANT. For autumn crop, plant tubers in spring (4–6 weeks before last frost date).

HOW TO PLANT. Plant whole tubers, or cut them into 2-ounce pieces, each with one or two eyes (growth buds). Plant 4"–6" deep, 24" apart, in rows 3'–3½' apart. Plant them where you can restrain their growth.

YIELD. About ⅓ bushel per 10' row.

CARE. Keep soil moist. Weed regularly.

PESTS AND DISEASES. Mites.

WHEN TO HARVEST. In autumn, after tops die back.

HOW TO HARVEST. Dig up tubers.

HOW TO STORE. Refrigerate unwashed in airtight container; use as soon as possible.

HORSERADISH

To many lovers of roast beef, a slab of medium-rare is nothing without the bracing heat of horseradish sauce. Its unique flavor comes from a perennial funny-looking root vegetable.

Horseradish is unusual because you plant the root almost on its side. Place it in a shallow trench with the wide end slightly higher in the soil.

The roots do most of their growing in late summer and early autumn. They're ready to harvest in late October or November, when they reach a good size— about 12 inches in length and 3 or 4 inches in diameter. You can dig them as soon as they're ready, or just leave them in the ground through the winter (if your ground does not freeze deeply), digging one up as needed. Once plants are established, they will probably grow back year after year from pieces of roots left in the ground.

For sauce, peel and grind the root, then mix three parts minced horseradish with one part vinegar and a dash of salt.

Horseradish root

Horseradish plant

JERUSALEM ARTICHOKES

Jerusalem artichokes are knobby perennial tubers of a kind of sunflower. "Jerusalem" is just a misunderstanding of *girasole,* the Italian word for sunflower. Sometimes, they are also sold as "sun chokes."

Whatever you call them, these tubers are among the world's easiest crops. In fact, they may take off and spread like weeds. Given full sun, they'll grow almost anywhere, surviving poor soil, drought, and neglect.

In early spring, plant whole tubers or cut them into chunks with one or two eyes (growth buds) apiece. Grow them where you can keep the plants from spreading uncontrollably, preferably surrounded by a 1-foot-deep metal strip in the soil.

Plants grow to 6 feet or more, putting out yellow blooms (smaller than common garden sunflowers) in late summer. When the leaves die in autumn, the tubers are ready to dig up; those dug after light frosts taste sweeter. Any tubers left in the ground will grow and become hard to eliminate.

Refrigerate the fragile tubers, or dig only what you can eat right away. Peel and cook them like potatoes, or eat them peeled and raw; either way, they taste rather like water chestnuts.

JICAMA

A familiar food in Mexico, jicama (pronounced *hee*-ca-mah) is almost as widely used in Hawaii, where it's known as "chop suey potato"—it develops underground like a potato. Sheathed in brown skin and weighing from 1 to 6 pounds, these white-fleshed tubers taste something like sweet water chestnuts.

Jicama needs a long, warm growing season and does well in areas such as southern California and southern Florida. The vines grow 25 to 30 feet long and need the support of a trellis. To promote the best tuber development, pinch off any flowers that appear on the vine. Apply a high-nitrogen fertilizer monthly.

Tubers should be mature, plump, and ready to dig up by August or September. You can just leave them in the ground until they're needed—right through winter where there are no frosts. In other areas, harvest them before the first frost hits, because it will cause them to rot.

Peel the light brown skin, and slice or dice the white flesh to eat raw (with dips or in salads) or to cook (in stir-fries and soups).

TYPE OF VEGETABLE. Annual; warm season.

EDIBLE PARTS. Tubers.

BEST SOIL. Fertile, well-drained, sandy loam.

WHEN TO PLANT. For autumn crop, sow seeds in spring (about 4 weeks after last frost date).

HOW TO PLANT. Sow seeds 2" deep, 4" apart, in rows along both edges of 2'-wide ridges; thin seedlings to 8"–12". Set up trellis.

YIELD. One tuber per plant.

CARE. Keep soil moist. Fertilize. Train vines on trellis. Pinch off flowers.

PESTS AND DISEASES. None of importance.

WHEN TO HARVEST. In autumn before frost; where there is no frost, harvest as needed.

HOW TO HARVEST. Dig up carefully.

HOW TO STORE. Keep whole tubers at room temperature for 2–3 weeks; wrap cut pieces in plastic, and refrigerate for 1 week.

KALE

Low in calories and loaded with vitamins and minerals, this frilly-leafed cabbage cousin is a dieter's delight. Use kale leaves as salad greens, chop them for garnishing soups and egg dishes, or steam them slightly and serve hot.

Kale is a cool-weather crop, hardy enough to survive moderately severe winters. You can plant it in late summer or autumn if your winter temperatures remain above 0° to 10°F/−18° to −12°C. A touch of frost sweetens its flavor; hot summer sun makes kale turn bitter.

Grow ordinary varieties, such as 'Red Russian' and 'Lacinato', or in a cramped garden try compact, short-stemmed 'Dwarf Blue Curled Vates' and 'Dwarf Siberian' (a variety with plumelike foliage). As a decorative addition to ornamental beds, walkway borders, or window boxes, plant flowering kale—its "flowers" are brightly colored edible leaves.

When the plants are a few inches high, thin to 12 to 18 inches apart. The thinned plants make delicious greens.

Plants can grow 2 feet high and equally wide, each plant producing prodigious crops of sweet leaves. Start harvesting outer leaves as soon as they grow large enough to use.

Decorative kale

'Winterbor' and 'Lacinato' kale

TYPE OF VEGETABLE. Annual; cool season.

EDIBLE PARTS. Leaves.

BEST SOIL. Fertile, pH 5.5–6.8.

WHEN TO PLANT. For summer crop, sow seeds in early spring. For autumn crop, sow seeds in late summer or autumn.

HOW TO PLANT. Sow seeds ¼" deep, 1" apart, in rows 1½'–2' apart; or broadcast seeds in wide bands. Thin seedlings to 12"–18" apart.

YIELD. 4–8 pounds per 10' row.

CARE. Keep soil moist.

PESTS AND DISEASES. Aphids, cabbageworms; damping off, fusarium wilt.

WHEN TO HARVEST. 55–75 days after sowing seeds. Harvest greens as you thin seedlings. Pick outer leaves as plants grow.

HOW TO HARVEST. Cut off outer leaves at base, or pull up entire plant.

HOW TO STORE. Refrigerate unwashed in plastic bag; use as soon as possible.

Type of vegetable. Annual; cool season.

Edible parts. Stems; leaves; leaf stems.

Best soil. Fertile, pH 5.5–6.8.

When to plant. For summer crop, sow seeds in early spring. For autumn crop, sow seeds in mid- to late summer.

How to plant. Sow seeds ¼"–½" deep, 1" apart, in rows 1½' apart; thin seedlings to 4"–8" apart.

Yield. 4–8 pounds per 10' row.

Care. Keep soil moist. Weed regularly.

Pests and diseases. *See* Cabbage, page 27.

When to harvest. 45–60 days after sowing.

How to harvest. Pull up whole plants.

How to store. *Stems:* Keep cool and damp for 2–4 weeks. To preserve, freeze. *Leaves and leaf stems:* Refrigerate unwashed; use as soon as possible. To preserve, freeze.

KOHLRABI

Hovering just above the ground like a tiny space ship, the kohlrabi's swollen stem resembles a small, airborne turnip. Kohlrabies offer a crisp texture and delicate flavor, but most gardeners are unaware of the culinary possibilities of this curious cabbage kin. The bulbous stems may look like turnips, but they are milder and less mealy, and kohlrabi leaves and leaf stems taste like tangy cabbage leaves.

Kohlrabi tastes best when 2 to 2½ inches across; larger than 3 inches, it may be hot and tough. Chill kohlrabies until crisp; then peel, slice, and serve them raw with hors d'oeuvres or in salads as a substitute for water chestnuts. To cook, steam or sauté slices, dice, or chunks, and steam leaves and leaf stems.

Popular varieties include 'Purple Danube', 'Early Purple Vienna', 'Early White Vienna', and 'Grand Duke'. Plant kohlrabies to harvest when weather is cool.

Type of vegetable. Annual; cool season.

Edible parts. Stems.

Best soil. Rich, pH 6.0–6.8.

When to plant. Cold-winter climates: Set out plants in spring. Mild-winter climates: Set out plants in spring through autumn where summers are cool, in autumn where summers are hot. Sow seeds in containers 6–8 weeks before you intend to set out plants.

How to plant. Set out plants 2"–4" apart in 5-inch-deep furrows spaced 4"–12" apart. Sow seeds ½" deep, 1" apart, in containers filled with 3" of potting soil.

Yield. 4–6 pounds per 10' row.

Care. Keep soil moist. Blanch with soil.

Pests and diseases. Thrips.

When to harvest. 4–7 months after setting out plants.

How to harvest. Lift out with spading fork.

How to store. Refrigerate unwashed; use as soon as possible. To preserve, freeze or dry.

LEEKS

Long honored by French chefs, leeks have admirers in this country as well. Since these mild-flavored onion relatives frequently fetch gourmet prices in the market, many cooks who use leeks grow their own. Popular varieties include 'Otina', 'St. Victor', 'Unique', and 'Longina'. 'Arcona' is a good storer. 'Titan' is an early-ripening variety.

'Broad London' leeks

Growing leeks takes patience—they spend 4 to 7 months fattening up to prime size. Though they prefer a mild, cool climate in full sun, leeks may do well in hotter climates if they're planted in partial shade.

As the plants grow, mound up soil around the stalks to blanch them—which makes the stem bottoms white and mild. Keep mounded soil just short of the leaf joints (where leaf joins stem), increasing the height of the mound as the plant grows. If soil is piled higher than the leaf joints, soil will work its way into the bulbs.

Leeks are ready to harvest when the stems are ½ to 2 inches thick. Lift clumps of soil containing plants with a spading fork, then shake the leeks to remove the soil. In cold-winter areas, harvest before the ground freezes. (If the ground doesn't freeze, you can leave leeks in place until needed.)

To prepare leeks for use, cut off the roots and all but 2 inches of the green leaves. Wash the leeks thoroughly, separating layers.

LETTUCE

The backyard lettuce gardener has a choice of five types of lettuce—leaf lettuce (also called loosehead lettuce), butterhead lettuce (sometimes known as Bibb lettuce), romaine (cos), crisphead (known as "iceberg") lettuce, and celtuce, which resembles a cross between celery and lettuce.

A short browse through a seed catalog or seed display rack reveals enough varieties of lettuce to keep your salad bowl crisp and colorful throughout the growing season. You can plant three or four varieties of quick-growing, easygoing leaf lettuce. Or try your hand at growing the slightly more difficult types: butterhead, romaine, crisphead, and celtuce.

The growing requirements for all lettuces are very much the same. Most of all, lettuce needs cool weather. In warm weather, it turns bitter and quickly goes to seed (it "bolts"). Lettuce grows readily in cool soil, so you can start sowing seeds in very early spring and make repeat sowings at 2-week intervals until late spring. Then delay additional plantings until the weather cools in late summer or autumn.

Plant lettuce in partially shaded areas that stay cool in warm weather or in the shade of taller vegetables such as broccoli or corn. Check with your Cooperative Extension Service for varieties that do especially well in your particular location.

Lettuce has rather shallow roots and will grow well in containers—all you need is a soil depth of 9 to 12 inches. Container-grown lettuce has the same growing requirements as garden lettuce.

The best soil for lettuce is fertile and well-drained. Keep the soil moist, but not soggy. Leaf lettuce is the least fussy about soil and will perform well even in rather poor soil as long as it drains well. Give leaf lettuce only light fertilization at planting time; heading types will respond to a second light fertilizing when plants are half grown.

The main differences in growing instructions among the five lettuce classes concern how much space to allow between seedlings when you are thinning and how to harvest them.

LEAF LETTUCE. The class that has the most varieties and is the easiest to grow is leaf lettuce. As the name suggests, this type produces loose bunches of leaves rather than a head. It comes in assorted colors (red, bronze, dark green, chartreuse) and in interesting textures (smooth, puckered, ruffly, frilled). The leaves on all varieties are exceptionally tender.

'Sierra' lettuce

You can enjoy the home gardener's exclusive rights to red, ruffly 'Ruby' or heat-resistant 'Red Sails' for color and sweet taste; super frilly 'Green Ice', which is slow to go to seed; apple green 'Black Seeded Simpson' or 'Simpson Elite'; dark green 'Oak Leaf', which has tender, thick midribs; 'Salad Bowl', with its deeply lobed bright green leaves; or 'Slo-bolt', which tolerates warm weather.

Because of its rapid maturation (40 to 50 days), leaf lettuce is a favorite where hot humid summers follow closely on the heels of spring. Those who live where spring is long and cool can enjoy a longer leaf-lettuce season by planting a succession of crops. You can plant in rows or tuck seeds into any bare spot—different varieties in different spots for interesting salads.

'Rosy' Batavian lettuce

Listing continues >

TYPE OF VEGETABLE. Annual; cool season.

EDIBLE PARTS. Leaves; stems.

BEST SOIL. Fertile, well drained, pH 6.0–6.8.

WHEN TO PLANT. COLD-WINTER CLIMATES: For spring crop, sow seeds or set out plants in spring (4–6 weeks before last frost date); make successive sowings or plantings until temperatures are 75°–80°F/24°–27°C. For autumn crop, sow or plant again in late summer and early autumn (until 6–8 weeks before first frost). MILD-WINTER CLIMATES: For autumn, winter, and spring crops, sow seeds or set out plants from autumn through midspring until temperatures are 75°–80°F/24°–27°C.

HOW TO PLANT. LEAF LETTUCE: Sow seeds ¼" deep, 1"–2" apart, in rows spaced 1'–2' apart; thin seedlings to 4"–8" apart. BUTTERHEAD AND ROMAINE: Sow seeds ¼" deep, 1"–2" apart, in rows spaced 1½'–2' apart; thin seedlings to 6"–8" apart. CRISPHEAD LETTUCE: Sow seeds ¼" deep, 1"–2" apart, in rows spaced 1½'–2' apart; thin seedlings to 12"–14" apart. CELTUCE: Sow seeds ¼" deep, 2" apart, in rows spaced 1½' apart; thin seedlings to 8"–12" apart. ALL LETTUCES: Set out plants in rows as described and at spacing of thinning.

YIELD. 4–10 pounds per 10' row.

CARE. Keep soil moist. Weed regularly.

PESTS AND DISEASES. Aphids, cabbage loopers, cutworms, flea beetles, leafhoppers, leaf miners, slugs, snails; downy mildew, fusarium wilt.

WHEN TO HARVEST. 40–90 days after sowing seeds. Harvest butterhead lettuce when loose head is formed; crisphead lettuce when heads are firm; leaf and romaine lettuce any time after leaves are large enough to use; celtuce when stem is formed, before it flowers.

HOW TO HARVEST. Pull off outer leaves of leaf lettuce. Cut off heads of heading types just below bases of heads.

HOW TO STORE. Refrigerate unwashed; use as soon as possible. Do not preserve.

THE QUILTED LETTUCE BED

With so many different leaf textures, shapes, and colors, lettuce plantings can be among the most attractive parts of the vegetable garden. Try mixing several different varieties in one bed, creating a quiltlike pattern. Simply alternating red- and green-leafed varieties in closely spaced rows yields a colorful show. Throw in several different varieties and some spring-blooming annuals, such as pansies or violas, and you'll have an eye-catching display.

Sow seeds according to the sidebar list instructions. Thin to 4 to 8 inches apart, depending on the variety, to give the lettuce room to spread.

Harvest the thinnings for salads, then harvest more mature leaves by either picking just the outer leaves or pulling up the whole plant. Some varieties, such as 'Grand Rapids' or 'Prizehead' can be cut off an inch or two above the ground and the plants will send out new leaves for a second crop.

BUTTERHEAD LETTUCE. The butterhead type forms small, tender, rather open (roselike) heads, that blanch to a creamy or butter yellow center. The heads mature in 65 to 80 days. Varieties include 'Bibb', 'Buttercrunch' (heat-resistant), 'Butter King' (disease-resistant, slow to bolt), 'Great Lakes' (heat-resistant, very productive), and 'Tom Thumb' (miniature, good in containers).

You can sow spring crops 4 to 6 weeks before the last frost date in spring. Sow autumn crops directly in the garden in late summer and early autumn.

Enjoy the thinnings, then pluck the outer leaves of maturing heads, or pull up the whole head when it reaches full size—or when you can't wait any longer. Lettuce is delicious at all stages.

ROMAINE. The staple of Caesar salad, romaine, also called cos, has upright clusters of big leaves that are exceptionally crisp and flavorful. 'Parris Island' and 'Valmaine' are two popular varieties. 'Little Gem' and 'Little Caesar' are dwarf varieties, ideal for gardens with limited space or for containers.

Growing instructions for romaine are the same as for butterhead. However, romaine takes 80 to 85 days to mature. This means you'll need a long stretch of cool-to-moderate weather to grow it. You can get a start by sowing seeds indoors in containers for early spring planting. Harvest by cutting off heads.

Romaine (cos) lettuce

CRISPHEAD LETTUCE. The most familiar lettuce, crisphead, is marketed as "iceberg" lettuce. It takes 80 to 90 days to mature. Crisphead lettuce can stand a little more heat than butterhead lettuce but still prefers cool weather for the best growth and flavor. Try 'Iceberg' for vigorous growth or one of several warm-climate varieties: 'Summertime' and 'Ithaca', which form good heads in warm weather; 'Premier Great Lakes', a variety resistant to tip burn and heat; 'Mini Green', a small, compact, heat-resistant variety; or 'Mirage', another good heading lettuce for warm climates.

Batavian lettuce, a form of crisphead, combines the best characteristics of leaf and iceberg lettuces. Handsome textured leaves give young Batavian the look of leaf lettuce. Then, as it matures, it forms a small head similar to iceberg but with better flavor and garden appeal. Red-tinged varieties include 'Sierra' (heat-resistant), 'Rosy', and 'Rouge Grenobloise'. 'Nevada' and 'Centennial' are green-leafed types with good heat tolerance.

Crisphead lettuce is ready for harvest when the heads are solid and the tops start to turn yellow (if green) or rose (if red). Cut the heads off the plants. Before eating them, trim the soiled leaves at the base, and rinse the heads in cool water. You can harvest Batavian lettuce when the leaves are young and tender, or you can wait until the head forms.

CELTUCE. The fifth type of lettuce you might want to add to your salad bowl is celtuce (*cel*ery and let*tuce*). This novelty looks and tastes like leaf lettuce when young, then sprouts stalks like celery as it matures. Like true lettuces, it loves cool weather and quickly bolts in hot spells.

Celtuce takes 90 days to mature, so start seedlings indoors for spring planting or wait for autumn planting. Sow seeds in moist, fertile, fast-draining soil. Keep the soil moist but not soggy. Thin seedlings to 8 to 12 inches apart.

You can eat the thinnings as you would leaf lettuce, and harvest the leaves of the plant, as it matures, to eat as salad greens. They taste like leaf lettuce. The mature stalks look and taste like celery and can be used raw or cooked as you would celery. Harvest by cutting individual stalks or pulling up the whole plant and cutting off the root.

MELONS

Palate-pleasing melons receive top marks for aroma, flavor, texture, and juiciness. That's an incentive to grow melons, but be prepared to pamper them a bit—they can be temperamental if not given the proper attention. To mature to full sweetness, melons need a spacious garden site in full sun, 2½ to 4 months of warm weather, rich soil, and generous amounts of water. (If you want to grow watermelons, see page 71.)

If you live in an area where summer days are often cool or foggy, you can still grow melons by planting early-ripening varieties and using some ingenuity to raise temperatures around the plants. Locating plants in hot pockets—near walls that reflect heat, in spots where breezes are blocked—will help raise the

ABOVE: 'Charentais' melon
TOP RIGHT: Cantaloupe

air temperatures. You may also want to cover the growing area with black plastic mulch, since warmth in the soil is as important as warmth in the air. Cut a 2-inch cross in the plastic for each four-leaf seedling or group of seeds, and set the plant through the opening and into the soil. Above all, cover young seedlings with floating row covers to get them off to a fast start (see page 125 for more information).

Another approach is to plant the seeds in your compost pile. Decomposition of the vegetable refuse creates heat that melon plants thrive on.

Container-gardening is a third possibility for gardeners who need to create a hot-summer climate for their melon plants. Miniature and bush melons can be grown in large containers. To save space, train the vines onto a welded-wire trellis. The fruit may need a cloth sling for support (see "Growing Melons on a Trellis," page 20).

Melons grow best in rich soil with good drainage. To prepare your soil, mix in bonemeal, well-rotted (fine-textured) manure, and organic soil amendment (compost, ground bark, peat moss, or nitrogen-stabilized sawdust) with average garden soil, in the ratio of one part amendment to three parts soil. In soils that are almost pure clay or sand, the ratio should be about one to one. Melons are very sensitive to fertilizer burn. If you use conventional fertilizers, mix them well with the soil before planting, and apply them sparingly.

Plant seeds or seedlings in spring, once the soil is warm, when danger of frost has passed and day temperatures are 60° to 75°F/16° to 24°C. Melons can be grown in

TYPE OF VEGETABLE. Annual; warm season.

EDIBLE PARTS. Fruits.

BEST SOIL. Rich, well drained, with high organic content, pH 6.0–6.8.

WHEN TO PLANT. Set out plants or sow seeds in spring. Sow seeds in peat pots 3–4 weeks before you set out plants. Set out plants in pots to protect sensitive roots.

HOW TO PLANT. Set out two plants per hill (mounds 1" high and 2'–3' across, spaced 4'–6' apart); or set out plants 2' apart in rows 3"–4" high, spaced 5' apart. Sow seeds 1" deep, four to five per hill, or 1" deep, 12" apart, in rows spaced as above; thin seedlings to two per hill.

YIELD. Two to three melons per vine.

CARE. Keep soil moist. Avoid getting leaves and fruit wet (especially if vines sprawl on ground).

PESTS AND DISEASES. Aphids, cucumber beetles, mites, squash vine borers; bacterial wilt, downy mildew, powdery mildew.

WHEN TO HARVEST. 70–115 days after sowing seeds. *CANTALOUPES:* when fruit slips easily off stem. *OTHER MELONS:* when they have a strong, sweet aroma and slight softening at the blossom end or when the skin turns from shiny to dull.

HOW TO HARVEST. Lift cantaloupes until they separate. Cut other melons from the vine with a knife or shears.

HOW TO STORE. Keep cool and damp for 2–4 weeks. To preserve, freeze.

'Freckles' crenshaw melon

hills, raised beds, or rows. To plant in hills, form the tilled soil into flat-topped mounds 1 inch high and 2 to 3 feet in diameter, with irrigation ditches encircling them. Sow four or five seeds 1 inch deep, in the hill. When seedlings begin to grow, thin to two.

To plant in rows, mound the tilled soil to a height of 3 to 4 inches above the soil surface and to a width of 12 to 15 inches. Make irrigation ditches along each side of the row.

When the seedlings are small, apply water near enough to them so that it reaches the tiny roots. When the plants are established, fill the ditches with water, keeping the foliage and fruit dry to prevent mildew and rot. Plants may wilt slightly on hot days. If they wilt badly, water deeply. In humid areas, use overhead irrigation early in the morning so the foliage will dry rapidly.

To make melons taste sweeter, hold off watering a week or so before you expect to harvest the ripe fruit. This gives melons time to develop flavor. But don't let the vines wilt; resume watering after the first harvest so the next crop will continue to put on size.

Cantaloupe is fully ripe when it pulls off the stem easily. With other kinds of melon, a strong, sweet aroma at the blossom (not stem) end is the best indicator of ripeness.

For sweetness and flavor, cantaloupes (muskmelons) are second only to watermelons. For cool-summer areas, choose varieties that mature quickly. 'Earligold', 'Sweet 'n' Early', 'Ambrosia', 'Burpee Hybrid', and 'Minnesota Midget' are popular.

Long-season melons—such as the green-skinned Persians, the pink-fleshed crenshaws ('Freckles' is early ripening), the yellow-skinned casabas, and the lime green honeydews require up to 115 days of 75°F/24°C temperatures to mature. Since these late melons also dislike high humidity, they grow best in the warm interior valleys of the West and Southwest.

Other melon varieties worth trying include hybrids developed in Europe and the Middle East: 'Charentais', 'Chaca', 'Charmel', 'Galia', 'Pancha', and 'Ha-Ogen'.

MUSTARD GREENS

The tender young leaves of mustard greens have a tang like watercress. Use them minced like parsley as a garnish for soups, fish dishes, and casseroles; add whole young leaves to lettuce and other greens for zesty salads; or cook them southern style with fatback or mixed with turnip greens.

'Kyong' mustard greens

Mustard greens thrive in cool weather; too much heat makes the leaves tough and their flavor strong. Plant seeds in spring as soon as the soil can be worked, even before the last frost date, and again in autumn before the first frost date. In mild-winter climates, you'll get a winter crop from autumn plantings. In moist soil, greens spring up about a week after you sow the seeds. When plants are 4 to 5 inches high, it's time to thin—and consume the discards. Harvest lower leaves when they are 6 to 8 inches long. (You can cook larger leaves than these.) Continue harvesting until hot weather.

Curly-leaf varieties, such as green-leafed 'Southern Giant Curled' and red-leafed 'Red Giant' ('Chinese Red'), make attractive additions to ornamental beds and deck or patio containers. 'Florida Broad Leaf' has smooth, easy-to-wash leaves; 'Tendergreen' is an early mustard with a spinach flavor and heat resistance. For Asian mustard greens, see page 19.

TYPE OF VEGETABLE. Annual; cool season.

EDIBLE PARTS. Leaves.

BEST SOIL. Fertile, well drained, pH 5.5–7.2.

WHEN TO PLANT. For spring crop, sow seeds in spring (4–6 weeks before last frost date). For autumn crop, sow seeds in autumn (6–8 weeks before first frost date).

HOW TO PLANT. Sow seeds ¼" deep, 1" apart, in rows spaced 1¼–2½' apart; keep soil moist; thin seedlings to 4"–6" apart.

YIELD. 3–6 pounds per 10' row.

CARE. Keep soil moist. Weed regularly.

PESTS AND DISEASES. Cabbage loopers, flea beetles; downy mildew.

WHEN TO HARVEST. 35–40 days after sowing seeds.

HOW TO HARVEST. Cut outer leaves or cut entire plant just below the head.

HOW TO STORE. Refrigerate unwashed; use as soon as possible. To preserve, dry.

OKRA

The slippery texture of stewed okra does not appeal to everyone. But when okra is quickly fried, sautéed, or steamed, it has a crisper texture that many love. Pretty rounds of sliced okra nicely flavor and thicken soups and gumbo.

Like corn, okra thrives on midsummer heat and tolerates almost any soil condition except poor drainage. Plant seeds only after the soil is warm (higher than 70°F/21°C) and the danger of frost has passed.

Okra's large, erect plants with tropical-looking leaves may grow to 6 feet. The prickly pods appear where leaf stems join the main stem. Apply a complete fertilizer when the first pods set and when the plants are shoulder high.

'Pentagreen' okra

Harvest the first crop when the pods are 2 to 4 inches long, and continue harvesting every 2 days. Wear gloves when harvesting pods. Even varieties such as 'Clemson Spineless' can irritate the skin.

If you have a small space, plant a dwarf variety such as 2½-foot-tall 'Dwarf Green Long Pod' or decorate a warm patio with one 'Burgundy' or 'Artist' (both red-podded) potted in a large tub. 'North & South' produces in cool weather. 'Cajun Delight' is early ripening and has less fiber than others.

TYPE OF VEGETABLE. Annual; warm season.

EDIBLE PARTS. Pods.

BEST SOIL. Fertile, pH 6.0–6.8.

WHEN TO PLANT. Sow seeds in spring and summer.

HOW TO PLANT. Sow seeds ½"–1" deep, 6" apart, in rows spaced 2½'–4' apart; thin seedlings to 12"–18" apart.

YIELD. 5–10 pounds per 10' row.

CARE. Keep soil moist.

PESTS AND DISEASES. Aphids, corn earworms, mites, nematodes.

WHEN TO HARVEST. 55–65 days after sowing seeds.

HOW TO HARVEST. Cut pods as they mature.

HOW TO STORE. Refrigerate unwashed; use as soon as possible. To preserve, can, freeze, or dry.

ONIONS

Raw or cooked, mild-tasting or pungent, onions greet your palate just about daily—from the merest hint in a soup or stew to the bold, tingling burst of flavor in a dressed-up hamburger. With such culinary demand awaiting them, it's not surprising that onions appear in so many home vegetable gardens.

Almost as if aware of their premium value to the cook, onions are quite temperamental about their cultural requirements. Still, their needs can be met in either a city balcony container garden or a suburban garden plot, since bulbs don't take much space.

KINDS OF ONIONS

Members of the lily family, most onions grow into flattish or spherical globes, but some are elongated, with tapering ends. Common kinds include storage, bunching, sweet Spanish, and torpedo onions. Onions may be sheathed in white, red, yellow, or russet skins.

Most of the small green onions (scallions) that are used in salads are simply immature onions. Some fastidious gardeners insist that only white varieties are suitable for scallions, but red, yellow, and russet onions taste just as exhilarating when young, crisp, and raw. If you should pull up an overmature scallion (one past its youthful delicacy and too strong to eat raw), simply use it in cooking as if it were a leek.

GROWTH NEEDS

Onions need fairly cool conditions to get off to a good start. Cultivated almost everywhere in the United States, onions tolerate frost well, and, where winters are mild, they're frequently started in autumn for a spring harvest. If your winter temperatures drop below freezing, plant onions in spring, as soon as the ground can be worked.

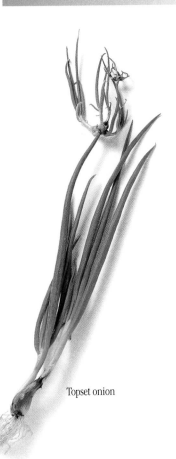

Topset onion

Listing continues >

Type of vegetable. Bulb; cool season.

Edible parts. Bulbs; leaves.

Best soil. Rich, well drained, loose, pH 6.0–6.8.

When to plant. COLD-WINTER CLIMATES: For spring and summer crop, plant sets or transplants in spring (4–6 weeks before last frost date). Sow seeds when soil temperature has warmed to at least 35°F/2°C, but preferably 50°F/10°C. In some areas, perennial onions (multiplier and Egyptian) can be planted in autumn. MILD-WINTER CLIMATES: For late spring to summer crop, plant sets or transplants in spring (4–6 weeks before last frost date). Sow seeds when soil temperature has warmed to at least 35°F/2°C. For spring crop, plant sets (for green onions only) or transplants in autumn. Sow seeds when soil temperature has cooled below 95°F/35°C.

How to plant. Plant sets with tops of bulbs ¾–2" deep, 2–4" apart, in rows spaced 1½–2' apart. Plant transplants with tops of bulbs 1"–2" deep, 3"–4" apart in rows spaced 1½–2' apart. Sow seeds ½" deep, ½" apart, in rows spaced 1½–2' apart; thin seedlings to 3"–4" apart. Apply liquid fertilizer.

Yield. 7–10 pounds per 10' row.

Care. Keep soil moist. Weed regularly. Apply fertilizer when plants have grown four to six leaves.

Pests and diseases. Thrips, wireworms; downy mildew.

When to harvest. 80–150 days after planting. Harvest green onions (scallions) whenever they are large enough to use. For mature onions, push leaves flat to ground when tops begin to fall over and turn yellow. Harvest when tops have fully turned brown.

How to harvest. GREEN ONIONS: Pull up plants. DRY ONIONS: Dig up bulbs, remove roots and stems, and dry in a cool, dark room.

How to store. GREEN ONIONS: Keep cool and damp for 4–12 weeks. DRY ONIONS: Keep cool and dry for 12–32 weeks. To preserve, can, freeze, or dry.

Proper variety selection is critical to success with onions, so it really pays to check with a local nursery or Cooperative Extension Service for recommendations and appropriate planting times. Onions form bulbs in response to day length. If you choose a type inappropriate for your area, it will make small premature bulbs or not bulb up at all. Long-day varieties need 14 to 16 hours of daylight and are grown in northern climates. They tend to be pungent and store well; examples are 'Early Yellow Globe', 'Ebenezer', 'Ruby', 'Southport White Globe', and 'Sweet Spanish'. Short-day varieties require 10 to 12 hours of daylight and are grown in southernmost climes (the Deep South, the Southwest, and southern California). They start making bulbs early in the year,

White onion plant

tend to be sweet, and are poor keepers; examples are 'Bermuda', 'California Red', 'Granex', 'Super Sweet', and 'Vidalia'. Intermediate-day types, requiring 12 to 14 hours of daylight, are suited to all growing areas; examples are 'Autumn Spice', 'Red Torpedo', and 'Ringmaker'. Bunching onions produce clusters of small onion bulbs.

Onions are finicky about soil: They want it fine textured, loose, and rich in organic matter. Before planting, rake the soil free of stones, clods, and sticks. Work in soil amendments and a complete fertilizer, such as 10-10-10, then rake the soil fine and smooth.

THREE WAYS TO START

You can start onions from seeds, sets, or transplants from the nursery, depending on how much time, money, and patience you wish to devote to them.

SETS. Sets are miniature, dormant onions (red, white, yellow, or brown) raised specifically for propagation. Easiest to manage, sets also produce quick results. You can have green onions as early as 3 weeks after planting.

But, unless you want an entire crop of green onions, plant only the smallest of the sets available. Large ones often grow too fast, bolting into flower as soon as the weather warms up and before the bulbs have had much chance to develop. (As soon as you notice bolting, pull up the onion; flowering drains away nourishment and causes the bulb to shrivel and toughen.)

In mild-winter areas, onion sets planted in October aren't so likely to bolt, since their growth during the cool winter months will be slower. But don't use sets in the warm winters of the southern latitudes, because sets are usually long-day varieties and will not grow a crop of bulbs properly.

For green onions, place sets 1 to 2 inches apart in furrows 1 to 2 inches deep, spaced 1 to 1½ feet apart. For big bulbs, simply push sets under the surface, aligning their pointed ends with the soil level, and space them 3 to 4 inches apart to allow for expansion.

TRANSPLANTS. The main advantage of using transplants instead of sets is that the onions are less likely to bolt before they're well fattened. After preparing the soil as you would for sets, position the plants so that the tops of the bulbs are about 1½ inches deep and 4 inches apart, in furrows spaced 1½ to 2 feet apart. At planting time it's a good idea to apply a mild dose of fertilizer—1 tablespoon of water-soluble fertilizer dissolved in 1 gallon of water; apply 1 cup of the solution per plant. You'll need to feed the plants again about 40 to 60 days after planting, with a side-dressing, as explained in "Continuing Care" further along.

SEEDS. Seeds are a slower way to grow onions than sets or transplants; they require more care initially, but you'll find more varieties available as seeds than as sets or transplants. After preparing the soil as for transplants, in furrows of similar spacing, sow one to five seeds per inch, burying them about ½ inch deep. Seeds germinate best at temperatures close to 65°F/18°C. After the young plants are established, thin to 1 inch apart for scallions or 3 to 4 inches apart for large bulbs.

CONTINUING CARE

No matter how you start your onions, follow up with loving care for good results. Keep young plants weed-free; with shallow roots, they can't reach far for nourishment to compete successfully with weeds. Cultivate carefully with a hoe, never working it deep enough to damage bulbs or roots. Keep the soil moist, especially during the onions' early, fast-growing phase in the cool months. Your object is to prevent any disturbance of even, rapid growth, so you'll have big, well-formed bulbs by the time warmer days come along, when the bulbs will swell and ripen.

Onions appreciate, sometimes require, a great deal of fertilizer. Give rows a second feeding of 10-10-10 (1 pound per 30 feet of row) as a side-dressing, 40 to 60 days after planting.

HARVESTING

Onion tops start to yellow and dry up when harvest time is approaching. When half of the plants have dropped their foliage naturally, push the rest of the foliage flat to the ground, a procedure called "lodging" (also recommended for garlic), with the back of a rake. Lodging forces the bulbs into their final maturing stage and ensures longer-lasting storage after harvest.

TOP: Red onions
BOTTOM: 'White Sweet' and 'Cippiola' onions

Roughly 3 weeks later, fully withered tops will indicate that ripened bulbs are ready to harvest. Use a spade or fork to dig up the onions. You can just leave them in the ground until needed—but be sure to use them before any new growth starts, such as a flowering stalk; like bolting, this new growth will starve the onion, causing it to toughen and shrivel.

Lay the harvested onions on newspapers outdoors in a dry, shady spot protected from dew or rain for about 10 days. Then brush off dirt, and trim away most of the stems and roots.

Some varieties (particularly some red and white onions) don't store well, but most yellow onions will keep several months or all winter if stored under proper conditions. Hang cleaned bulbs in mesh bags in a dark, indoor place (such as the garage) where temperatures remain 35° to 50°F/2° to 10°C. If new roots appear, the air is too humid; if onions sprout, the temperature is too warm. In either case, rotting will probably ensue, so use the onions quickly.

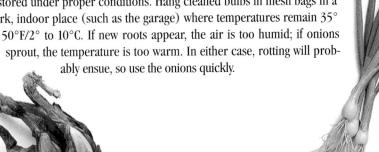

Potato onions

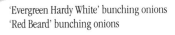

'Evergreen Hardy White' bunching onions
'Red Beard' bunching onions

TYPE OF VEGETABLE. Biennial grown as annual; cool season.

EDIBLE PARTS. Roots.

BEST SOIL. Fertile, pH 6.0–6.8.

WHEN TO PLANT. For autumn crop, sow seeds in spring.

HOW TO PLANT. Sow seeds ½" deep, 1" apart, in rows 1½–3' apart; thin seedlings to 2"–4" apart.

YIELD. 10 pounds per 10' row.

CARE. Keep soil moist. Weed regularly.

PESTS AND DISEASES. Army worms, cabbage root maggots, flea beetles, leafhoppers, nematodes.

WHEN TO HARVEST. 100–130 days after sowing.

HOW TO HARVEST. Dig up roots with spade or fork.

HOW TO STORE. Keep cool and damp for 8–16 weeks. To preserve, freeze.

TYPE OF VEGETABLE. Annual; warm season.

EDIBLE PARTS. Seeds.

BEST SOIL. Well-drained, coarse loam, pH 5.8–6.2.

WHEN TO PLANT. For late summer crop, sow seeds in spring after last frost date.

HOW TO PLANT. Sow shelled seeds of Virginia and Runner peanuts 1½–2" deep, 6"–8" apart, in rows spaced 3' apart. Sow seeds of Spanish and Valencia peanuts 1½–2" deep, 4"–6" apart, in rows spaced 2' apart.

YIELD. 1½–3 pounds of nuts in shells per 10' row.

CARE. Keep soil moist. Weed regularly.

PESTS AND DISEASES. Armyworms, cutworms.

WHEN TO HARVEST. 110–150 days after sowing seeds, when leaves turn yellow.

HOW TO HARVEST. Dig up plants with fork. Dry for 2–3 weeks; then pull shells from plants.

HOW TO STORE. Place shelled or roasted nuts in paper or plastic bags in cool, dry place.

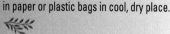

PARSNIPS

Parsnips were popular in the bygone era of root cellars because they stored so well. Modern storage methods have made them less well known. Why not revive the past by simmering a savory stew with a few garden-fresh specimens of these delicately sweet, creamy white carrot cousins?

Like carrots, parsnips need a deep, light, loose soil to develop straight, slender roots. Add sand and well-rotted compost to the soil to help parsnips grow and to make them easy to dig up. Till the soil to a depth of 18 inches, because parsnips grow as long as 15 inches. Usually you plant them in early spring, as soon as the soil temperature has reached 50°F/10°C, and harvest them in autumn and winter. Apply a fertilizer 4 to 6 weeks after sowing seeds.

Cold increases the sugar in mature parsnips, so don't harvest until the first frost occurs. Or you may leave them in the ground through winter, digging them up as needed, but mound soil over the crowns in autumn. Dig up the parsnips before they sprout in the spring, because overmature roots become woody.

PEANUTS

You won't find peanuts growing on trees like other nuts but, instead, hidden underground. Peanuts flower aboveground but produce seed pods underground from pegs, stemlike appendages from the flowers, that burrow down into the soil.

The four basic classes of peanuts are Virginia and Runner types with two large seeds per pod, Spanish with two or three small seeds per pod, and Valencia with three to six small seeds per pod. Order seeds from a mail-order catalog or nursery. Varieties for northern climates include 'Early Northern', 'Early Spanish', and 'Valencia'.

Peanuts need a long, warm growing season, coarse soil, and ample moisture. Sow peanut seeds with shells removed but with skins intact. On the coarse, sandy soils common in the South, dust the soil with gypsum (calcium sulfate) when the plants begin blooming. This provides extra calcium to develop well-filled pods.

Peanuts are ready to harvest when the plants' leaves turn yellow—in late summer or autumn before a hard freeze occurs. With a spading fork, dig up and turn over entire plants. Hang them to cure in a warm, dry, well-ventilated, dark place. Pull the peanuts from the plants in 2 to 3 weeks, when the hulls are dry.

'Jumbo Virginia' peanuts

PEAS

So delightful is the taste of fresh garden or English peas that two out of five gardeners find room for peas in their gardens. Some kinds are for shelling, some have edible pods, and some can be relished either way. (For the vegetables known as southern, or field, peas, see page 61.)

A cool-weather crop, garden peas will even withstand light frosts. Where winters are cold, plant peas in early spring as soon as you can work the soil. Where winters are mild, you can sow a crop of peas in early spring for a spring crop and again in the autumn for a winter or early spring harvest.

ABOVE: 'Green Arrow' peas
TOP RIGHT: 'Oregon Sugar Pod' peas

Garden peas grow on a vine and climb with modified leaves called tendrils. Dwarf varieties, such as 'Green Arrow' and 'Little Marvel', range in height from 1½ to 2 feet and will stand best with some support. The tall varieties, such as 'Alderman', grow 6 to 8 feet high and need poles or string or chicken-wire trellises to climb. Tall varieties give harvests of longer duration than dwarf kinds.

Shelling peas are old-time favorites of gardeners. Besides dwarf and tall, they come in early, midseason, and late-ripening varieties. Edible-pod peas, also known as sugar peas or snow peas, are available in dwarf and tall varieties. 'Sugar Snap', 'Sugar Ann', 'Super Sugar Mel', and other varieties of this type combine the qualities of shelling peas and edible-pod peas: you can eat the immature pods, or eat pods and peas together as you would string beans (the most widely used way), or wait for the peas to mature and harvest them for shelling. Traditional snow peas, popular in Asian cooking, are usually eaten before the peas fully swell. 'Mammoth Melting Sugar' and 'Oregon Sugar Pod' are tall vining varieties, 'Dwarf Gray Sugar' a bushy one. In France, tiny peas called *petits pois* are considered a delicacy because of their tenderness and sweet,

Full-grown 'Precovelle' *petits pois* (right) are smaller than other peas (left)

succulent flavor. These aren't just immature versions of shelling peas. They're genetically smaller—2 to 3 inches long at maturity, with six to nine small, round peas. Two common varieties are 'Waverex' and 'Precovelle'.

Peas like well-drained soil that is rich in organic matter but limited in nitrogen. (Too much nitrogen will produce mostly foliage.) If your soil is lacking organic matter, prepare the soil by digging a trench 1 or 2 feet deep and mixing in large amounts of compost, leaf mold, bonemeal, and manure.

Before sowing seeds, soak them overnight in water. Keep the soil moist, but avoid overwatering while the seeds are germinating. (Overwatering in cold soil will cause them to rot.) Put up poles or trellises at planting time.

Begin harvesting peas for shelling when the pods have swelled to almost a round shape and before the pods lose their bright green color. Harvest edible pods when the pods are 2 to 3 inches long, before the seeds begin to swell. For the freshest taste, harvest peas every 2 days. This also keeps the plants producing.

TYPE OF VEGETABLE. Annual; cool season.

EDIBLE PARTS. Harvested seeds; pods of some varieties.

BEST SOIL. Rich, pH 5.5–6.8.

WHEN TO PLANT. COLD-WINTER CLIMATES: For spring crop, sow seeds in spring (6–8 weeks before last frost date). For autumn crop, sow seeds about 12 weeks before first frost date in autumn. MILD-WINTER CLIMATES: For spring crop, sow seeds in spring (6–8 weeks before last frost date). For autumn and winter crops, sow seeds from late summer through autumn.

HOW TO PLANT. Sow seeds 1"–2" deep, 1" apart, in single rows spaced 2'–4' apart, or in double rows spaced 6" apart with 2½'–3' between double rows. Thin seedlings to 2"–4" apart. Set up stakes or trellises for vines at planting time.

YIELD. 2–6 pounds per 10' row.

CARE. Keep soil moist. Weed regularly.

PESTS AND DISEASES. Aphids, cucumber beetles; powdery mildew.

WHEN TO HARVEST. 55–70 days after sowing, when peas for shelling are full size and pods are bright green or when edible-pod peas are just beginning to form.

HOW TO HARVEST. Pick from lower parts of vines as peas mature.

HOW TO STORE. Refrigerate unwashed; use as soon as possible. To preserve, can, freeze, or dry.

PEPPERS IN CONTAINERS

Small-fruited peppers, such as 'Tabasco', 'Serrano', and 'Chiltepin', are very attractive container plants with an abundance of colorful fruit, prolific bloom, and compact habits. For a novel color display, try the Thai pepper 'Rainbow', which has purple foliage and metallic blue fruit.

PEPPERS

What a variety of sizes, shapes, colors, and flavors of peppers are available to home gardeners! Choose from short and chunky, long and skinny, cone-shaped, round, or crumpled—in nearly all shades of the rainbow. Choose flavors from mild and sweet to sizzling hot and pungent. Use them cooked by themselves and with other foods or raw in salads and appetizers.

As garden plants, peppers are somewhat demanding about conditions but well worth the effort it takes to get them to produce. Besides a sunny location, fertile soil, ample moisture, and protection from strong winds, peppers also need warm days and slightly cooler nights.

'Purple Flame' bell pepper

Sweet peppers grow best when daytime temperatures range between 70° and 75°F/21° and 24°C. Hot peppers prefer slightly warmer temperatures. They thrive when daytime temperatures are between 70° and 85°F/21° and 29°C. For sweet and hot peppers, if night temperatures fall below 60°F/16°C or stay above 75°F/24°C, blossoms often fall off and fruit set is poor.

Sweet peppers grow on stiff, rather compact, large-leafed bushes, mature in 60 to 80 days, and can be grown almost anywhere except at high elevations and in extreme northern areas. Taller, more spreading hot pepper plants have smaller and narrower leaves than sweet pepper varieties. Hot peppers ripen later and are best suited to areas with long, warm growing seasons, but they can be grown in northern states. Other than liking slightly warmer weather, hot peppers require the same care as sweet peppers.

SWEET PEPPERS. The best-known sweet peppers are bell peppers, so named because of their bell shape. Frequently these peppers are harvested when green in order to make the plants more productive. When left on the plants to mature, bell peppers turn red or yellow, depending on the variety. Varieties of bell peppers differ in size, shape, and color of fruit at maturity, resistance to disease, and earliness of ripening.

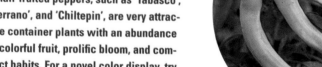

'Yellow Banana' sweet pepper

A quartet of non–bell peppers with names and flavors that delight diners may be scarcely known to most gardeners. Worth seeking out and growing, these peppers have thinner flesh, are less watery, and have a more concentrated sweet-pepper flavor than big bell peppers. They are also strong garden plants that produce heavily and continuously from the start of harvest until the first heavy frost of autumn. (Don't give up on plants that stop bearing during hot weather. Keep the plants alive, and they should produce again when the weather cools.)

Pimiento peppers, relatively small peppers with thick, sweet flesh, are used for flavoring sauces and dips and in salads and appetizers.

Pointed Italian frying peppers are 4 to 7 inches long and yellow green to red when mature. As the name implies, they are used for frying or cooking with various meats.

Sweet Hungarian yellow peppers are slender, pointed, and 4 to 6 inches long. In some areas they produce more reliably in hot weather than bell peppers do. They are usually harvested when yellow, but they turn red when mature. Only fully red, ripe peppers are used for drying, either in the sun or in a dehydrator.

Cherry peppers are globe-shaped, about 1½ inches wide, and sweet. They are harvested for pickling whole, either when green or when they turn red at maturity.

HOT PEPPERS. With flavors from mild to searing hot, hot peppers range in size from 1¼-inch-long 'Tabasco' peppers to 7-inch-long 'Pasilla' peppers. Their colors include green, red, and shades of brown. Hot peppers are used for making sauces, for pickling, and for making dried seasonings. You can select some varieties by degrees of hotness; for example, there are 'Anaheim Mild' and 'Anaheim Hot' varieties. For a really hot pepper, try 'Habanero'—it's said to be 50 times hotter than 'Jalapeño'.

Some hot peppers, such as 'Hungarian Wax Hot' and hot cherry peppers, look just like their sweet counterparts. Read labels carefully at planting time to avoid confusing hot and sweet peppers, or you'll be in for a surprise at harvesttime.

To harvest all kinds of peppers, cut them carefully from the plants with pruning shears.

LEFT TO RIGHT: 'Pico de Gallo', 'Thai', and 'Coban' hot peppers

POTATOES

Potatoes have come a long, roundabout way to your garden. Carried by Spanish explorers from South America to Europe, they were received as a curiosity. However, Irish farmers discovered their food value and made potatoes popular—so popular that this crop that was native to South America is called "Irish potatoes." Irish settlers then brought potatoes to the colony of New Hampshire in the early 1700s, and eventually farmers in the United States developed many varieties.

Potatoes have all the virtues: easy to grow, long-lasting if properly stored, thrifty, nutritious, heartily satisfying, and wonderful to eat, especially with butter or sour cream.

Like its relative, the tomato, the potato produces an abundance of sprawling, bushy vines above the ground. But, unlike tomatoes, potatoes fatten up under the soil as tubers (swollen underground stems).

In a home garden, potatoes aren't likely to trouble you with the many pests and diseases that beset a commercial grower—as long as you start with certified disease-free seed potatoes. Available from some nurseries, from farm supply stores, from seed and feed stores, and from mail-order sources in numerous varieties, they come with red, brown (russets), blue, or "white" (actually most are pale yellow) skins. Most potato varieties are round or oblong, but fingerlings are long and narrow. Some kinds mature faster than others; most varieties take about 3 months.

ABOVE: Potatoes in a broad spectrum of colors
LEFT: 'All Blue' potatoes

Listing continues >

TYPE OF VEGETABLE. Annual; cool season.

EDIBLE PARTS. Tubers (thickened underground stems).

BEST SOIL. Fertile, well-drained, sandy loam, pH 4.8–5.4 (may get scabby in higher pH).

WHEN TO PLANT. COLD-WINTER CLIMATES: For summer crop, plant cuttings of early-maturing varieties in spring (4–6 weeks before last frost date). For autumn crop, plant late-maturing varieties in late spring. MILD-WINTER CLIMATES: For summer crop, plant in late winter or early spring (4–6 weeks before the last frost date). For winter-into-spring crop, plant in late summer or early autumn.

HOW TO PLANT. Use certified seed potatoes (specially grown disease-free potatoes). Cut seed potatoes into blocky chunks, each with two eyes (growth buds). Allow chunks to callus for 2 days. Plant in furrows 4" deep, 12"–18" apart, in rows spaced 2½'–3' apart; cover potatoes with 2" of soil; add 2" more soil when sprouts emerge.

YIELD. 10–20 pounds per 10' row.

CARE. Keep soil uniformly moist. Weed regularly. Mound up soil around vines as vines grow to keep growing tubers protected from sunburn.

Continues next page >

PESTS AND DISEASES. Aphids, Colorado potato beetles, flea beetles, leafhoppers, wireworms.

WHEN TO HARVEST. 90–120 days after planting. Harvest tender "new" potatoes when vines start to flower. Harvest mature potatoes (for storage) when tops die.

HOW TO HARVEST. Dig beneath plants with spading fork or shovel. Keep tool 8"–10" from plant to avoid injuring potatoes. Lift plant gently, shake off loose soil, and pull potatoes from vines.

HOW TO STORE. Keel cool and damp for 12–20 weeks. To preserve, can, freeze, or dry.

POTATOES IN POTS

You can produce quite a few potatoes in a large container, such as half a wine or whiskey barrel. Fill the bottom of the container with about 6 inches of soil. Place three seed potatoes, evenly spaced, in the bottom of the pot, and cover with 3 to 4 more inches of soil. As the foliage appears, fill the pot with more soil until just the tips show. Continue to fill the pot as the potatoes grow, until the soil level is 1 to 2 inches below the rim of the pot. Water and fertilize the plants regularly. Harvest when the tops start to die down.

Two days before planting, cut the seed potatoes into chunks about 1½ inches square, each with at least two "eyes," from which sprouts will emerge. Allow them to dry (or "callus") partially before planting to help prevent them from rotting.

Plant in spring as soon as the ground can be worked—or in midwinter if frosts aren't too severe. Potatoes need plenty of growing room compared to most backyard crops. They want full sun and fertile, sandy, fast-draining soil. If the soil is heavy or waterlogged, the tubers may become deformed or rot.

Set the chunks 12 to 18 inches apart in 6- to 8-inch-wide, 4-inch-deep furrows, spaced 2½ to 3 feet apart. (Closer spacing will result in higher yields of smaller potatoes.) Cover chunks with 2 inches of soil.

At planting time, fertilize in bands along both sides of each furrow, keeping fertilizer about 2 inches away from seed potatoes but at the same soil level. Use a 10-10-10 fertilizer at about 8 to 12 pounds per 100 feet of row—half this amount if manure was previously tilled into the soil. Too much nitrogen will encourage excessive aboveground vegetation and poor tuber development.

After sprouts emerge, add another 2 inches of soil to the furrow. As the potato vines grow, continue adding soil, mounding a ridge of soil up and over each row, until the ridges are about 4 inches high and 18 inches wide. Keep the ridges formed as the plants mature, since the soil cover helps ensure the best temperature and moisture for the tubers developing below. It also keeps the tubers protected from the sun, which would turn any exposed areas green and inedible.

You can harvest a few new potatoes from around the edge of each plant in late spring or early summer, about the time the plants flower. New potatoes aren't just small potatoes—their sugar hasn't converted to starch, as it will in fully developed tubers, and their skins are thin and tender. That's why new potatoes are deliciously sweet and why they're best when used immediately after harvest.

TOP LEFT: Red potatoes
ABOVE, TOP: Seed potato cut into chunks
ABOVE, BOTTOM: Soil mounded around plants
4–6 inches tall

When most of the potato foliage has turned yellow to brown, water the plants for the last time, then wait 7 to 10 days, and cut away the vines. This sets or hardens the potato skins, so they won't peel or bruise too easily. In another 5 to 7 days, preferably when it's cool and overcast, dig up the potatoes with a spading fork. Gather the harvest in burlap bags or baskets. To heal any injuries, store potatoes for 2 weeks in a dark place with high humidity and a temperature of 50° to 60°F/10° to 16°C. Loosely cover stacked bags or baskets with burlap.

Keep only healed specimens for further storage; unblemished potatoes are best for long storage. Don't expose them to light for any length of time. Further storage should be in a well-ventilated, dark, and dry location, such as a basement, where the temperature is about 40°F/4°C. (If much warmer than that, potatoes are likely to sprout; if much cooler, their starch may turn to sugar, sweetening the flavor.) In these conditions, potatoes should keep well for 3 to 6 months.

Before cooking, cut off and discard any green portions; these are poisonous.

PUMPKINS

Carve its shell, cook its flesh, and snack on its seeds—the versatile pumpkin can be enjoyed by the whole family.

Depending on the variety grown, the fruits range in size from tiny jack-o'-lanterns, such as 'Jack Be Little', to giants (actually squashes), such as 'Prizewinner' and 'Big Moon', weighing more than 100 pounds. Some, like 'Lumina' and 'Baby Boo', have white skin. You can eat the seeds of all kinds, but the easiest to prepare are ones without hulls; get them by planting 'Lady Godiva' or 'Triple Treat'.

Pumpkin vines need lots of room to grow. Even the bush types can spread over 20 square feet.

In most areas, sow seeds outdoors in late spring (when soil has warmed to 65°F/18°C). In areas with a short growing season, give plants a 2- to 3-week head start by sowing seeds indoors in peat pots. Water the plants generously, but keep the leaves dry to prevent leaf diseases.

For a monogrammed jack-o'-lantern, scratch a name onto the fruit in mid- to late summer, before the shell is hardened. As the pumpkin matures, the inscription will callus over and become easily readable. Harvest pumpkins when they are ripe, usually after the first autumn frost kills the vines.

'Lumina' pumpkin

TYPE OF VEGETABLE. Annual; warm season.

EDIBLE PARTS. Fruits; seeds.

BEST SOIL. Rich, pH 6.0–7.5.

WHEN TO PLANT. For autumn crop, sow seeds in late spring.

HOW TO PLANT. Sow hills of five or six seeds of vining pumpkins 1" deep, 6'–8' apart; thin seedlings to two per hill. Sow cluster of three or four seeds of bush pumpkins 1" deep, 2' apart, in rows spaced 3' apart; thin seedlings to one to two plants per cluster.

YIELD. 10–20 pounds per 10' row.

CARE. Keep soil moist, weed regularly.

PESTS AND DISEASES. Cucumber beetles, squash bugs, squash vine borers; powdery mildew.

WHEN TO HARVEST. 90–120 days after sowing seeds, when shell is hard.

HOW TO HARVEST. Cut with pruning shears.

HOW TO STORE. Keep warm and dry for 8–24 weeks. To preserve, can, freeze, or dry.

RADISHES

Radishes are a surefire success for children. They're hardy, they take up little space, and they offer bright, crunchy bouquets for the kitchen in as little as 3 weeks after seeds are sown.

Most people limit their mind's-eye picture of a radish to the typical supermarket variety—small, round, and rosy to deep red. But you'll also find radish varieties in a parade of different colors, shapes, and sizes.

Some radish surprises include colors of burnished gold, deep purple, white, and even black. The seed mix called 'Easter Egg', a kid favorite, includes purple, lavender, pink, rose, scarlet, and white radishes (all are white inside). Besides forming bite-size nuggets, these roots may stretch to the size of foot-long carrots, or resemble miniature turnips or cucumbers. Flavors vary widely, too, from delicate and mild to sizzling hot. Don't expect the large varieties—especially winter radishes—to grow as fast as the small round ones. Many medium and long varieties take 50 to 70 days to mature. (For *daikon*, see "Japanese Radish," page 21.)

Large and small, round and long, red and white radishes

TYPE OF VEGETABLE. Annual, cool season.

EDIBLE PARTS. Roots.

BEST SOIL. Fertile, well drained, pH 5.5–6.8.

WHEN TO PLANT. For spring crop, sow seeds during spring. For autumn crop, sow seeds in autumn. MILD-WINTER CLIMATES: For winter crop, sow seeds in autumn and winter.

HOW TO PLANT. Sow seeds ½" deep, 1" apart, in mounded rows (4"–6" high) spaced 8"–18" apart; or broadcast seeds in wide beds. Thin seedlings to 1"–4" apart.

YIELD. 2–5 pounds per 10' row.

CARE. Keep soil moist. Weed regularly.

PESTS AND DISEASES. Cabbage root maggots, flea beetles.

WHEN TO HARVEST. 22–70 days after sowing.

HOW TO HARVEST. Pull up small radishes. Pull or dig up large radishes.

HOW TO STORE. Refrigerate unwashed; use as soon as possible. Do not preserve.

Listing continues >

'Easter Egg' radishes

Appreciative of cool weather, radishes sown in autumn will thrive through winter if your climate is mild. Otherwise, plant in early spring, leaving space for successive sowings until summer (most varieties do not do well in really hot weather). Radishes can be intercropped with carrots beneficially (see page 29).

Give radishes a sunny spot and well-pulverized soil. Till the soil several inches deeper than the expected length of the radishes you're planting, so they can grow without interference from clods or stones and you can harvest them easily. The soil should be loose, light, and rich in organic matter. Rake it smooth, and form it into raised beds 4 to 6 inches high, 8 to 18 inches apart, to aid drainage and let air enter the soil easily.

Sow seeds ½ inch deep and 1 inch apart down the center of each ridge. Cover the seeds lightly, and keep the soil reasonably moist throughout the season. Seedlings will appear in 4 to 6 days. After their roots begin to swell, thin out every other plant, eating thinnings that are large enough. Begin checking the root development shortly before the expected harvest date. Harvest radishes as soon as they're mature, before they become tough, woody, and perhaps hollow inside.

Successive sowings every 7 to 10 days should keep your salads amply supplied during spring and fall and, where it's possible, during winter.

TYPE OF VEGETABLE. Frost-hardy perennial.

EDIBLE PARTS. Stalks.

BEST SOIL. Fertile, pH 5.0–6.8.

WHEN TO PLANT. In late winter to early spring when dormant crowns are available.

HOW TO PLANT. Set out crowns so tops are 1" below soil surface in hills 3'–4' apart.

YIELD. 1–1½ pounds per plant.

CARE. Keep soil moist. Fertilize. Remove flower stalks. Mulch.

PESTS AND DISEASES. Aphids, flea beetles, leafhoppers.

WHEN TO HARVEST. In spring, starting in second year.

HOW TO HARVEST. With sideways twist and tug, pull off leaf stems near base.

HOW TO STORE. Keep cool and damp for 2–3 weeks. To preserve, can or freeze.

R HUBARB

Does your mouth water at the thought of rhubarb pie? If you'd like to grow some of your own rhubarb, plant it and be patient—it can take 3 to 4 years to get the first full harvest.

In the meantime, you can enjoy the color and shape of the developing plants: broad, pink-veined leaves on tall, smooth red or green stalks. Rhubarb is so attractive that you may decide to plant some in ornamental beds.

A perennial, rhubarb shoots up new leaves in spring and dies back each autumn. *Caution: Don't eat the leaves; they're poisonous.* Rhubarb does best in areas where the ground freezes in winter, but it can be grown as a cool-season annual in mild-winter climates. Where summers are hot, plant rhubarb in partial shade. In the Deep South, start from seed; you'll harvest a few stalks in spring and the remainder in autumn. Planting time is usually in spring when the dormant crowns (clumps of roots with growth buds attached) are available.

Fertilize rhubarb every year with high-nitrogen fertilizer, and cover plants with a compost mulch in autumn.

You may be able to harvest a few stalks during the second year after planting, but bigger harvests that last for 8 to 10 weeks will come in the third and fourth years. Remove any flower stalks that appear. Using a sideways twist and tug, gently pull off the leaf stems near their base when they reach 10 to 15 inches long. Don't cut the stems with a knife—they will decay. Never harvest more than one-third of the leaves. The leaves that remain on each plant make food to replenish the crowns. Stop harvesting in late spring or when the stalks start to become thinner.

ROQUETTE

Whether you call it roquette (French), arugula (Italian), or rocket (English), it's a salad green with a spicy tang somewhere between that of cress and horseradish. It's

expensive in gourmet markets, but fortunately no spring or autumn crop could be easier to grow.

In a sunny garden spot, either sow seeds 2 inches apart in rows about 16 inches apart or scatter the seeds in a patch. When the seedlings have four or five leaves, thin them to about 6 inches apart, and eat the thinnings.

Harvest entire plants when they are still young and tender. Unharvested plants will eventually shoot up and bloom, producing tender flower buds and white flowers. At this time, harvest only the flower buds and flowers, which taste just like the young leaves. (The older leaves turn sour and tough.)

Because the leaves of roquette have considerable bite, try mixing your first harvest with more bland lettuce leaves. If you like the tang, you may eat roquette straight after that. It's delicious with a simple dressing of vinegar or lemon juice and oil.

TYPE OF VEGETABLE. Annual; cool season.

EDIBLE PARTS. Leaves; flower buds; flowers.

BEST SOIL. Fertile, pH 5.5–6.8.

WHEN TO PLANT. For spring crop, sow seeds in spring (4 weeks before last frost date). For autumn crop, sow seeds in late summer and autumn.

HOW TO PLANT. Sow seeds ¼" deep, 2" apart, in rows 16" apart; thin seedlings to 6" apart.

YIELD. A 10' row should give enough leaves for a family of four.

CARE. Keep soil moist. Weed regularly.

PESTS AND DISEASES. None of importance.

WHEN TO HARVEST. 40 days after sowing seeds.

HOW TO HARVEST. Pull up entire plant.

HOW TO STORE. Refrigerate unwashed; use as soon as possible. Do not preserve.

RUTABAGAS

The big, yellow "superturnips" you see at the market in autumn are rutabagas. These cool-season, frost-hardy roots are a lot like turnips, except for their color.

Slow-growing rutabagas are almost always planted in early summer to midsummer for an autumn harvest. The large plants need plenty of space to allow their roots to reach their full weight of 3 to 5 pounds each, although you may want to harvest them when they are smaller. Recommended varieties of rutabagas include 'Altasweet', 'American Purple Top Yellow', and 'Laurentian'.

Sow seeds in rows about 1½ feet apart. Water generously, and thin several times. Full harvest begins about 90 days after sowing seeds, when the roots are 3 inches wide. After they reach full size, they can stay in the ground to be harvested as needed. Rutabaga greens are edible, but you may prefer to use only the tender thinnings. Older leaves tend to be coarse.

Cook and serve the roots as you would turnips. Sliced, rutabagas make tasty additions to soups and, when cooked and served as a side dish, a spirited complement to pork or beef.

TYPE OF VEGETABLE. Annual; cool season.

EDIBLE PARTS. Roots; young leaves.

BEST SOIL. Fertile, well drained, pH 6.0–6.8.

WHEN TO PLANT. COLD-WINTER CLIMATES: For summer crop, sow seeds in early spring. For autumn crop, sow seeds in early summer to midsummer. MILD-WINTER CLIMATES: For winter-into-spring crop, sow seeds in early autumn.

HOW TO PLANT. Sow seeds ½" deep, 1" apart, in rows spaced 1½'–3' apart; or broadcast seeds in wide beds. Thin seedlings to 5"–12" apart.

YIELD. 8–30 pounds per 10' row.

CARE. Keep soil moist. Weed regularly.

PESTS AND DISEASES. Armyworms, cabbage root maggots, flea beetles.

WHEN TO HARVEST. 90–120 days after sowing.

HOW TO HARVEST. Dig up roots with garden fork.

HOW TO STORE. Keep cool and damp for 8–16 weeks. To preserve, freeze.

Type of vegetable. Biennial, grown as annual; cool season.

Edible parts. Roots.

Best soil. Rich, well-drained, sandy loam, pH 6.0–6.8.

When to plant. For summer or autumn crop, sow seeds in spring (2–4 weeks before last frost date).

How to plant. Sow seeds ¼"–½" deep, ½" apart, in rows spaced 1½'–2½' apart; thin seedlings to 2"–4" apart.

Yield. 3–7 pounds per 10' row.

Care. Keep soil moist. Weed regularly.

Pests and diseases. Armyworms, flea beetles, leafhoppers.

When to harvest. 140–150 days after sowing seeds.

How to harvest. Dig up roots with garden fork.

How to store. Refrigerate in plastic bag.

SALSIFY

If it looks like a parsnip and tastes like an oyster, it has to be a salsify root. Reactions to the "oyster plant" are as strong and varied as the food for which it's nicknamed. For fanciers of oysters who enjoy growing root vegetables, salsify is worth trying.

Plants are slow growing (up to 150 days) but undemanding. If you start seeds in the spring as soon as the soil is workable, small roots should be ready to dig by mid-summer; or they can be left in the ground to be harvested as needed.

When left in the ground through the winter months in mild climates, the roots will produce large, purple, dandelion-like flowers in spring and, in moist soil, lots of volunteer salsify plants for the second year's crop.

Grown well, young salsify roots are delicate in flavor and very tender. As they age, lengthening to 10 inches or so, their flavor gradually becomes quite strong and their texture somewhat fibrous.

'Sandwich Island Mammoth' is a popular variety.

Type of vegetable. Bulb; cool season.

Edible parts. Bulbs; young green shoots.

Best soil. Fertile, pH 5.0–6.8.

When to plant. For summer crop, plant in early spring (2–4 weeks before last frost date). Mild-winter climates: For winter crop, plant in autumn (at least 6 weeks before first frost date).

How to plant. Plant cloves so that tops are ½" deep, 4"–8" apart, in rows spaced 2'–4' apart.

Yield. Several cloves per plant.

Care. Keep soil moist. Weed regularly.

Pests and diseases. Thrips.

When to harvest. 60–120 days after planting.

How to harvest. Pull up clumps of shoots.

How to store. Keep cool and dry for 12–32 weeks. To preserve, can, freeze, or dry.

SHALLOTS

Prized for their flavor—a combination of mild onion and pungent garlic—shallots are grown for their dry bulbs and young green shoots. The bulbs are divided into cloves that grow on a common base.

In mild-climate areas, shallots are often planted in the autumn, harvested during the winter, and raised primarily for the green portion. In colder zones, shallots are planted as early as possible in the spring and grown for both green shoots (summer) and dry bulbs (autumn).

Use cloves (sections of bulb) purchased by mail order or from seed stores, or bulbs you buy in a grocery store and separate into cloves. Place the cloves in the ground with the fat base downward and tips covered with ½ inch of soil. You'll have green shoots in about 60 days and new bulbs in 90 to 120 days.

At bulb maturity, the shoots yellow and die. Harvest by pulling up clumps and separating the bulbs. Let the outer skin dry for about a month before using the bulbs. You can store shallots for as long as 8 months in a cool, dry place.

Mature shallot bulbs

Dutch shallots

SORREL

Scarcely known in the United States, sorrel is a staple in French cuisine, where it is known as *oseille,* and in eastern European and Jewish cuisines, where it's called *schav*.

Sorrel tastes like a sharp, sprightly spinach but is a much better garden performer. A hardy perennial, it is indifferent to heat and mild winters, and it produces leaves all year. (Plants go dormant in winter if the ground freezes, but they revive earlier in spring than other vegetables.)

Sorrel plants and seeds are not easy to find. Search herb sections of nurseries for young plants, and explore seed racks and catalogs for the seeds. Set out nursery plants when they are available. Sow seeds early in the spring. The following spring, divide the plants to increase your supply. A dozen plants will supply plenty of sorrel for a family of four.

With its lemony tang, sorrel is good raw or cooked. You can use the tender leaves in place of lettuce on sandwiches or hamburgers. Cook sorrel in an omelet, sauté it with mushrooms, or blend it into gazpacho.

TYPE OF VEGETABLE. Hardy perennial.

EDIBLE PARTS. Leaves.

BEST SOIL. Fertile, well drained, pH 5.0–6.8.

WHEN TO PLANT. For spring to autumn crops, plant in spring (about 2 weeks after last frost date).

HOW TO PLANT. Set out plants 8" apart in rows spaced 1½' apart. Sow seeds ¼" deep, 1" apart, in rows spaced 1½' apart; thin seedlings to 8" apart.

CARE. Keep soil moist. Weed regularly. Cut off flower stalks in summer.

PESTS AND DISEASES. None of importance.

WHEN TO HARVEST. 60 days after sowing seeds, or when leaves are big enough to use.

HOW TO HARVEST. Pick tender leaves when big enough to use.

HOW TO STORE. Refrigerate unwashed; use as soon as possible. Do not preserve.

SOUTHERN PEAS

Southern (or field) peas—cowpeas, crowder, black-eyed, cream, and purple-hull—come in an array of shapes, sizes, and colors. They can be long or round, smooth or wrinkled, solid color or speckled. And they are packed with vitamins and protein.

Originally brought to the United States from Africa as part of the slave trade in the early 1700s, southern peas flourished in the long sweltering summers in much of the Deep South. Soon these peas became a delicious staple in southern cuisine.

Although referred to as "peas," these plants grow and look much like bush snap beans. Southern peas prefer a long warm season, but you can grow them in cooler regions of the country, although the yield will be paltry. Where the growing season is short, you'll have the best chance of success with early-bearing dwarf or bush varieties.

Wait until early summer nights are warm before sowing seeds. For southern peas the soil need not be as rich as for most vegetables; a few varieties can grow even in poor soil. Make successive sowings in summer until 11 weeks before the first frost date in autumn.

Water these plants by soaking the soil, but don't overwater, and avoid sprinkling—it may encourage mildew.

After young pea plants are fairly well established, fertilize them once only with a 5-10-10 side-dressing, at 3 pounds per 100 feet of row. Giving too much nitrogen will hinder good seedpod

TYPE OF VEGETABLE. Annual; warm season.

EDIBLE PARTS. Seeds.

BEST SOIL. Average, well drained, pH 5.5–6.8.

WHEN TO PLANT. For summer crop, sow seeds in spring (2–4 weeks after last frost date), when soil has warmed.

HOW TO PLANT. Sow seeds 1" deep, 1" apart, in rows spaced 2'–3½' apart; thin seedlings to 3"–6" apart.

YIELD. 5–8 pounds per 10' row.

CARE. Water soil regularly. Weed regularly. Fertilize once.

PESTS AND DISEASES. Aphids, Mexican bean beetles, nematodes, thrips; powdery mildew.

WHEN TO HARVEST. 50–120 days after sowing.

HOW TO HARVEST. Hand-pick or cut with pruning shears.

HOW TO STORE. *SOFT PEAS:* Refrigerate in plastic bag. *DRY PEAS:* Store in jars.

development. (Southern peas are leguminous plants and, if the seeds are inoculated, have nitrogen-fixing bacteria on their roots.)

Peas are most flavorful if they are picked when the pods are still green, their seeds fully grown but soft to the touch. Shell and cook these soft peas, or freeze or can them for future use. The pods will shell more easily, however, if they are left to ripen fully. At that stage the pods turn yellow, tan, or purple. Let the peas dry or harden on the vine, then shell and store them dry in jars.

To cook dried southern peas, simmer them, with a slab of bacon, in three times their volume of water until they are tender (1 to 1¼ hours). They are delicious served with rice or ham. Or top each portion with a sweet tomato and green pepper salsa.

SPINACH

Two thousand years before Popeye, spinach grew in the gardens of ancient Persia. A favorite today among greens, it lends its leaves to everything from soup to quiche, tasting wonderful raw or cooked. And it offers not only flavor but a wealth of vitamins and minerals as well.

For the gardener, spinach has only one irksome tendency—it bolts quickly into flower if the weather gets too warm or if days lengthen too much before harvest. To pursue just the right pace of rapid, steady growth, spinach needs the cool of spring or autumn—or even winter, where the climate is mild and nearly frost-free. Temperatures should average about 60° to 65°F/16° to 18°C, never rising above 75°F/24°C. If you live in a hot region, or want to grow a summertime crop, try instead one of the taste-alike alternatives, New Zealand or Malabar spinach, described further along in this section, amaranth (tampala), described on page 18, or sorrel, described on page 61. None of these is a true spinach, but they have the flavor of spinach. To prolong harvests as long as possible into warm weather, try bolt-resistant varieties such as 'Italian Summer', 'Teton', or 'Nordic IV'.

New Zealand spinach

Spinach does best in rich, well-drained soil and full sun. To prolong the harvest, plan to make successive sowings at 2- to 3-week intervals. Thin seedlings to 3 to 4 inches apart when they are well established. As plants grow larger and begin touching, thin out every other plant, and eat the thinnings.

When spinach has put out 6 to 8 leaves (varieties come with either flat or crinkled leaves), it's ready for harvest. Either cut off the entire plant at its base, or cut or pinch (don't pull) off just enough outer leaves for one meal. Wash thoroughly, because the leaves are usually sandy or gritty.

NEW ZEALAND SPINACH. New Zealand spinach, a native of New Zealand, was discovered in the 18th century by British explorers. A spreading, low-growing, and vigorous annual, it tolerates some cool weather but can't survive frost. It can even grow as a perennial in regions of the Deep South.

Soil for New Zealand spinach should be rich. Though it can stand poorer conditions, this kind of spinach won't produce really succulent leaves unless it's well nourished.

Presoak the seeds overnight in cool water to speed germination. Sow seeds in the garden in late spring, when the soil temperature reaches 60°F/16°C. Thin the seedlings to 12 to 18 inches apart when they are established. Pinch back runners to encourage leafy growth.

When leaves reach 3 to 4 inches long, begin harvesting them by plucking off the last 3 inches of stem tips. To promote growth and prolong the harvest until frost, pick leaves at least once a week while the leaves are young and tender. Overmature leaves may be tough and bitter.

MALABAR SPINACH. Similar to New Zealand spinach, but a native of India, Malabar spinach is a tender perennial vine. It won't survive frost, and to thrive it requires night temperatures that stay above 58°F/14°C.

Malabar spinach prefers rich soil. Sow the seeds in early summer; thin established seedlings to 12 inches apart. When the young vines are about 1 foot tall, train them on wires or a trellis. After the vines reach a height of 2 feet, pinch out a few inches of stem tip (harvesting any young, tender leaves) to encourage the plants to branch and form more stems (vines reach a maximum height of about 4 feet).

As the leaves reach full, succulent size, pick them individually. Since they're bigger and thicker than leaves of true spinach, you'll need fewer per serving.

Malabar spinach

SPROUTS

Growing sprouts is truly gardening without tears—no mucking about in the soil, no worries about weather, weeds, and insects, and you'll be enjoying your crop within days instead of weeks.

Grow alfalfa, cress, chia, mustard, or radish seeds for their tiny sprouts, which form green leaves—great for salads and sandwiches. For a more substantial crunch that's delicious in breads, entrees, or salads, try sprouts of lentils, mung beans (used in Asian cooking), or fenugreek seeds; you harvest these before the leaves open or turn green. For variety, sprout a mixture of similar-size seeds. Cress, mustard, or radish sprouts add peppery bite to alfalfa, for instance.

When you shop for seeds to sprout, be certain to buy seeds that are for sprouting and not for planting. Seeds for planting in gardens are often treated with poisonous chemicals to prevent them from rotting in the soil.

A 1- or 2-quart glass jar with a screen lid or cheesecloth cover is a good container for sprouts. (Cress seeds do better in a shallow container.) Use 1 tablespoon of alfalfa seeds to fill a quart jar with sprouts. For others, plan on using 2 to 3 tablespoons of seeds per quart jar. Discard any broken seeds of large-seeded sprouting vegetables, such as beans; don't bother for small-seeded sprouts. Discard any unhealthy looking seeds.

Soak seeds overnight in two to three times their volume of water. The next day drain the water through the screen or cheesecloth, and place the jar on its side, out of direct sunlight. Rinse and drain two or three times a day for about a week.

Give alfalfa, mustard, chia, and radish sprouts indirect sun to turn their leaves green; harvest when the leaves open. Keep fenugreek and mung bean sprouts in the dark to prevent them from developing a strong flavor. Lentil sprouts can grow in the light or dark. Harvest fenugreek, lentil, and mung when the sprouts are ½ to 1 inch long. Cover and refrigerate sprouts until you are ready to use them (up to 2 weeks).

Another way to sprout seeds is to line any shallow nonmetallic container with cheesecloth or white paper towels, and sprinkle the seeds in a solid layer over the surface. Cover the seeds with water overnight; the next morning drain and cover the container with clear plastic wrap. Add water as necessary to keep the sprouts moist. Snip or pull off sprouts when you're ready to use them.

TYPE OF VEGETABLE. Annual; warm season.

EDIBLE PARTS. Fruits.

BEST SOIL. Rich, well-drained, sandy or clay loam, pH 5.5–6.8.

WHEN TO PLANT. For summer and autumn crops, sow seeds in spring.

HOW TO PLANT. Sow seeds of vining squash 2"–3" deep, 12"–18" apart, in rows spaced 6'–8' apart; thin seedlings to 3'–8' apart. Or plant seeds of vining squash in hills (groups of four or five seeds), 5'–6' apart, in rows 7'–12' apart; thin established seedlings to two per hill. Sow seeds of bush squash 2"–3" deep, 12" apart, in rows spaced 3'–5' apart; thin seedlings to 2'–4' apart.

YIELD. 10–80 pounds per 10' row.

CARE. Water deeply to keep soil moist; avoid overhead watering. Weed regularly.

PESTS AND DISEASES. Aphids, cucumber beetles, mites, nematodes, squash bugs, squash vine borers; powdery mildew.

WHEN TO HARVEST. *SUMMER SQUASH:* 50–65 days after sowing. *WINTER SQUASH:* 60–110 days after sowing.

HOW TO HARVEST. Cut stems 2" from fruits with a sharp knife.

HOW TO STORE. *SUMMER SQUASH:* Keep cool and damp for 2–3 weeks. To preserve, can, freeze, or dry. *WINTER SQUASH:* Keep warm and dry for 8–24 weeks. To preserve, can, freeze, or dry.

SQUASH

Squash is a rewarding crop for novice and experienced gardeners. Few other vegetables produce such a bountiful harvest for so little effort.

The two basic types are summer squash and winter squash. The major differences between them are in the stage at which the fruits are harvested and in their ability to last well in storage. Summer squashes are planted for a warm-weather harvest and eaten when the fruits are small and tender—skins, immature seeds, and all. Winter squashes, with fruits that are slower to mature and usually bigger, are grown for late summer harvest and winter storage, although some can be harvested when immature and eaten like summer squashes. The skin of mature fruits is hard and inedible. Ordinarily, you scoop out the seeds and pulp before baking the squash. The seeds may be saved, dried, and roasted to eat.

Few vegetables are easier to grow than squash. With plenty of organic material added to the soil, regular watering, and occasional fertilizing, squash will fruit with reckless abandon (it will happily grow on a compost pile). Your biggest job, especially for zucchini, will be keeping the crop picked.

ABOVE: 'Golden Scallop' summer squash
TOP LEFT: 'Early Butternut' winter squash

One word of caution about watering squash. Avoid splashing water on the leaves, stems, and flowers. Squash plants are susceptible to mildew. Water them by flooding or soaking the soil after its surface has dried out.

SUMMER SQUASH. Summer squash yields prodigious crops from just a few plants and continues bearing for several weeks. The vines are large—2½ to 4 feet across at maturity—and need plenty of room. If space is limited, look for "bush" varieties—they have short vines but are still big plants.

Summer squash used to mean slender green zucchini, pale green scallop (pattypan) squash, and yellow crookneck and straightneck squash. But in recent years, plant breeders and seed companies have expanded this popular group of vegetables by developing several new types.

Zucchini now comes in a variety of shapes and colors: baseball-shaped with light green stripes; top-shaped and dark green (a cross between scallop squash and zucchini); and cylindrical and golden. You won't have much problem finding golden zucchini's beacon-yellow fruits under its foliage. Even after cooking, the skin retains its deep yellow color. Golden zucchini has a distinct zucchini flavor with slightly less bite than the green-skinned kinds.

'Ronde de Nice' summer squash in blossom

Harvest the ordinary and golden zucchini fruits when they are 4 to 6 inches long (or even smaller). Harvest the round zucchini when it's 3 to 4 inches wide, the zucchini–scallop squash hybrid when it's 2 to 3 inches across.

Straightneck squashes are yellow and smooth-skinned; crookneck squashes are yellow and may be warty; scallop squashes are white, light green, or dark green, flat, and smooth-skinned, with scalloped edges.

It's usually best to harvest straightneck squashes when they are less than 5 or 6 inches long, crookneck and scallop squashes when they are 2 to 3 inches wide. If you allow summer squashes to grow larger than this, test them for tenderness with your thumbnail (it should pierce the skin easily). If your summer squashes become large and tough, hollow them out and cook them stuffed, or shred them for zucchini cake or bread.

WINTER SQUASH. Winter squash is planted and grown just like pumpkin, which it resembles both in the size of its vine and in its fruiting characteristics. It comes in a wide array of colors, shapes, and sizes.

Acorn squash is shaped like an oversize acorn with fluted sides. Dark green or golden yellow, acorn squash ranges in size from 5 to 7½ inches long and from 4 to 6 inches wide.

Butternut squash is shaped like a fat zucchini with a stubbed toe. The tan-skinned fruit is 8 to 10 inches long and 4 to 5 inches wide.

Resembling an oversize banana with pink or gray skin, banana squash can grow up to 20 inches long and 5½ inches wide.

'Emerald Buttercup' winter squash

'Carnival' winter squash

Hubbard squash is roughly pear-shaped, sometimes with a pointed rather than rounded narrow end. The fruit grows from 10 to 15 inches long and 8 to 10 inches wide. The skin is warty and can be dark green, blue gray, or red orange.

Buttercup squash's "turbans" are 4 to 5 inches long, 6 to 8 inches wide, and dark green, gray green, or orange in color.

Included among the winter squash novelties is 'Turk's Turban', a large (8 to 12 inches wide), turban-shaped squash. It comes in an array of colors—orange, red, brown, white, and dark green. You can either eat this squash or use it for autumn decorations indoors.

Another novelty type, spaghetti squash, looks like just a fat, yellow-skinned zucchini. Once cooked and cut open, this 10- to 12-inch-long squash offers a surprise. Its unusual flesh is made up of long, spaghetti-like strands.

Melon squash, a third novelty type, looks like an extra-large butternut squash; it grows 24 to 30 inches long and sports an orange skin when ripe. The flavor is sweeter than that of most winter squash, more like a yam than a melon. It takes a long time to mature and will grow best where watermelons do well.

Harvest winter squash in late autumn after the vines have dried but before the first heavy frost. The skins of the fruits should be hard and unscratchable when tested with your thumbnail. Stems are thick; cut them with a sharp knife, leaving a 2-inch stub on the fruit.

ORGANIC GARDENS

For many gardeners, growing the healthiest food means growing vegetables organically, without relying on strong pesticides or chemical fertilizers. Luckily, organic gardeners have an increasing number of alternative, nontoxic pest controls (see pages 112–113) and natural soil amendments and fertilizers (see pages 96 and 108) to work with. More and more gardeners see organic techniques as a commonsense approach to problem solving.

TYPE OF VEGETABLE. Annual; warm season.

EDIBLE PARTS. Seeds.

BEST SOIL. Rich, well drained, pH 5.8–6.2.

WHEN TO PLANT. For summer crop, sow seeds in spring (4 weeks after last frost date).

HOW TO PLANT. Sow seeds ½" deep, 6"–12" apart, in rows spaced 2½'–3' apart; thin seedlings to 12"–18" apart.

CARE. Water generously. Protect flower heads from birds.

PESTS AND DISEASES. Aphids, cucumbers beetles, mites.

WHEN TO HARVEST. 68–80 days after sowing.

HOW TO HARVEST. Cut flower heads with about 1' of stem. Dry and remove seeds.

HOW TO STORE. Keep (roasted or unroasted) in paper bag in cool, dry place.

SUNFLOWERS

No vegetable garden should be without sunflowers. They're so easy to grow and so beautiful, you can always find room for at least one. Plant a few boisterous seeds at the ends of rows, on the outsides of melon hills, or wherever there's an open wet spot.

Many people use the seeds from these towering plants for nutritious snacks, some grow them to provide winter feed for birds, and others just enjoy their blooms.

Probably the most common sunflower variety grown is 'Mammoth'. Living up to its name, its 8- to 10-inch flower heads peer down from giant stalks, which often reach more than 10 feet high. Shorter varieties, such as 'Sunspot', bear flowers similarly large on 3- to 6-foot stalks. There are also varieties with lemon yellow, orange, mahogany, deep red, and multicolored blooms. Many of these bear multiple flowers instead of one large bloom and are usually not grown to harvest the seeds.

Easy to raise, sunflowers grow wild in some areas of the country. Sow seeds in a sunny location in spring, when the soil temperature has warmed to at least 60°F/16°C and the weather is warm.

As the seeds ripen, cover the flower heads with cheesecloth or paper bags to keep birds from eating your crop. In summer, when the seeds are mature and fairly hard, cut off the flower heads with 1 foot of stem attached, and spread them to dry in a warm, well-ventilated spot. When the seeds are thoroughly dry, remove them from the heads, and store them in a cool, dry place.

TYPE OF VEGETABLE. Perennial grown as annual; warm season.

EDIBLE PARTS. Roots.

BEST SOIL. Fertile, pH 5.0–6.5.

WHEN TO PLANT. For summer crop, plant slips in spring when soil temperature has warmed to 70°F/21°C.

HOW TO PLANT. Set out slips 10"–18" apart, on ridges 8"–15" high, spaced 3'–4' apart.

YIELD. 8–12 pounds per 10' row.

CARE. Allow soil to dry slightly between waterings. Do not overfertilize. Let vines sprawl.

PESTS AND DISEASES. Aphids, flea beetles, leafhoppers, nematodes, wireworms.

WHEN TO HARVEST. 110–120 days after setting out sprouts.

HOW TO HARVEST. Dig roots carefully, dry roots in sun, then cure.

HOW TO STORE. Keep cool and damp for 20 weeks.

SWEET POTATOES

You can grow sweet potatoes in your garden if you live where summers are long and hot. The plants are both attractive, with heart-shaped or lobed leaves, and productive.

There are two classes of sweet potatoes—those with soft, sugary, yellowish orange flesh, incorrectly labeled "yam" in grocery stores ('Beauregard', 'Centennial', 'Georgia Jet', 'Vardaman', and bush-type 'Puerto Rico'), and those with firm, dry, whitish flesh ('Yellow Jersey', 'Nemagold').

It's best to buy certified disease-free slips (rooted cuttings), but you can start your own cuttings indoors or in a hotbed 4 to 6 weeks before planting time. To start cuttings, place sweet potatoes in a container and cover them with 4 inches of moist sand. For the first 3 to 4 weeks, keep them at 80° to 85°F/27° to 29°C. When sprouts appear, reduce the temperature to 70°F/21°C until the sprouts are several inches long and ready to transplant.

Carefully pull or cut the rooted sprouts from the starter potatoes when it's time to set them out. Plant the slips in the garden in ridges or raised beds in late spring when the soil temperature has warmed to 70°F/21°C. Increase the heat around the plants with floating row covers in cool-summer areas.

If the tops are killed by frost, harvest the sweet potatoes immediately. Dry them in the sun, and then put them in a warm (about 85°F/29°C), humid place to cure for several weeks. Store them in a cool place (not below 55°F/13°C) until you're ready to use them. Their flavor improves with storage.

SWISS CHARD

Swiss chard is easy to grow and virtually indestructible. Though it's closely related to beets, this plant is grown not for its root but for its succulent stalks and tangy leaves.

There is no denying that Swiss chard is a delicious, nutritious vegetable, but it's also a very beautiful plant with brightly colored stems and lush foliage. Try growing it in containers or ornamental beds, mixed with spring-flowering bulbs (such as daffodils or tulips), annuals (such as pansies, violas, or primroses), or herbs (such as chives and parsley). Your garden will be a showstopper.

Sow seeds early in spring (2 to 4 weeks before the last frost date) in most climates, and start harvesting overcrowded

Red Swiss chard

seedlings soon after. Stalks mature in about 8 weeks and keep shooting up until the ground freezes in autumn. In mild-winter climates, plants produce for up to a year if you remove bloom stalks as they form; however, the leaves often get bitter tasting in hot weather.

To harvest, cut off outer stalks near the base, allowing central stalks and leaves to grow. If you want to use the whole plant, slice it off a couple of inches above the ground; new leaves will eventually sprout.

Some Swiss chard varieties include 'Lucullus', with yellowish green leaves and broad, yellowish white stalks; decorative 'Rhubarb', with bright crimson stalks and red-veined leaves; 'Fordhook Giant', with broad, pearl white stalks; 'Perpetual', with smooth, dark green leaves; and 'Bright Lights', a multicolored mix. All are extremely colorful additions to the vegetable or ornamental garden.

TYPE OF VEGETABLE. Annual; cool season.

EDIBLE PARTS. Leaves; stalks.

BEST SOIL. Fertile, well-drained, sandy or clay loam, pH 6.0–6.8.

WHEN TO PLANT. COLD-WINTER AREAS: For summer and autumn crops, sow seeds in early spring. MILD-WINTER AREAS: For spring and early summer harvest, sow in late winter or early spring. For autumn and winter harvest, sow in late summer to early autumn.

HOW TO PLANT. Sow seeds ½" deep, 2" apart, in rows spaced 1½–2½' apart; thin seedlings to 12" apart.

YIELD. 8–12 pounds per 10' row.

CARE. Keep soil moist. Weed regularly.

PESTS AND DISEASES. Aphids, cabbageworms, flea beetles, leaf miners, nematodes.

WHEN TO HARVEST. 50–60 days after sowing.

HOW TO HARVEST. Cut off outer stalks near base or slice off whole plant 2" above base.

HOW TO STORE. Refrigerate unwashed; use as soon as possible. To preserve, freeze or dry.

TOMATILLOS

A tomatillo is a large green cherry tomato with a husk. This tough, prolific tomato relative is easy to grow. There are two ways for the gardener to get seeds to plant: Scrape them out of fresh fruit when it's available at grocery stores, or order them from a seed catalog.

Sow tomatillo seeds directly in the garden, or start them in containers. Most seeds germinate in warm, moist soil in about 5 days. Seedlings are ready to transplant in about 3 to 4 weeks. Set them out in spring (4 to 6 weeks after the last frost date, when the soil has

warmed), and space them about 10 inches apart in fertile soil with full sun. Bury the stem almost up to the bottom leaves to encourage rooting. Water well.

Tomatillos sprawl all over the ground unless you stake or trellis them. Once mature, the plants need infrequent watering—every 5 to 10 days.

Harvest the fruits when they're walnut size (or smaller if they seem fully grown) and deep green. The husks around ripe fruit will turn dry and brown and will split. Don't remove the papery husks until you're ready to eat the fruit.

You can use raw tomatillos in salads and cooked tomatillos in salsas and preserves.

TYPE OF VEGETABLE. Annual; warm season.

EDIBLE PARTS. Fruits.

BEST SOIL. Fertile, well drained, pH 5.5 to 6.8.

WHEN TO PLANT. For summer crop, sow seeds in spring.

HOW TO PLANT. Sow seeds ⅛" deep, 2" apart, in rows spaced 2' apart; thin seedlings to 10" apart. Set up supports for vines.

YIELD. 1–2 pounds per plant.

CARE. Water every 5–10 days. Weed.

PESTS AND DISEASES. *See* "Tomatoes," page 68.

WHEN TO HARVEST. 120 days after sowing.

HOW TO HARVEST. Pull or cut fruit from plant.

HOW TO STORE. Refrigerate unwashed; use as soon as possible. To preserve, can, freeze as purée, or dry.

TOMATOES

What makes home-grown tomatoes so great? Taste and texture are surely at the top of the list. Commercially grown tomatoes that are picked green, before flavor develops, often consist of bland mealy flesh encased in a tough skin. They've been bred for long storage and easy shipping at the expense of zesty sweet taste and smooth fleshy texture.

Home gardeners, however, can choose from among dozens of varieties with real old-fashioned tomato flavor. What's more, gardeners can pick vine-ripened tomatoes at the peak of their flavor. No tomato tastes better than a juicy one plucked from the vine, rinsed with the garden hose, and eaten right on the spot.

CHOOSING TOMATOES

SIZES, SHAPES, AND COLORS. A wide choice of sizes, shapes, and colors awaits the adventuresome tomato gardener.

Tomatoes range in size from the pop-in-the-mouth cherry type, such as 'Sweet 100', 'Tiny Tim', 'Gardener's Delight', 'Camp Joy', and 'Sugar Bunch', to the 1- to 2-pound giants, such as 'Big Beef', 'Beefeater', 'Brandywine', and 'Beefmaster'. Between these extremes are medium-size tomatoes such as 'Ace', 'Early Girl', 'Better Boy', 'Celebrity', and 'Flor-america'.

Besides the usual round, red tomatoes, you can grow small yellow ones shaped like pears or plums or larger ones, such as 'Lemon Boy'. These have mild, sweet flavor, and some have low acid content. Or you can grow orange-colored tomatoes, such as 'Husky Gold' or 'Burpee's Jubilee'. There are even pink tomatoes: 'Oxheart' produces

ABOVE: 'Enchantress' tomatoes
TOP LEFT: A harvest of large and small tomatoes

large fruits that can weigh 1 pound each, and 'Ponderosa' has mild-tasting 1½-pound fruits. For even more unusual salad additions, try some of the heirloom varieties, such as 'Cherokee Purple', which is pinkish brown with green stripes on its shoulders, or 'Marvel Stripe', which is yellow with green stripes.

If you want to grow special tomatoes for canning or to make your own tomato sauce or paste, you'll find types available for processing, such as 'La Rossa', 'Roma' (plum-shaped), 'San Rimo', 'Royal Chico', and 'Viva Italia'. These have a high amount of solid matter and ripen over a short period for early harvest.

DETERMINATE AND INDETERMINATE PLANTS. The number of tomatoes a plant produces is often (though not always) related to whether it's a determinate or an indeterminate tomato. Determinate tomatoes are shorter-growing types, which reach only 3 to 5 feet; their crop tends to ripen over a shorter period than the crop of indeterminate tomatoes.

The vines of indeterminate tomatoes keep on growing until frost kills them; some varieties, like 'Better Boy' and 'Big Boy', can reach 12 to 14 feet in height. Indeterminate vines tend to produce larger crops over a longer period than the bush determinate types. Those extra-large tomato plants, such as 'Big Boy', however, make you wait an extra-long time—so long that they really can't be grown where the summer growing season is short.

TYPE OF VEGETABLE. Annual; warm season.

EDIBLE PARTS. Fruits.

BEST SOIL. Fertile, well drained, pH 5.5–6.8.

WHEN TO PLANT. For summer crop, set out plants in spring (1½–7 weeks after last frost date). Sow seeds in flats 5–7 weeks before you intend to set out plants.

HOW TO PLANT. Space seedlings 1½'–4' apart in rows spaced 3'–4' apart. Remove lower leaves, and cover half to three-quarters of stem with soil.

YIELD. 15–45 pounds per 10' row.

CARE. Water and weed regularly. Stake large, sprawling varieties. Protect plants set out early from frost.

PESTS AND DISEASES. Aphids, cutworms, flea beetles, leaf miners, nematodes, tomato hornworms, whiteflies; fusarium wilt, verticillium wilt.

WHEN TO HARVEST. 50–90 days after setting out plants.

HOW TO HARVEST. Cut or gently pull fruit from stem.

HOW TO STORE. Refrigerate unwashed; use as soon as possible. To preserve, can, freeze as purée, or dry.

OTHER FACTORS. Early ripening is an important characteristic to gardeners in areas with short growing seasons or chilly summers, such as the cool Northwest. Reliable varieties in cool-summer areas include 'Stupice' and 'Oregon Spring'. Where summers are very short, try 'Northern Exposure' and 'Early Girl'. You can also use floating row covers or other techniques to extend the season (see pages 124–125).

Seed packets, catalog descriptions, and tags on packs of seedlings give the maturity dates. Keep in mind that the dates are only rough averages of the time that will elapse between transplanting and the first ripe fruit under good growing conditions.

Disease resistance is another element to look for when searching for the great garden tomato. Seed packets and pack tags bear initials to tell you if the plants have some inbred resistance to one or more of the big four tomato troublemakers: "V" for verticillium wilt; "F" for fusarium wilt; "N" for nematodes (which cause root knots); "T" for tobacco mosaic virus.

It would be a boon to have a failproof list of tomatoes that taste great, ripen early, produce reliably and bountifully, and resist diseases. But climate and soil differences make it impossible to list even one or two varieties in each size, shape, and color of tomato available that will do well everywhere. For instance, beefsteak-type tomatoes—the gorgeous behemoths—usually thrive in the South, Midwest, and East but flop in the West because they need long, humid summers and warm night temperatures (65° to 70°F/18° to 21°C). Your local garden center and Cooperative Extension Service—not to mention neighborhood gardeners willing to share their expertise—are the best guides to selecting great garden tomato varieties for your area.

GETTING STARTED

Start your own tomatoes from seeds, or purchase seedlings from a nursery or garden center. The seedlings should be sturdy—not weak, spindly, or overmature. If you grow your own seedlings, start them indoors 5 to 7 weeks before you plan to set them out (at least 10 days after the last frost date in spring). Expose tender seedlings, including purchased tomato plants, to cool outdoor air gradually. This is called "hardening off" the plants before setting them out in the garden, and it will decrease transplant shock.

If you have heavy clay soil or very sandy soil, it's a good idea to dig in ample organic matter before planting. Add compost, peat moss, or ground bark at the rate of one part organic matter to two parts soil.

Unlike most other plants, tomato seedlings prefer deep planting. You can bury as much as half to three-quarters of the stem after removing the leaflets. Roots will form along the buried part of the stem and strengthen the plants.

If you're going to stake the plants, set the seedlings out 2 feet apart in rows spaced 3 to 4 feet apart. If they will not be staked, set them out 1½ to 4 feet apart in rows spaced 3 to 4 feet apart. Remember that indeterminate vine types need the greatest amount of space. Pinch off the suckers that form at the notch between a branch and the main stem to get earlier ripening and larger tomatoes. Let a few suckers develop, to get more fruit and greater protection against sunscald.

Gardeners in cool-weather zones (where summers are cool or short) can give their plants a faster start by covering the soil with black plastic sheeting or by planting tomatoes in bottomless containers made of old automobile tires. These devices can speed the growth of roots by raising the soil temperature.

If you set out plants early in the season, be prepared to cover them with hotcaps or other protective devices (see pages 124–125) to give them protection from frost.

Listing continues >

Hand-picking is an effective way to control the dread tomato hornworm (see page 117 for other techniques). However, these pests are not easy to see because their color blends in well with tomato foliage. Here's a trick learned from a retired criminologist, who uses ultraviolet light to detect fingerprints. Buy a small, hand-held, battery-powered flashlight that uses fluorescent bulbs. Replace the fluorescent bulb with an ultraviolet bulb—a good old black light from the 60s (you'll find everything you need in a hardware store). Now go hunting for hornworms at night with your new light. Voilà! The critters glow in the dark.

'Sweet 100' tomatoes

CONTINUED CARE

Watering tomatoes is relatively simple: water often enough to keep the soil in the root zone damp but not soggy. This may mean watering seedlings every 1 to 2 days until they become established. During dry spells you should water well-established plants deeply about every 10 days.

It's wise to support tomatoes on stakes or in wire cages. This not only keeps plants neat and avoids fruit rot by keeping the fruit from touching the soil but also allows better air circulation through the plant to prevent foliage diseases. In extremely hot areas, don't use metal supports—they may burn plants.

If you use stakes, choose sturdy ones at least 1 inch thick and 6 feet tall. Hammer the stakes into the ground 1 foot from the plant at the time of planting. To avoid any damage to stems, tie the tomato vines to stakes or other supports with strips of cloth or other soft ties. (For ideas for tomato supports, see page 107.)

If the soil is well prepared, you probably won't have to fertilize tomatoes until the fruit starts to develop. At that time, you can apply a low-nitrogen fertilizer that is high in potassium and phosphorus. Avoid giving a high-nitrogen fertilizer, which would encourage lush foliage at the expense of fruit production.

Harvest tomatoes when they reach the size and color you prefer. Be sure to harvest the last of the crop before the first frost in autumn.

DEALING WITH PROBLEMS

Hot weather can cause plants to stop setting fruits, especially when temperatures go above 100°F/38°C. If that happens where you live, you can decrease the temperature around your plants a few degrees with a protective cover. Use nursery shade cloth draped over stakes, or construct a simple wooden framework to support a lath or bamboo shade. These devices also prevent sunscald on fruit.

On the other hand, tomatoes do need warm temperatures to pollinate reliably: 65°F/18°C for late varieties, 60°F/16°C for early varieties. Fruit-setting hormones that you apply to the flowers may be worth the expense where summer nights are cool, but they are not always effective. You can also encourage pollination by tickling the blossoms once or twice during the hottest part of each day.

Blossom-end rot, which looks just like its name—a hard, brown, leathery spot on the blossom end of the fruit—is another common problem. Though this malady is still somewhat of a mystery, it is associated with wide fluctuations in soil moisture and perhaps a calcium deficiency. Try to maintain even soil moisture by watering regularly and mulching. You might also want to apply a fertilizer with calcium as a precaution if you've had a problem with blossom-end rot in previous years in the same garden soil. Adding lime to acid soil helps. Gypsum (calcium sulfate) may be added to any soil to provide calcium.

Tomato hornworms are fat, green 4-inch worms that love tomato leaves but also eat green or ripe fruit. Control is simple, if brutal: Pick them off, and stomp on them.

GROWING TOMATOES IN CONTAINERS

Though any tomato plant can grow in a container that's large enough, the dwarf and miniature varieties are best suited for pots with a soil capacity of 1 cubic foot. Try varieties such as 'Patio', 'Sweet 100', 'Small Fry' (grows like a small tree, needs to be caged), 'Pixie', 'Early Salad' (good for a hanging basket or trellis), 'Tumblin' Tom' (hanging basket), and dwarf 'Champion'. Put a stake in each pot at the time of planting, and tie the stem to the stake as the plant grows.

Standard-size tomatoes need a container with a capacity of 3 cubic feet.

'Brandywine' heirloom tomatoes

HEIRLOOM VEGETABLES

Heirloom vegetables are the varieties that your grandparents, great-grandparents, and maybe even great-great-grandparents used to grow. While modern vegetable hybrids have their strengths, including uniformity, pest resistance, and vigor, heirloom varieties also have their virtues, such as adaptation to local climates, exceptional flavor, and unique appearance. Growing and preserving heirloom varieties helps maintain a diverse genetic reserve, which society may need someday if modern hybrids should fail. Besides, these old varieties are part of gardening history.

Many heirloom varieties are mentioned in our descriptions of individual vegetables. If you want explore the world of heirloom vegetables more fully, send for a catalog from one of the seed companies that specialize in old varieties. Addresses for several are listed on pages 126–127.

TURNIPS

Edible from top to bottom, turnips offer good nutrition in a package of very few calories. With most kinds, you can eat the leaves when they're young and tender and the roots when they reach maturity. With some varieties you eat only the leaves.

Turnips are frost hardy and like cool weather. You can sow seeds in early spring for a harvest before the weather gets hot, and sow again in late summer and autumn for a harvest when the weather cools down.

Some people prefer the roots from the autumn harvest because they are most flavorful and tender then. Turnips protected from frost by a straw mulch can stay in the ground in autumn until you're ready to dig them up and use them, but harvest them before the ground freezes solid.

Turnips aren't fussy about care, but they like rich soil.

Grow the ones you want for leaves closer together than the ones you want for roots. As the greens grow, pick the outer leaves. Harvest the roots when they're 2 to 3 inches wide; they become tougher and more pungent as they grow fatter.

TYPE OF VEGETABLE. Annual; cool season.

EDIBLE PARTS. Roots; leaves.

BEST SOIL. Rich, pH 5.5–6.8.

WHEN TO PLANT. For summer crop, sow seeds in spring. COLD-WINTER CLIMATES: For autumn crop, sow seeds in mid- to late summer. MILD-WINTER CLIMATES: For autumn crop, sow seeds in autumn.

HOW TO PLANT. Sow seeds ½" deep, 1" apart, in rows spaced 1'–3' apart (roots) or 6"–12" apart (greens); or broadcast seeds, and rake to cover. Thin seedlings to 2"–6" apart (roots) or 1"–4" apart (greens).

YIELD. 8–12 pounds of roots per 10' row.

PESTS AND DISEASES. Cabbage root maggots, wireworms.

WHEN TO HARVEST. 30–60 days after planting.

HOW TO HARVEST. *ROOTS:* Dig with garden fork. *GREENS:* Cut tender outer leaves.

HOW TO STORE. *ROOTS:* Keep cool and damp for 8–12 weeks. *GREENS:* Refrigerate unwashed; use as soon as possible. Do not preserve.

WATERMELONS

Gardeners with plenty of space and a hot summer in store should take the opportunity to grow this big, jolly blimp of a melon with its sweet, siren pink (or bright golden) flesh. It's a delight, especially for children.

'Cherokee Moon and Stars' watermelon

A favorite of the South and West, watermelons need plenty of summer heat. Large varieties may require 95 days of sun drenching, but you can buy smaller, earlier-ripening "icebox" types, the yellow-fleshed 'Golden Crown' and red-fleshed 'Sugar Baby'. Every year seems to bring new varieties, adapted to more areas. Compact bush varieties, such as 'Bush Sugar Baby' and 'Bush Baby II', can even be grown in small gardens. If you don't like seeds, plant seedless varieties, such as 'King of Hearts', 'Sweet Heart', or 'Redball Seedless'. Want a speckled watermelon? Try 'Moon and Stars', an heirloom variety that has dark green skin spotted with yellow.

Sow five or six seeds per hill when the soil has warmed to 70°F/21°C; thin seedlings to one or two per hill. Keep the soil moist, but avoid overhead watering. If you live in a cool-summer or short-season climate, cover the seedlings with floating row covers to speed them along (see page 125). Feed with a complete fertilizer every 4 to 6 weeks. A mulch of straw helps keep the soil moist and warm and reduces chances of rotting. For fatter melons, thin fruits to three or four per vine when they're small.

A watermelon is probably ripe if it makes a dull "thunk" when thumped, if its underside has turned from white to pale yellow, and if the tendril opposite the stem of the melon has withered.

TYPE OF VEGETABLE. Annual; warm season.

EDIBLE PARTS. Fruits.

BEST SOIL. Rich, pH 6.0–7.5.

WHEN TO PLANT. For summer crop, sow seeds in spring.

HOW TO PLANT. Sow five or six seeds 1"–2" deep, in hills spaced 6'–8' apart; thin seedlings to one or two per hill. Or sow seeds 1"–2" deep, 12" apart, in rows spaced 6'–7' apart; thin seedlings to 2'–3' apart.

YIELD. 8–40 pounds per 10' row.

CARE. Keep soil moist, leaves and fruit dry.

PESTS AND DISEASES. Aphids, cucumber beetles, mites; fusarium wilt, powdery mildew, verticillium wilt.

WHEN TO HARVEST. 70–95 days after planting.

HOW TO HARVEST. Cut fruit from vine with pruning shears.

HOW TO STORE. Refrigerate unwashed; use as soon as possible. To preserve, can.

GROWING
BERRIES

Berry gardening lets you enjoy sweet vine-ripened fruit at its peak without paying gourmet market prices. Truly nothing can compare to the flavor of fresh-picked strawberries, raspberries, and grapes. That's an incentive for many vegetable gardeners to include a berry plot in their plans.

Details on growing specific berries—both the most popular and less well known ones—are given in the descriptions of individual types on the pages that follow. Berries are perennials, so the climate maps for vegetables on pages 7–8, giving spring and fall frost dates, are less relevant than knowing which regions of the country are most suitable for particular fruits. Accompanying the descriptions of berries on the following pages are small maps detailing the best growing areas for that crop. Since varieties of strawberries are adapted for almost all regions, however, no map is offered of their growing areas.

USING THE SIDEBAR LISTS

Accompanying each individual description is a sidebar list that tells you at a glance how the berries grow on the plant, the type of soil they prefer, a summary of when and how to plant the berries, what care the plants require during growth and dormant seasons, and common pests and diseases you may have to combat. For ideas on how to control berry pests and diseases, see pages 112–119. Finally, the sidebar indicates the yield of berries that you can expect, when and how to harvest the crop, and how to store any that you don't eat right away.

Use the sidebar lists as guides to determine whether you want to grow a particular berry, as well as quick reference sources for cultivation facts.

CHOOSING A SITE

Because berries live and bear for many years, it's important to select a location where you won't have to disturb them. Choose a spot with full sunlight, free air circulation, and good soil that drains well.

Try to plant berries where perennial weeds have been eliminated. If you plant where you have had a garden in the past, be sure to avoid soil where tomatoes, potatoes, peppers, or eggplants have grown in the past 3 years. These vegetables encourage a fungus disease—verticillium wilt—to build up in the soil; it can kill most cane and bush berries.

CHOOSING WHICH BERRIES TO GROW

The maps and sidebar lists can help you decide which berries to plant in your garden, based on your personal taste preferences and local conditions in your area. While the descriptions offer general guidelines about climate conditions, varieties, and seasonal care, be sure to consult your local Cooperative Extension Service, which can provide advice more precisely geared for your particular region.

PRUNING

Like other fruiting plants, most berries require regular, frequent pruning. The individual descriptions of berries tell how and when to prune and how to train vines on trellises or other supports, if appropriate. Drawings accompany the instructions, for quick reference. Pruning varies within a berry crop depending on type, in some cases. Be sure to follow the instructions for the type you are growing. Proper pruning is an essential element if you want to ensure that your plants remain healthy and provide continuing bountiful harvests.

Clusters of pale pink gooseberries peek out from their green, lobed foliage

PLANTING BLACKBERRIES

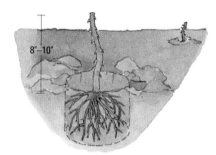

Plant trailing blackberries in holes, widely spaced to allow them room to grow. After planting, cut back canes to 8–10 inches long. Leave 9–10 feet between rows of plants.

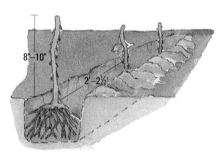

Plant erect blackberries in trenches. After planting, cut back canes to 8–10 inches long. Leave 6–10 feet between rows of plants.

█ Best climate areas.

█ Suitable for selected varieties.

Plants do best where summers are cool and moist and winters are cold, but not colder than −15°F/−26°C. Some kinds do well where summers are warm and moist. Some varieties of thornless blackberries, boysenberries, and youngberries are hardy only to 0°F/−18°C.

BLACKBERRIES

Blackberries have much the same growth cycle and cultural needs as raspberries, their close cousins. They send up canes the first year and produce berries on them the second. They prefer areas with cool, moist summers, though some kinds are native to the warm, moist regions of the Southeast and can tolerate warmer climates, and there are also some hardy varieties (see map below for the areas of best adaptation).

Included in the blackberry category are cane berries known as dewberry (native to the South), loganberry, boysenberry, youngberry, and olallieberry. Berries range in color from jet black to red and in taste from sweet to tart, with a variety of flavors.

Blackberries develop in two distinctly different forms. Varieties typical of the West Coast, so-called trailing blackberries, such as 'Boysen', 'Cascade', 'Logan', and 'Olallie', produce long vine-like canes that need to be trellised. Blackberries of the Midwest and East, varieties such as 'Darrow', 'Arapaho', and 'Navaho', grow upright, on shorter canes. Crosses between trailing and erect types are called semierect.

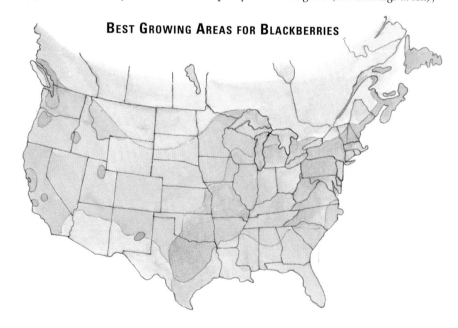

In general, blackberries have wicked thorns, though many thornless varieties have been developed. Different varieties do best in different parts of the United States and Canada, so it pays to get local recommendations from a nursery or your Cooperative Extension Service. Though most kinds are self-pollinating, some varieties in the South need a second variety as a pollinizer.

PLANTING

Blackberries thrive in rich, well-prepared soil and a sunny location. Most kinds are fairly hardy, but some can't take hard freezing unless you completely cover their canes with mulch. To avoid verticillium wilt, don't plant blackberries in soil where you have raised potatoes, eggplants, peppers, or tomatoes in the last 3 years.

For best chances that your blackberries will produce well, start with certified stock from a reliable nursery. At planting time, set the plants 1 inch deeper into the ground than they grew in the nursery. Give blackberries plenty of room to grow (see drawings at left),

BEST GROWING AREAS FOR BLACKBERRIES

TRAINING BLACKBERRIES

Weave long canes of trailing blackberries through wires for support.

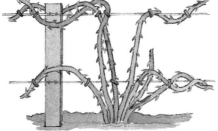

Selectively tie long canes of erect blackberries upright or along wires.

and set up a trellis, such as two wires strung between posts, to support them. Use 3-by-3s or 4-by-4s for the posts or round posts 3 or 4 inches in diameter, made of rot-resistant wood, such as redwood or cedar. Anchor the posts well. Then string 10- or 11-gauge smooth galvanized wire between them (see drawings above).

Unless they get ample rainfall, you need to give blackberries water liberally during their growing season until the harvest is complete. Then reduce watering.

Blackberries have perennial roots but biennial canes. Canes grow to their full length or height in the first year. In that year they are called "primocanes." After flowering and fruiting in the second year, the canes, now called "floricanes," die and should be cut down.

PRUNING

ERECT BLACKBERRIES. In the summer of the first year, pinch or cut the tops of new canes (primocanes) down to 2 to 2½ feet tall to promote branching. In early spring of the second year, as new growth starts, cut back the side branches to 12 to 15 inches long, and remove any dead or diseased canes (see drawings below). (New canes will be growing from the ground and will need to be topped during the summer when they are taller than 2 to 2½ feet.) After you've picked all the berries, cut to ground level all 2-year-old canes that have fruited.

Listing continues >

PRUNING ERECT BLACKBERRIES

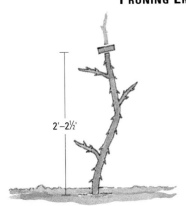

2'–2½'

Prune erect blackberry cane to 2–2½ feet in summer of first year after planting. In later years, top new canes from ground this way during summer.

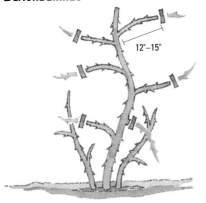

12"–15"

In early spring of second year, trim side branches to 12–15 inches long, and remove dead or diseased branches. In later years, prune all year-old canes this way.

GROWTH HABIT. Berries borne in clusters on 2-year-old canes.

BEST SOIL. Rich, well-drained, sandy loam, pH 5.5–6.8.

WHEN TO PLANT. COLD-WINTER CLIMATES: In early spring before new growth starts. MILD-WINTER CLIMATES: In early spring or autumn.

HOW TO PLANT. *ERECT BLACKBERRIES:* Set out bare-root plants 2'–2½' apart in trenches 5"–6" deep, spaced 6'–10' apart. *TRAILING BLACK-BERRIES:* Set out bare-root plants in holes 5"–6" deep, spaced 5'–8' apart, in rows 9'–10' apart. Set up trellis to support canes. *ALL BLACKBERRIES:* Cover crowns with 1" of soil. Cut canes back to 8"–10".

YIELD. 1 quart of berries per plant.

CARE. Keep soil moist. Weed regularly. Tie trailing kinds to trellis. Prune (see instructions in text).

PESTS AND DISEASES. Aphids, borers, mites, strawberry root weevils; verticillium wilt.

WHEN TO HARVEST. In spring or summer, when berries are full size and fully colored.

HOW TO HARVEST. Pull berries gently from stems.

HOW TO STORE. Refrigerate unwashed; use as soon as possible. To preserve, can or freeze.

PRUNING TRAILING BLACKBERRIES

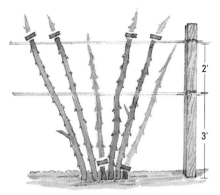

At beginning of second year of growth, tie trailing blackberry canes to trellis, and prune to height of 5–6 feet; prune weak and diseased canes to ground.

TRAILING BLACKBERRIES. Let the canes grow unpruned along the ground the first year. At the end of the first season, if your winters are cold, cover the canes with mulch to protect them from freezing. If your winters are mild, no mulch is needed. At the start of growth in the second year, tie the year-old canes to a trellis, either cutting off their tops at 5 feet (see drawing at left) or weaving long canes onto the trellis (see top left drawing on page 75). Remove weak, dead, or diseased canes. After the harvest is over, cut to the ground all canes that bore fruit. New canes that grew during the summer will be tied to the trellis the next year.

BLUEBERRIES

Today's backyard blueberries descend from solid Yankee stock. Members of the heath family (and therefore cousins of azaleas, rhododendrons, and cranberries), their forebears were wild, upright-growing bushes from New England. Hybrids that would produce well in gardens were first achieved in 1909; before that, if you wanted blueberry pancakes for breakfast, first you had to roam the countryside and harvest blueberries wherever they grew.

Today, you can raise blueberries in many areas of the United States and Canada (see map below), provided you can give plants certain conditions. Northern highbush blueberries, such as 'Bluecrop', 'Patriot', and 'Jersey', need cold winters. Some of the newer southern highbush blueberries, such as 'Cape Fear' and 'Georgia Gem', are better adapted to mild-winter areas. Rabbiteye blueberries, such as 'Tifblue' and 'Woodard', are best adapted to the mild-winter regions of the South and West. There are also very hardy, dwarf hybrids (they grow about 1½ to 3 feet high), such as 'Northblue', 'Northsky', and 'Tophat', which are ideal for containers and confined areas and best adapted to cold-winter climates.

In addition to producing delicious fruit, blueberry plants excel in the landscape, adapting successfully in both sun and shade, and producing colorful fall foliage.

Native types occur and plants grow with the least amount of effort in green areas of map. Highbush varieties do best where winters are cold and summers are not too hot and dry. Southern highbush blueberries are more widely adapted. Rabbiteye varieties do best where winters are mild and summers are warm, especially in southeastern states.

BEST GROWING AREAS FOR BLUEBERRIES

PLANTING

Blueberries need a very acidic soil (pH between 3.5 and 5.0) that is rich in organic matter. To increase soil acidity, you can mix 1 pound of soil sulfur per 100 square feet of soil. Maintain acidity by using fertilizers formulated for acid-soil plants. Most soils will benefit from the addition of generous amounts of peat moss or other organic material.

Plant blueberries in the autumn or winter if your winter is mild (compared to New England's), otherwise in early spring. Buy 2- or 3-year-old certified plants that are 1 to 3 feet high. To allow for essential cross-pollination, choose two or three different varieties to raise together. Prune transplants to three or four of their strongest shoots, and prune off the plump fruit buds.

Prepare to plant by digging holes 12 to 18 inches deep and as wide as they are deep, spaced 4 to 6 feet apart, in rows 8 to 12 feet apart (see drawing bottom left). Blend the soil with organic matter before backfilling and setting in the plants. Put down a thick mulch around each plant to help shallow roots to retain moisture and to keep down weeds.

During the critical first 3 years, blueberries need at least 1 inch of water per week in the growing season. Don't fertilize at all the first year, and fertilize only lightly the second and third years. Use a fertilizer blended for azaleas and rhododendrons or use ammonium sulfate, and divide it into several applications during the growing season in the second and third years. After that, apply fertilizer just once a year, in early spring.

PRUNING

Blueberries produce fruit on short branches (called spurs) for several years. In early spring of the first 2 years, when the plants are dormant, remove flower buds and prune lightly to remove low canes, drooping stems, and crossing branches. Thereafter (see drawing bottom right) remove not only drooping stems and crossing branches but also broken stems and branches and old twiggy stems—especially stems that are more than 5 or 6 years old. After 3 years, also cut back the tips of vigorous canes, leaving six to eight buds, to promote side branching, and cut back long stems to a length where their fruit can be harvested easily. The goal is to keep canes well spaced so that berries have ample exposure to sunlight, to force side branching, and, in later years, to keep bushes from growing too tall. Leave intact all vigorous stems that bear well, if they come up from the ground or from the base of the plant.

GROWTH HABIT. Berries borne along 1-year-old branches of bushes.

BEST SOIL. Well-drained, sandy loam with abundant organic matter, pH 3.5–5.0.

WHEN TO PLANT. *HIGHBUSH VARIETIES:* In early spring before growth starts. *RABBITEYE VARIETIES:* In late autumn or winter.

HOW TO PLANT. *HIGHBUSH VARIETIES:* Set out bare-root plants in holes 12"–18" deep, 4'–5' apart, in rows spaced 8'–10' apart. *RABBITEYE VARIETIES:* Set out bare-root plants in holes 12"–18" deep, 4'–6' apart, in rows spaced 10'–12' apart.

YIELD. 2–7 pounds per plant.

CARE. Keep soil moist. Mulch heavily with organic matter. Weed regularly. Prune in late winter or early spring before growth starts. Cover berries with netting to protect them from birds.

PESTS AND DISEASES. Leafhoppers, mites, nematodes; powdery mildew.

WHEN TO HARVEST. 60–80 days after bloom, when berries are entirely blue and taste sweet.

HOW TO HARVEST. Pull berries gently from stems.

HOW TO STORE. Refrigerate unwashed; use as soon as possible. To preserve, can or freeze.

PLANTING BLUEBERRIES

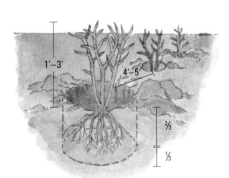

Plant blueberries in holes that are a third deeper than the roots. Space the rows 8–12 feet apart.

PRUNING BLUEBERRIES

In third and subsequent years, remove old and crossing branches, shorten vigorous growth.

CURRANTS

Though prized in Europe for jams and jellies, currants are cultivated much less in the United States and Canada. Since they need a cold climate, currants are grown primarily in the Pacific Northwest and British Columbia, the northern United States, and adjacent southern Canada (see map on next page).

The small, tidy bushes offer striking beauty in spring and summer, their grapelike clusters of berries glistening amid the new foliage. Red currants, such as 'Red Lake', 'Wilder', and 'Perfection', are most common, but white ('White Imperial') and black varieties ('Consort', 'Coronet', and 'Crusader' are immune to rust) also exist.

ABOVE: White currants
TOP LEFT: Black currants

Currants need to be cooked to be palatable, so they are usually used in jam or jelly. Because they ripen all at once, harvesting can be a sizable job.

Caution: In some areas it is illegal to plant currants, which can be hosts to white pine blister rust. Check with your local Cooperative Extension Service.

PLANTING

Plant bare-root currants in spring or autumn in fertile, well-drained soil. Dig holes 5 to 6 inches deep, spaced 3 to 4 feet apart, in rows 6 to 10 feet apart (see drawing bottom left). Cut back all but the three strongest stems, making each cut just above an outward-facing bud.

PRUNING

Currants bear fruit on 1-year-old stems and on spurs (short side branches) on 2- and 3-year-old stems. Prune them during winter dormancy. The first year, cut back stems to short stubs with three to four buds per stem. (Black currants don't need to be cut back.) The top bud on each stem should face outward. The second year, cut back all but five to eight main stems; shorten those to one-third of their length, cutting above an outward-facing bud (see drawing bottom right). The third year, remove crowded stems, leaving eight to nine sturdy stems; cut these to half their length. Thereafter, each year remove all stems more than 3 years old and any weak, diseased, or drooping stems. If growth is dense, younger branches may need thinning to six to eight per bush.

GROWTH HABIT. Berries borne in clusters on 1- to 4-year-old branches of bushes.

BEST SOIL. Fertile, well-drained, sandy to clay loam, pH 5.5–6.8.

WHEN TO PLANT. Spring or autumn.

HOW TO PLANT. Set out bare-root plants in holes 5"–6" deep, 3'–4' apart, in rows spaced 6'–10' apart. Cut back all but three strongest stems.

YIELD. 4–6 quarts per plant.

CARE. Water and weed regularly. Fertilize yearly. Prune yearly (after fourth year) in early spring before growth starts.

PESTS AND DISEASES. Aphids, borers, mites.

WHEN TO HARVEST. In summer, when berries are soft and fully colored.

HOW TO HARVEST. Pull berries gently from stems.

HOW TO STORE. Refrigerate unwashed; use as soon as possible. To preserve, dry.

PLANTING CURRANTS

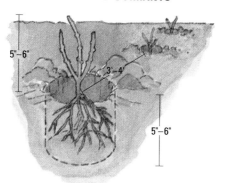

5"–6"

3'–4'

5"–6"

Plant currants in holes, and cut back to three strongest stems.

PRUNING CURRANTS

On established plants, remove old and crowded growth, shorten stems.

BEST GROWING AREAS FOR CURRANTS AND GOOSEBERRIES

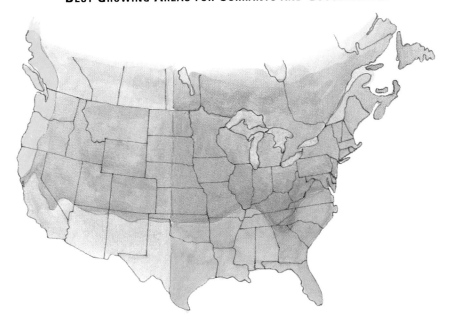

■ Best climate areas.

□ Good climate: need to water in summer.

▨ Tolerable climate: need to water in summer.

■ Not adapted: summers too long and hot for currants and generally for gooseberries, although gooseberries have been grown successfully in parts of area.

■ Not adapted: summers too hot and dry.

Currants and gooseberries both do best where winters are cold and summers are not hot and dry; they are hardy to about −40°F/−40°C. Currants generally need colder weather and cooler summers than gooseberries.

Red gooseberries

GOOSEBERRIES

The elusive gooseberry seldom turns up in the grocery store, so gooseberry gourmands have to grow their own.

The most widely grown gooseberries are varieties of the American species, *Ribes hirtellum*. They are attractive shrubs with pretty spring flowers, lobed leaves that turn bright colors in fall, and colorful fruit. Some varieties, such as 'Fredonia', 'Poorman', 'Pixwell', and 'Welcome', have pink to red berries; others, such as 'Oregon Champion', have green ones. You can eat them fresh (they're tarter than other berries) or cooked in pie or jam. Plants are usually thorny, but some varieties, such as 'Welcome', are almost thornless.

Easygoing as long as the climate is cool enough, gooseberries are grown mostly in the northern United States and in Canada but also in some areas of the South (see map above).

Caution: In some areas it is illegal to plant gooseberries, which can be hosts to white pine blister rust. Check with your local Cooperative Extension Service.

PLANTING

Plant bare-root gooseberries in spring or autumn in fertile, well-drained soil. If your summer gets very hot, plant them against a north wall. Dig holes 5 to 6 inches deep, spaced 3 to 4 feet apart, in rows 6 to 10 feet apart (see drawing on page 80, top left). Cut back all but the three strongest stems, making each cut just above an outward-facing bud.

Because gooseberries bear for as long as 20 years, plan a permanent location for planting them.

Listing continues >

GROWTH HABIT. Berries borne in clusters on 1- to 4-year-old branches of bushes.

BEST SOIL. Fertile, well-drained, sand or clay loam, pH 5.5–6.8.

WHEN TO PLANT. Spring or autumn.

HOW TO PLANT. Set out bare-root plants in holes 5"–6" deep, 3'–4' apart, in rows 6'–10' apart. Cut back all but three strongest stems.

YIELD. 4–6 quarts per plant.

CARE. Water and weed regularly. Fertilize yearly. Prune every year (after fourth year) in spring before growth starts.

PESTS AND DISEASES. Aphids, mites.

WHEN TO HARVEST. In summer, when berries are soft and fully colored.

HOW TO HARVEST. Pull berries gently from stems.

HOW TO STORE. Refrigerate unwashed; use as soon as possible. To preserve, can.

PLANTING GOOSEBERRIES

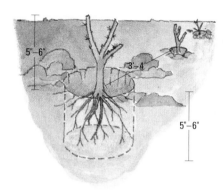

Plant gooseberries in holes, and cut back to three strongest stems.

PRUNING GOOSEBERRIES

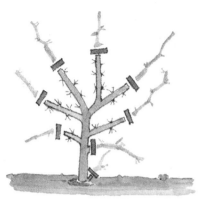

At second year of growth, remove old and crowded stems, shorten vigorous ones.

PRUNING

Gooseberries bear fruit on 1-year-old stems and on spurs (short side branches) on 2- and 3-year-old stems. The first year, prune the stems to short stubs with three to four buds per stem. The second year, remove all but six to eight main stems; shorten those to one-half their length (see drawing directly left). The third year, remove weak stems, shorten main stems to one-half their length, and shorten side shoots to 1 to 3 inches. Thereafter, each year remove weak and diseased stems and all stems more than 3 years old.

'Concord' grapes

'Flame Seedless' grapes

GRAPES

From antiquity until today, viticulture—growing grapes—has flourished as one of humanity's few enduring traditions.

Though grapes are much glorified as the source of wine, this discussion focuses on only those varieties called table or dessert grapes—the kinds used mainly for eating fresh or for making jellies.

Besides their sumptuous contribution to fruit bowls and jelly jars, grapes bring exceptional beauty to a garden. Vines create a fascinating filigree of heart-shaped leaves, twisting canes, and curling tendrils. Their glistening fruit comes in a color range from pale gold green through shades of red and purple to deep blue black. Extraordinarily long-lived, vines may endure for 100 years and more.

Grapes can be grown nearly everywhere in the United States—in many different types of soil and in widely varying climates—and in certain regions of western and eastern Canada (see map on next page). Derived over the centuries from wild species of the Near East and North America, varieties grown today number roughly 8,000.

THREE CLASSES OF GRAPES

Grape varieties fall into three major classes. Two encompass native North American vines: American grapes *(Vitis labrusca)* and muscadine grapes *(Vitis rotundifolia)*. Both are also known as "slipskin" grapes because of the way their skins easily peel free. The third class is European grapes *(Vitis vinifera)*.

In addition, numerous hybrids of European and American grapes have been bred over the years to bring out traits of hardiness or fruit quality.

AMERICAN GRAPES. Also called "foxgrapes," American grapes adapt best to cold-winter areas. They are native to the eastern portion of North America, from New York and adjacent Canada south to Georgia and west to the Mississippi valley. American grapes tend to be the most resistant to grape-marauding pests and diseases, many of which are indigenous to the plants' native soil. Their most famous representative is 'Concord', a blue-black table grape (also used for wine, grape juice, jelly, and jam) that ripens in late autumn. Other popular American varieties include 'Delaware' (red) and 'Niagara' (white).

Like the other two major classes, American grapes display the full color palette of blues, reds, purples, and pale greens. Some seedless varieties are available. And you can

BEST GROWING AREAS FOR THE THREE TYPES OF GRAPES

■ American grapes
■ Muscadine grapes
■ European grapes

Different varieties of grapes are adapted to different regions of United States. European varieties do best in mild-winter areas of California and Arizona. Muscadine grapes do best in southern United States where winter temperatures do not fall below 10°F/–12°C. American and hybrid grapes do well in just about every cold-winter area. Varieties within each type may be limited to only a portion of the area shown.

choose early, midseason, or late-ripening vines to match the length of your growing season. (For all grapes, the ripening range lies between late summer and late autumn.)

MUSCADINE GRAPES. The muscadine species originates and grows best in the southeastern United States. Muscadines are grown there by many home gardeners.

Muscadine vines, with few exceptions, bear only female or only male flowers on one vine. To bring about fruiting, you must plant all-female vines near a vine with either male flowers or "perfect" flowers (male and female combined). One male vine can pollinate a dozen female vines.

The older they get, the more profusely muscadines produce. Clusters are relatively short, containing as few as five large grapes. Grapes drop individually to the ground when ripe; the traditional harvest method is to shake them loose onto a tarpaulin.

The best-known and oldest muscadine variety is 'Scuppernong', originally found growing wild in Virginia; it ripens early, turning bronzy green. Other popular muscadines include 'Carlos' (bronze, self-fertile), 'Cowart' (black, self-fertile), and 'Fry' and 'Higgins' (both bronze, female vines).

EUROPEAN GRAPES. These account for the immense commercial crops of California, where the climate resembles that of their native Mediterranean-to-Middle Eastern habitat. They also grow in parts of Arizona and New Mexico. European grapes generally are not found east of the Rockies, for they're susceptible to freezing in the North and to Pierce's disease in the South.

Though more celebrated as wine grapes, European varieties such as 'Red Malaga', 'Thompson Seedless' (pale green), 'Cardinal' (dark red), and 'Emperor' (red) make delicious table or canning grapes.

To guard against crop devastation by phylloxera (a root-attacking louse), European vines are often grafted to the far more resistant American rootstocks. Hybridizing American and European varieties has been another approach to adapting European grapes to American climates and hazards.

Listing continues >

GROWTH HABIT. Berries borne in clusters on branches of woody perennial vines.

BEST SOIL. Fertile, well-drained, deep, sandy loam, pH 5.5–6.5.

WHEN TO PLANT. COLD-WINTER CLIMATES: In early spring, when bare-root plants are available, before new growth starts. MILD-WINTER CLIMATES: In winter.

HOW TO PLANT. Set out bare-root plants in holes that are wide and deep enough for roots. *AMERICAN AND EUROPEAN GRAPES:* Space holes 8'–10' apart in rows 10'–12' apart. *MUSCADINE GRAPES:* Space holes 12'–15' apart in rows 20' apart. Set up supports for vines.

YIELD. 7–28 pounds or more per plant.

CARE. Water and weed regularly. Prune yearly.

PESTS AND DISEASES. Aphids, grape berry moths, leafhoppers; downy mildew.

WHEN TO HARVEST. In late summer or autumn, when grapes are sweet and fully colored. It takes 4–5 years after planting for full harvest.

HOW TO HARVEST. Cut bunches from vines. Shake muscadine grapes from vines onto cloth.

HOW TO STORE. Refrigerate unwashed; use as soon as possible. To preserve, can or dry.

PLANTING

Grapes prefer well-drained soil. If you're planting a vulnerable European variety, avoid "old vineyard soil." Pests or diseases may still contaminate the soil in which grapes were raised during the previous 3 years.

Consult your Cooperative Extension Service to find the varieties best suited to your local conditions. For example, you need to grow early-ripening American grapes in a cold-winter area where the growing season is quite short. (The earliest ripening grapes need at least 140 frost-free days; European varieties need many more.)

The vines need a full quota of sun and free air movement. It's better to plant them on a slope than in low-lying basins where trapped air will increase the danger from frost or mildew.

Plant bare-root grapes during dormant season (December to May, depending on the severity of your winter). About 3 weeks before the last expected frost, set out 1-year-old vines, after trimming their roots to 6 inches (this forces growth of feeder roots). Place them as deep in the soil as they grew in the nursery, spreading the roots in all directions (see drawing top left). Cut top growth back to two or three buds. (In some areas, it's recommended that you plant grapes deeper than they grew in the nursery, leaving just one bud exposed.) This promotes deep rooting and one strong cane for the future trunk.

Space European or American varieties 8 to 10 feet apart in all directions. Rampant-growing muscadines need more room; place them 12 to 15 feet apart, in rows 20 feet apart.

CARE

Keep weeds and grass removed from the planting area. If you use a mulch, avoid using one rich in nutrients, such as compost. Keep the vines irrigated regularly if rainfall is lacking.

After growth starts in the first spring, spread ½ cup of 10-10-10 or similar fertilizer per vine in an encircling band 12 to 18 inches from the trunk of each vine. In the second year, apply 1 cup of fertilizer when buds swell in spring; in the third year, apply 1 to 1½ cups of fertilizer as the buds swell in spring. After the third year, apply 1 to 2 cups of fertilizer each spring. Spread the fertilizer in bands from 2 to 3 feet from the trunk of each plant.

TRAINING AND PRUNING

To have productive grapes, you must continually train (or direct) the vines to grow in the shape you want, and regularly prune the vines to achieve that shape.

Vines won't produce a full crop for 4 or 5 years. During the first few years of a grapevine's life, the object of training and pruning is to promote a thick, strong trunk that divides into a branching framework to bear future crops.

There are many ways to train grapevines. This discussion covers one of the most common: training grapes on a two-wire trellis. The technique can be used for American, European, and muscadine grapes and is essentially the same for the three classes during their first 2 years of growth.

For other training methods, consult your Cooperative Extension Service or a book on growing grapes.

THE FIRST 2 YEARS. Set stout posts in the ground 15 to 20 feet apart (farther apart for the more vigorous grapes, such as muscadines) so that they project 5 feet above the soil. String sturdy wire—10 or 11 gauge—across the post tops and also at the 2½-foot level (see drawing bottom left). Four "arms"—canes of each grape plant—will be trained on these wires.

PLANTING GRAPES

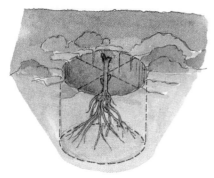

Plant bare-root grapevine, and cut back to two or three buds, leaving one bud exposed above-ground.

TRELLIS FOR GRAPES

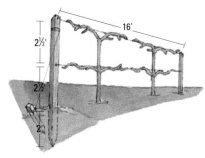

Support grapevines on two-wire trellis.

In the first growing season, let each vine sprawl undisturbed. The more leaves it develops, the more food it manufactures to help root development.

In the first winter's dormancy, cut growth back to the single sturdiest cane. This will be the future trunk. Tie this strong cane as upright as possible to the post or lower trellis wire; then cut the cane back to the bud that's closest to the lower supporting wire (2½ feet above the ground).

During second spring, new growth will come from the uppermost buds. As they send forth shoots, select the strongest upright shoot and tie it to the post or to the top trellis wire. This creates a trunk. Remove other shoots, except for the two strongest lower shoots to form arms along the lower wire.

During the second summer, when the strong trunk shoot reaches the top wire, pinch out the tip. Let two shoots grow just below the pinched-off tip, and train them along the top wire. Meanwhile, tie the arms selected in spring along the lower wire. These arms may form laterals (new canes growing out from them) during the summer. Pinch back the laterals to 10 inches.

During the second winter's dormant period, prune or pinch off all growth on the trunk and arms. The vine's basic structure is now established so pruning in subsequent years can be aimed at fruit production.

SUBSEQUENT YEARS. New canes will grow on the arms during the third summer. Tie them to the wires or posts for support. Prune any new growth from the trunk.

By the third winter, the trunk and arms are thicker, the arms are longer, and they have many lateral canes. Canes have grown from buds where old canes were cut off.

There are two basic approaches to pruning table and dessert grapes from the third year on: spur pruning and cane pruning. The choice depends on the variety.

Spur pruning works for most European grapes ('Thompson Seedless' and 'Lady Finger' are among the exceptions) and for muscadine grapes. The object is to create short spurs, each of which develops two bearing canes (armlike branches). After bearing, these canes are cut back and new spurs grow out. This method is illustrated in the drawings on page 84.

TRAINING AND PRUNING GRAPES

First summer: allow unhampered plant growth.

First winter: prune to select trunk, and tie it to support.

Second spring: select strongest shoot for trunk, two strong lower shoots for arms; prune off others.

Second summer: after growth reaches top wire, pinch off trunk to form upper arms; pinch lateral canes from arms back to 10 inches.

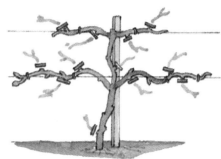

Second winter: prune all lateral canes, and tie arms to wires; remove any other branches from trunk.

Third summer: as new canes grow from all four arms, prune any growth from trunk.

Listing continues >

SPUR PRUNING GRAPES

Spur prune lateral canes during dormancy fourth (or later) winter to space them on arms, and cut them back to two buds.

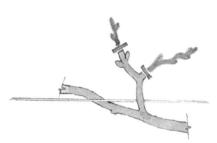

Close-up of spur-pruned lateral: prune spur in winter, after its branches bore fruit the previous summer; totally remove lower branch, cut upper one back to two buds.

To spur prune, you select the strongest of the previous year's canes coming from each arm of the vine. Cut off all weaker canes from the arms, so that the stronger canes are 6 to 10 inches apart. Cut these stronger canes back to their lowest two buds (see drawing top left). The shortened cane is now called a spur. From each spur, two new fruiting canes will grow during the third summer.

During the fourth (and subsequent) winters, shorten one of the two canes that grew from each renewal spur, cutting back until eight to fifteen buds remain on it. They will become the fruiting canes for the following summer. Then shorten the second cane that grew from each renewal spur, cutting it back to a stub with just two buds; it is a new renewal spur, which will produce the canes that bear fruit in the fifth summer (see drawing middle left).

In the fourth and subsequent summers, fruiting canes will develop from buds borne on canes that grew in the previous summer. The purpose of pruning is to remove old (or weak or extra) canes, creating space and ample nourishment for the new fruiting ones. By limiting the crop, you gain improved fruit quality, maximum size, and uniform clusters.

In the fifth winter and each following year, cut off the old fruiting canes. You can distinguish new from 1-year-old canes by looking at the bark: New canes have smooth, tight bark; 1-year-old branches have rough, loose bark. Each renewal spur will have sent out two shoots; prune the lower shoot as a fruiting cane (eight to fifteen buds long), the upper shoot as a renewal spur with two buds. Keep four spurs on each arm as renewal spurs, and keep the same number of fruiting cane shoots.

Cane pruning is used for 'Thompson Seedless', 'Lady Finger', and a few other European grapes and for most American grapes, such as 'Concord', 'Delaware', 'Niagara', and 'Pierce'. These kinds produce sparsely when cut back to short spurs, since most of their fruit is borne from buds farther out on the canes—the part that's cut off when branches are spur pruned.

In cane pruning, one strong lateral shoot near the trunk on each arm is cut back to two buds (it will serve as a renewal spur), and another strong lateral is cut back to twelve buds and tied to the wire support (see drawing bottom left). All other shoots are removed. New fruit-bearing canes will grow from the twelve buds in the summer. Those canes are removed at their base the next winter. Meanwhile the renewal spurs will have produced several new shoots from which new fruiting canes can be selected. Choose the longest and strongest shoot on each spur, cut it to twelve buds, and tie it to the supporting wire. Choose the next best shoot on each spur, and cut it to two buds for the next renewal spur.

CANE PRUNING GRAPES

Cane prune each arm to a shoot of twelve buds, which will produce fruit-bearing canes, and a renewal spur of two buds.

RASPBERRIES

Red raspberries

A soft blushing red is the color most people usually associate with raspberries, but the juicy little nuggets also come in purple, black, and even yellow.

Raspberries grow from perennial roots that produce biennial stems, called "canes." The canes grow to full size the first year—called the "primocane phase"—and bear fruit the second year—called the "floricane phase." Canes that have borne their fruit then die, while new primocanes emerge to produce the next year's crop.

Ordinarily, raspberries bear their fruit in summer. One group of raspberries, the fall-bearing (or everbearing) kind, has a different pattern. These plants bear a crop of fruit in the autumn of their first year of growth. The fruit is borne on the upper third of the new canes, the primocanes. The summer of the second year, these canes bear a second crop of fruit on the lower part of the canes (now called floricanes). After this second crop, the canes die. Red and yellow raspberry varieties may be either summer-bearing or fall-bearing.

Raspberries thrive where the climate is fairly cool in summer, winters are cold, and there is adequate rainfall during the growing season (see map below). Irrigation can take the place of summer rainfall. Heat—both humid and dry—is raspberry's enemy. ('Bababerry' is one everbearing variety that produces well in warm-summer, mild-winter areas.) You can moderate the effect of heat by choosing a cool planting location. The less favorable your overall climate is, the more erratic your results are likely to be. Since raspberries differ widely in their adaptability to local conditions, check with your local Cooperative Extension Service for the best varieties for your climate.

Listing continues >

GROWTH HABIT. Berries borne in clusters on 1-year-old canes.

BEST SOIL. Rich, well-drained, sandy loam, pH 5.5–6.8.

WHEN TO PLANT. In early spring.

HOW TO PLANT. Plant raspberries 1"–2" deeper in soil than they were in nursery. *RED AND YELLOW RASPBERRIES:* Set out bare-root plants 2'–2½' apart, in rows spaced 6'–10' apart. Cut back all other canes to 5"–6". *BLACK AND PURPLE RASPBERRIES:* Set out bare-root plants 2'–3' apart, in rows spaced 6'–8' apart. Note: Cut back all canes to the ground.

YIELD. 1 quart or more per plant.

CARE. Keep soil moist. Weed regularly. Prune yearly (see text).

PESTS AND DISEASES. Borers, rose chafers; anthracnose, verticillium wilt.

WHEN TO HARVEST. In summer or autumn, depending on variety. Pick berries when they slip off their stems easily.

HOW TO HARVEST. Gently pull ripe berries from their short stems.

HOW TO STORE. Refrigerate unwashed; use as soon as possible. To preserve, can or freeze.

BEST GROWING AREAS FOR RASPBERRIES

Plants do best where winters are cold and summers are not too hot and dry; hardy from 0° to –35°F/–18° to –37°C.

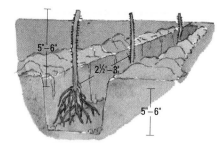

Plant red and yellow raspberries in trenches.

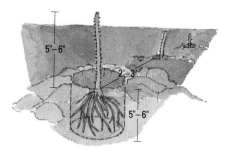

Plant purple and black raspberries in holes.

TRAINING RASPBERRIES

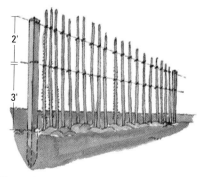

Tie raspberry canes to trellis of two horizontal wires for support.

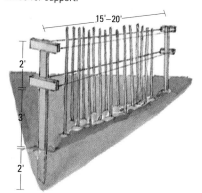

Use hedgerow of four wires on crossbars to keep raspberry canes in bounds.

PLANTING

The planting site for raspberries should be sunny, with good air circulation and rich, well-drained soil. In hot climates, place the plants where they will receive afternoon shade.

Buy only certified virus-free plants from a reputable nursery, or you may face disease problems. Avoid planting raspberries where you have previously raised tomatoes, potatoes, peppers, or eggplants, for those vegetables may have tainted the soil with a potentially harmful fungus disease, verticillium wilt.

Plant bare-root stock during the dormant season. Set red and yellow raspberries 2½ to 3 feet apart in rows 6 to 10 feet apart (see drawing top left). Plant purple and black raspberries in slightly raised mounds 2 to 3 feet apart in rows spaced 6 to 8 feet apart (see drawing upper middle left); the plants will develop into clumps of canes.

CARE

During the first year of growth, tie new canes of red and yellow raspberries to a trellis of two wires strung between posts, or confine the canes in a hedgerow (see drawings lower middle left and bottom left). You can grow black and purple raspberry plants either freestanding or on a trellis.

Once raspberries are established, caring for them is fairly simple. Twice a month during the growing season, cultivate around the plants (but no deeper than 2 inches) to remove weeds. Putting down a layer of mulch will discourage weeds and also help keep the soil moist. If the soil is rich or has been enriched before planting, you probably won't need to fertilize. But if the plants grow poorly or their foliage is not deep green, apply a complete fertilizer the next spring before the start of growth.

PRUNING

The main care that raspberries need is pruning. It differs for red and yellow varieties between summer-bearing and fall-bearing types and between those and the purple and black varieties.

Clean up prunings to prevent the spread of disease. Shred or burn the debris.

SUMMER-BEARING RED AND YELLOW RASPBERRIES. Do not prune the canes of summer-bearing red or yellow varieties during the first summer's growth. Early in the second spring—after frost danger is past, but before buds start to swell—cut to the ground any weak, broken, or diseased canes, until healthy canes are thinned to 6 to 8 inches apart (whether planted in a row or a hedgerow). Prune the tops of remaining canes at a height of 5 to 5½ feet for rows, 4 feet for hedgerows (see drawing on page 87, top right).

Yellow raspberries

After you have harvested the crop in summer, cut to the ground all canes that bore fruit. The remaining canes will bear fruit in the second summer.

During the second summer, new canes will grow to bear the following year's crop; tie the new canes to the trellis or confine them within the hedgerow.

FALL-BEARING RED AND YELLOW RASPBERRIES. Let the first year's canes come up and bear fruit in autumn. After you harvest the fruit, cut off the top third of each cane that bore fruit (see drawing middle right).

During the second year, after 1-year-old canes have borne a summer crop of fruit on the lower parts of canes, cut those canes to the ground. As new canes emerge during summer, tie them to the trellis or confine them in the hedgerow. In autumn, after you harvest the crop, cut off the top third of all canes that bore fruit (see drawing bottom right). Or you can follow the example of growers who cut fall-bearing canes to the ground yearly in fall after fruiting is finished (in cold regions wait until late winter). You'll sacrifice one of the crops but gain easier maintenance and a prolonged crop in summer. With this pruning method, raspberries can be grown in large containers.

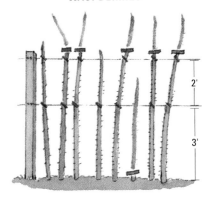

For summer-bearing red and yellow raspberries, early in second spring before growth begins, thin weak canes, top vigorous growth.

Black raspberries

PURPLE AND BLACK RASPBERRIES. During the first summer's growth, "top" black and purple raspberries (remove the tops of the stems), to force the plants to grow lateral branches. For freestanding plants, top the black varieties down to 2 feet tall and the purple varieties down to 2½ feet tall. For plants grown on a trellis, top black varieties to 2 to 2½ feet tall, purple ones to 2½ to 3 feet tall (see drawing bottom left).

Early in the second spring, before new growth starts, remove all weak canes (those less than ½ inch thick) and any dead, diseased, or broken canes. Leave six to eight sturdy canes in a hill or canes spaced 6 to 8 inches apart in a row. If all the canes are less than ½ inch thick, remove all but the two strongest from each plant. Also shorten the lateral (side) branches to 8 to 10 inches for black raspberries and 12 to 14 inches for purple raspberries (see drawing bottom center). The side branches will bear fruit.

After you pick the crop, cut to the ground all canes that bore fruit. During the second summer, top all new canes as described for the first summer's growth.

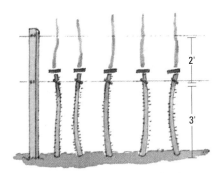

For fall-bearing red and yellow raspberries, after harvesting first year's autumn fruit, remove top third of canes.

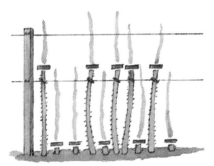

Prune fall-bearing red and yellow raspberries after summer crop of second year. Prune to ground canes that bore summer fruit. Prune top third of those that did not bear fruit in summer; they will bear fruit next summer.

PRUNING PURPLE AND BLACK RASPBERRIES

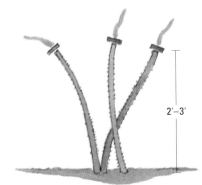

Prune purple and black freestanding raspberries during first summer, to encourage growth of lateral branches.

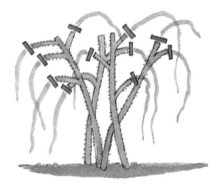

During second spring, remove weak canes, shorten lateral branches.

STRAWBERRIES

Since tiny *fraises des bois* were first found carpeting their native woodlands of southern and central Europe, strawberries have enraptured artists and epicures alike. In illuminated manuscripts of the 15th century, strawberries shown with the Madonna and Child symbolized Christ's wounds and the promise of eternal life. Today, strawberries are one of the most widely cultivated small fruits, with a botanical history that goes back to the writings of ancient Rome.

Strictly speaking, strawberries aren't fruits at all: the juicy red flesh is actually the swollen tip of the flower stalk. The true fruits of this popular perennial are those tiny seed capsules that stud the flesh like pins in a pincushion.

Because strawberries are very sensitive to subtle shifts of environment, such as the length of daily exposure to sunlight, nurseries have developed a seemingly endless procession of varieties. There is one adapted to almost every climate in United States. But a variety that produces copiously in one state may prove disappointing in a neighboring state, even when the general climate appears to vary only slightly. For reliable choices for your garden, be sure to consult your local Cooperative Extension Service.

Varieties also offer differences in sweet-to-tart flavors, susceptibility to freezing, berry sizes and shapes, and rosy to deep red colors. Some, called "everbearing," have been especially developed to bear fruit over a long season.

ABOVE: *Fraises des bois*
TOP LEFT: 'Seascape' everbearing strawberries

CHOOSING A LOCATION

Most varieties will thrive in any good garden soil; some are more robust than others in adverse conditions. Strawberries prefer rich, well-drained soil that never is waterlogged yet retains enough moisture to supply constant growth.

Avoid planting strawberries at sites where you have raised potatoes, eggplants, tomatoes, peppers, or raspberries in the previous 3 years—any of these may have infected the soil with verticillium wilt. To guard against invasion by weeds or white grubs, don't plant strawberries where a lawn has grown recently.

If you live in a cold-winter climate, or wherever late frosts are likely, try to plant strawberries on relatively high or gently sloping land. Because their blossoms are vulnerable to frost damage, it is important to plant strawberries where cold air will drain away from them.

Select a site that receives full sun all day in the growing season.

GROWTH CYCLE

Strawberries begin to grow and bloom early in spring, fruiting later in spring or early summer. The length of the harvest depends on both variety and climate. Being perennial, strawberries go dormant in winter and grow back the following spring to bloom and fruit again.

To get plants off to a strong start, pinch off the earliest blossoms that form. Strawberry plants slowly decline in vigor after 2 to 3 years and should be replaced often, with either runners or new plants. Many gardeners grow them as annuals, replanting every year. This works particularly well in mild-winter areas, where strawberries can be planted in fall and where diseases quickly overtake old plants.

June-bearing strawberries produce one crop in late spring or early summer; generally they are the highest quality strawberries you can grow. Everbearing varieties (day-neutral strawberries) peak in summer and continue to produce into autumn, often until the first frost. Though they bear for a longer time, they tend to be less vigorous than June-bearing varieties and may produce fewer fruits.

PREPARING THE SOIL AND THE PLANTS

In most parts of the country, strawberries are planted in early spring, 3 to 4 weeks before the last expected frost. Where winters are mild, you can also plant strawberries in early summer, early autumn, and winter.

Thoroughly till or spade the soil until it is loose and free of rocks and lumps. If the soil contains a generous amount of organic matter, you should need no fertilizer. But if a soil analysis indicates the need, spread and mix in 1 pound of 10-10-10 fertilizer per 100 feet of row before planting.

It's best to plant certified disease-free strawberries from a reliable nursery. These will probably be 1-year-old plants that have been kept in cold storage. Keep their roots moist, and, just before planting, trim the roots to 6 inches for easier management.

METHODS OF GROWING

In setting plants into the ground, it's essential to position the base of the crown at soil level. Gently fan out the roots, and firm the soil around them. They must be completely buried.

There are three common arrangements for strawberry plants: in hills, in an intensive spacing called "matted rows," and in a modification of the latter system called "spaced matted rows."

"Mother" strawberry plants produce a number of "daughters" by sending out runners. Depending on which planting system you follow, you either leave the daughter plants alone, train them, or thin them out to coax lusher growth of the mother.

HILL SYSTEM. The hill system is popular west of the Rockies. It results in a relatively smaller yield than the matted row system but produces big, beautiful berries from large and vigorous mother plants. Though the hill system is also more costly, using more plants, the harvest may seem well worth the price. Hills are the preferred arrangement for any everbearing variety.

Set plants 12 to 14 inches apart on long mounds spaced 28 inches apart; the mounds, or hills, are 5 to 6 inches in height and width and are irrigated from the furrows that separate them (see drawing top right). Remove all runners as soon as they appear; this encourages more vigorous growth of the crown of each mother plant.

MATTED ROW SYSTEM. In matted row planting, you place mother plants 18 to 24 inches apart, in rows spaced about 4 feet apart (see drawing middle right). Allow runners to set roots freely in all directions within the bed, but keep the bed to a width of 18 to 24 inches. Trim off any runners that extend beyond this limit (see drawing lower right). Each year remove older plants to keep plants spaced at least 6 inches apart. Obviously, you'll need fewer plants initially than for hill planting.

SPACED MATTED ROW SYSTEM. In spaced matted row planting, each mother is allowed only a few runners, usually six. Daughter plants are carefully placed by hand, so that they root 6 to 8 inches apart in rows 18 to 24 inches apart. This method requires a bit more work, but the result is usually a higher yield of larger and lovelier berries, with fewer disease problems.

Listing continues >

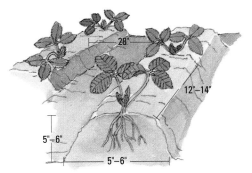

Hill planting system: set plants on long, low mounds, and remove all runners.

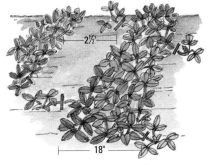

Matted row system: start plants far apart on level ground (upper drawing), but allow runners to root, forming dense mat of plants (lower drawing). Cut off any runners that grow beyond boundaries of row.

CARE

During the first year, no matter how you have arranged your plants, pinch off the early blooms. This practice ensures that ample nourishment will strengthen the mother plants. Early runners left the first year will bear the best fruit the following year.

Since strawberries have shallow roots, weed control and adequate irrigation during dry spells are important. For most varieties, cultivate frequently (about once a week) for the first 6 weeks. Cultivation keeps the soil loose to allow daughter plants to root easily, as well as uprooting competing weeds. Avoid cultivating so deeply that you endanger the strawberry roots.

Though many strawberry varieties can survive drought, it takes plenty of water to produce prime fruit. Allow at least 1 inch of water per week (rainfall included), more in dry weather.

Cultivate everbearing varieties for only 10 days to 2 weeks after planting, then apply a clean mulch, such as sawdust, taking care not to mix it with the soil. Pay special attention to irrigation, because the berries develop during the months when the soil is most likely to dry out.

In areas with very cold winters, mulching strawberries to prevent winter damage is vital. When periods of freezing and thawing alternate, the ground may heave, uprooting plants. In late November, when temperatures have dropped to freezing several times, loosely sift mulch to cover plants completely. Straw is a commonly used material.

The following spring, as new growth starts, brush the straw into the alleys between rows (be absolutely sure to clear the mulch off the strawberry leaves). The mulch will

Drip irrigation waters strawberries efficiently

Strawberry bed is mulched with straw to hold moisture in and covered with netting to keep birds out

help keep the fruit clean and hold down weeds; also, you can heap it over plants again whenever a late frost threatens—but remember to clear it away again the next day.

Another precaution against late spring frost damage is to turn on sprinklers whenever the ground-level temperature drops to 32°F/0°C. A protective layer of ice will form on the plants, insulating them from lower temperatures and usually preventing excessive frost damage.

If birds frequent your garden, you'll probably have to protect emerging berries with plastic netting or floating row covers.

Let strawberries ripen to a full red color before you harvest them; then pick immediately. You'll probably have to do this every day during the season's peak. To avoid bruising the fruit, harvest by cutting the stems carefully. Ripe fruit will keep for a day or two in the refrigerator.

After the harvest, you can choose whether to renovate the bed for another season's crop or simply to dig up the plants and turn them under. Before renovating, remove any mulch clinging to the foliage; then mow or clip the leaves to within an inch of the crowns. Thin out older plants, and remove and burn any plants that show signs of insect infestation or disease.

To stimulate a renewal of top growth, apply ½ to ¾ pound of a high-nitrogen fertilizer per 100 feet of row. If plants are too crowded, thin them, after new growth starts, to 6 to 8 inches apart. Keep the soil weed-free and adequately wet. Fertilize in autumn, and mulch at the onset of winter, just as you did in the first year. A new crop will develop the following spring or summer, perhaps somewhat less grand and abundant than the first.

ABOVE RIGHT: 'Chandler' strawberry plants in traditional planter with pockets
BELOW: Strawberry plants grow thickly in matted row bed

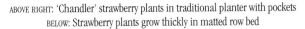

STRAWBERRIES FIT ANYWHERE

Unlike most other berries, strawberries are ideal for the small-space garden and for growing in containers. Their low, clumping growth habit and attractive lobed foliage make them perfect plants for tucking in among flowers, as a ground cover in front of a shrub border, or in the herb garden. In addition to the classic strawberry pot with small pockets on the sides, look for a variety of container opportunities—you'll find many. Strawberries don't require much space, and the fruits dangle beautifully over the edge of the pot. You can even plant strawberries in the sides of moss-lined hanging baskets or vertical planters. Truly versatile plants, strawberries can grace your garden wherever there's the smallest space.

VEGETABLE
GARDEN BASICS

Understanding general gardening procedures is essential for a successful food garden. The purposes of this chapter, therefore, are to explain the basic techniques you will need to create a thriving vegetable garden and to serve as a handy reference throughout the growing season.

Because any garden begins with the soil, this discussion starts (on pages 94–99) with the general soil types and how each may be modified or improved so roots will have the conditions they need to produce good plants and crops. Garden soils are notoriously individual, but this section will help you to understand your particular soil and its needs, so that you can grow the crops you want.

After you've prepared the soil, your next step is planting. Pages 100–103 describe planting from seeds, setting out young plants, and planting perennials during the dormant season.

Knowing when, how, and how much to water your vegetables is important if you are to achieve maximum success. Turn to pages 104–105 for information on a number of ways in which you can deliver water to plants. The methods you choose will depend on water availability in your area, the size of your garden, your climate—and your personal preference.

To keep water available to your crops and, at the same time, suppress weeds, mulching is recommended. For ideas on various mulch materials and methods, see page 106.

As your garden grows, four maintenance jobs almost inevitably emerge: (1) supporting plant growth, (2) supplying nutrients vital to your crops, (3) controlling those ubiquitous garden interlopers, weeds, and (4) dealing with pests and diseases that may afflict vegetables. You'll find various ideas for supporting the vining crops on page 107. Look on pages 108–109 for the basics about fertilizers: the nutrients plants need, times to fertilize, kinds of fertilizers, and methods of application. For advice and cautions on various types of weed control, see pages 110–111. And, should you find a chewed leaf, a wilted branch, or a strange "bug" among your crops, check the illustrations, descriptions, and control suggestions for pests and diseases on pages 112–119.

When success brings you more fresh produce than you can use at once, turn to pages 120–121 for harvesting and storage ideas. Check the specific information in the descriptions of individual vegetables and berries as well.

Finally, a few garden situations—planting in containers or on hillsides, increasing yields in a limited space with the French intensive method of gardening, and using protective devices to get a jump on the season or to defy poor weather conditions—require special techniques. You'll find these described on pages 121–125.

Bamboo poles with crosspole at top support climbing vegetables

PREPARING THE SOIL

Just as a well-constructed house depends on a solid foundation, a successful garden starts with fertile, well-prepared soil. What's your soil type? Can it be improved? Should you fertilize? What type of fertilizer should you use? The answers to these questions follow.

SOIL STRUCTURE

Soil is a mass of mineral particles, living and dead organic matter, air, and water. The size and shape of the mineral particles in the soil determine its characteristics. The smallest mineral particles are clay particles (less than $1/12,500$ of an inch in diameter); the largest are sand particles ($1/25$ to $1/50$ of an inch). Silt particles are intermediate in size (up to $1/500$ of an inch). Most soils contain a mixture of sand, silt, and clay. A "loam" soil contains about the same proportion of each plus organic matter.

Clayey soil probably causes more consternation among gardeners than any other type. When wet, it's gummy and unworkable; when dry, it cracks apart. Because it's composed of many tightly packed particles with great surface area for holding, clay soil holds water and nutrients well. But the pores are so small that drainage is poor, so plants do not grow easily in it.

Sandy soil, at its worst, is the exact opposite of clay. Large particles and large pore spaces between them make for well-aerated soil, but water pours through, taking nutrients with it.

Silt soil drains better than clay and holds more water and nutrients than sand.

Because loam is a mixture of clay, silt, and sand, it preserves the best characteristics of each and is considered the ideal soil. It drains well, holds ample nutrients, retains moisture, and provides enough air for root growth.

You cannot feasibly change the ratio of sand, silt, and clay in your soil, but you can make a clayey soil drain better or a sandy soil hold more water and nutrients by adding organic matter (see page 96). A little organic matter changes the structure of soil and improves its ability to produce garden vegetables.

NUTRIENTS IN THE SOIL

Because plants get most nutrients essential for growth from the soil, it is a good idea to have your soil tested (see "Soil testing," page 96) before you prepare it for planting. The test will tell whether your soil will provide the primary nutrients—nitrogen, phosphorus, and potassium—that plants must have in order to thrive. These are the three soil-derived nutrients that plants need in the largest amounts and the three most likely to be lacking in a particular soil.

If your soil lacks one or more of these nutrients, or if they are present in only small amounts, you'd be wise to add fertilizer (see pages 108–109) as well as soil amendments (see page 96) at recommended rates. A complete fertilizer, containing nitrogen, phosphorus, and potassium, is usually incorporated into the soil at planting time.

NITROGEN. Plants use large quantities of nitrogen, an essential component of all protein. It promotes green, leafy growth. Any that isn't used by the plants is easily lost through the leaching action of rainfall and irrigation or is quickly used by microscopic soil organisms.

Because nitrogen promotes rapid growth of plant stems and leaves and gives plants a deep green color, it is especially needed by leaf crops. Signs of nitrogen deficiency are a yellowing and dropping of older leaves and stunted growth (smaller leaves, fewer flowers, and smaller fruits).

If plants have too much nitrogen, they grow so fast that they may become weak and spindly and produce leaves and stems instead of flowers and fruit.

Chemical sources of nitrogen include ammonium nitrate, ammonium sulfate, calcium nitrate, and urea. Organic sources of nitrogen are blood meal, hoof and horn meal, cottonseed meal, fish meal, fish emulsion, and animal manures.

SOIL PARTICLES

Clay
Less than $1/12,500$ in.

Silt
Up to $1/500$ in.

Fine sand
Up to $1/250$ in.

Medium sand
Up to $1/50$ in.

Largest sand particles
$1/12$ in.

SOIL TYPES

Clay

Sand

Loam

Size of mineral particles determines texture of soil and designates its type. Loam, a mixture of particle sizes and organic matter, is considered ideal garden soil.

SOIL PH

A soil's acidity or alkalinity is expressed in terms of pH, on a scale from 1 to 14. A pH of 7 is neutral; lower than 7 is acid, and greater than 7 is alkaline. The ideal vegetable and berry garden soil is slightly acid to neutral (pH 6 to 7), but you can grow excellent crops in slightly alkaline soil (pH 7 to 8).

Acid soil is most common in areas of heavy rainfall. If soil pH is less than 5.5, you can add ground limestone (lime) to neutralize the acidity and add calcium to the soil. If you can find it, add dolomitic limestone, which contains both calcium and magnesium. Check with your local soil laboratory, Cooperative Extension Service, or nursery for the amounts of lime necessary to raise your soil's pH to an optimum level. Liming is usually done based on a soil test (see page 96).

Alkaline soil is common in areas with low rainfall, poor drainage, and natural limestone deposits. Often alkaline soils are also too salty. To reduce mild alkalinity, fertilize with an acid-type fertilizer. To reduce salinity on well-drained soil, irrigate the land slowly for 24 to 48 hours to wash excess mineral salts down below the root zone.

If your soil remains moderately alkaline after you leach and apply an acid-type fertilizer, you may need to add sulfur to neutralize the alkalinity. Large-scale chemical treatment of extremely alkaline soils is expensive and complex; instead, you may decide to garden in raised beds filled with good soil (see "Raised beds" on page 98).

PHOSPHORUS. To get plants off to a fast start, work in a fertilizer high in phosphorus as you prepare the soil. This plant nutrient encourages root formation, flowering, and fruiting. It doesn't move very far in the soil, so apply it before planting when you can mix it deeply into the soil. When you set out transplants, water them with a high-phosphorus solution.

Dull green leaves with a purple tint are the visible sign that a plant is deficient in phosphorus. (Purple veins in tomato seedlings are common.) In general, when this nutrient is lacking, plant growth is stunted. Too much phosphorus in the soil is not likely to hurt your vegetables, but excessive soil phosphorus may pollute local water sources, creating environmental concern. A soil test can tell you the precise phosphorus level.

Chemical sources of phosphorus include phosphoric acid and super-phosphate. Bonemeal is a good organic source of phosphorus, but it often takes years to break down and become available to plant roots. All composts and manures contain some phosphorus.

POTASSIUM. Essential to all plant processes, potassium promotes root growth and seed production. A deficiency of this vital nutrient results in slow growth overall. Leaves may have mottled yellow tips and edges; older leaves may look scorched at the edges. Excess potassium can cause salt burn.

Chemical sources of potassium include potassium chloride, potassium nitrate, and potassium sulfate. Organic sources of potassium are granite dust, pulverized granite, potash rock, green sand, and wood ashes. Ashes, however, are also very alkaline, so don't use them in high pH soil.

Yellowed leaves are a sign of nitrogen deficiency.

SECONDARY NUTRIENTS. Calcium, magnesium, and sulfur are called secondary nutrients because garden soils are not as likely to be deficient in these elements. Some soil laboratories also test for the secondary nutrients.

Calcium is part of plant cell wall structure, and magnesium is part of the chlorophyll molecule. If you treat an acid soil with dolomitic limestone, you'll also be adding both calcium and magnesium. Some fertilizers contain calcium and magnesium as well. Blossom-end rot of tomatoes is the most common manifestation of calcium deficiency in the home garden. Tomatoes turn black on the lower end of the fruit just before they ripen, ruining the crop. You can try liming the soil and using fertilizers high in calcium, such as calcium nitrate, but the problem is usually caused by inadequate or irregular watering. Calcium uptake is very dependent on adequate moisture when the fruit is ripening.

Sulfur, like nitrogen, is part of plant protein, but most vegetables need much less sulfur than nitrogen. The strong flavor of onions and the odor of cole crops come from aromatic sulfur compounds. Many fertilizers contain sulfur. Organic amendments usually add adequate sulfur to soils. Sulfur deficiencies are most likely in sandy soils low in organic matter. If your soil fits that description, use a fertilizer that contains some sulfur.

MICRONUTRIENTS. Micronutrients are just as important to healthy crop growth as primary and secondary nutrients; they simply are needed in "micro" amounts. Most mineral soils contain adequate supplies of some or all of the essential micronutrients: iron, zinc, copper, manganese, molybdenum, boron, and chlorine. However, their availability to plants can be affected by soil pH, organic matter, clay content, moisture, and other conditions. Deficiencies are most likely to occur in vegetables grown in containers in a potting mix that does not contain soil. The premium fertilizers usually contain trace amounts of the micronutrients most likely to be lacking.

1 Spread amendment layer evenly over surface of soil.

2 Mix amendment into soil, using either rotary tiller or spade.

3 Rake tilled soil smooth to break up clods, remove stones, and level surface.

SOIL TESTING

Before tilling or amending your soil, find out whether the soil has problems, whether alkalinity, acidity, or nutrient deficiency. Then you can tell how to correct them. A soil test will pinpoint any problems.

Inexpensive soil test kits, available at garden supply stores or through mail-order catalogs, are quick but provide only a crude estimate of your soil's condition. Check with your Cooperative Extension Service or state university for more dependable soil analysis and recommendations for your area.

SOIL AMENDMENTS

A few gardeners are fortunate enough to have an ideal soil, but most must improve the texture of their soil with organic soil amendments. Organic matter helps soil in several ways. It changes the physical structure of the soil to allow a healthy balance of air and water to enter. It increases the moisture-holding capacity of sandy soils, and acts as a buffering agent to prevent rapid changes in the soil pH. And it increases soil fertility by releasing some nutrients, particularly nitrogen, as the organic matter decomposes.

How much organic amendment should you add? Mix in a quantity that is at least 25 percent of the final volume of soil. For an even, deep mixture of amendments and soil, try to work in 3 to 4 inches of amendment at a time to a depth of 9 to 12 inches. Double digging (see next page) will greatly improve poor soil. If your soil is so poor that it will need extensive (and expensive) amending, consider bringing in new soil and planting in raised beds (see page 98).

Descriptions of some common soil amendments and their uses in various soil types follow. Keep in mind that amendments don't work forever. Because the organic material is constantly decomposing, you'll need to replenish the soil before every planting.

Wood products, such as sawdust and bark, work well in clay soils because they physically separate the fine clay particles without holding moisture. Wood products quickly use up nitrogen as they decompose, so if you're using raw wood products, add nitrogen to the soil. If you don't, plants won't have enough nitrogen for growth.

Manure in all its forms improves most soils and acts as a mild fertilizer. Fresh manure is high in nutrients and salts. It must be aged before you use it, or it will burn plants; composting is a good way to age it. Some manures, especially steer and poultry manure, may have high concentrations of soluble salts. It's important not to add too much steer manure to the soil, because the excess salts can harm seedlings and transplants. Apply manures at least 1 month before planting to allow time for decomposition and leaching of salts. Apply steer manure at a rate of ½ to 1 pound per square foot.

Peat moss, a fairly expensive but excellent acidifying soil amendment, is ideal to improve sandy soils because it holds water and nutrients well. Most peat moss sold in bales is air-dried; wet it thoroughly before mixing it into the soil.

Compost is one of the best soil amendments, as well as one of the least expensive. Directions on page 99 tell you how to build a compost pile.

Green manure is a term is used by agriculturalists to describe a cover crop that usually is grown during the winter to be tilled into the ground in the spring. In the autumn, you plant any of the fast-growing members of the grass family (cereal rye, barley, or oats) or the legume family (clover, vetch, broad beans, or peas). In the spring, about a month before planting time, till the crop into the ground. Though the top growth may be sparse, the well-developed root system will add organic matter to the soil as it decays. For garden areas not planted in summer, grow a summer cover crop of buckwheat, lespedeza, or Sudan grass.

SPADING AND TILLING

Turning the soil makes it crumbly for seed germination and root growth, while deterring weeds. If your soil has not been worked recently, it's best to turn over the soil thoroughly and then, well ahead of planting time, blend in amendments and fertilizers. If your soil has good texture and has been gardened before, you can apply amendments and fertilizers and mix them into the soil without prior tilling. Working and conditioning the soil—whether in one or two steps—can be done by hand or with a power tiller. Fall tilling is recommended unless your garden is prone to wind or water erosion.

Turning over the soil by hand is a hard job (you may get in shape as well), but the task will seem easier if you use the proper tool. A spade—square bladed, sharp, and straight in the shank—or a garden fork is the ideal tool for breaking up the soil (see drawings at right). A shovel, with its rounded blade, is the best tool for mixing or turning materials once you've loosened the soil. The point of the shovel helps you to slide it into the material, and the concave blade keeps the material from falling off as you lift and turn the shovel.

In spading up small areas, many gardeners make the mistake of turning each spadeful of earth completely over. If you do this, any weeds, leaves, or other debris in the soil may form a one-spade-deep barrier that cuts off air and water. Instead, you should turn the dirt on its side (against the previous spadeful) so the original surface is vertical to the ground.

For really big jobs, rent or buy a power tiller. If the soil is firmly packed, you may have to start tilling at a shallow depth, then go over the area a second time, or even a third, with the tiller at a deeper setting each time.

Timing is critical in successful soil preparation. If the soil is gummy wet, wait until it dries enough to crumble when you squeeze a handful into a ball. Tilling soil when it's too wet can destroy its structure, causing it to turn into hard clods later. If it's brick hard, water deeply, and wait until the soil dries to the moist-but-crumbly stage. If your spade slides in easily and soil doesn't stick to it, the soil is at the right stage for tilling.

RAKING AND LEVELING

Smoothing out the soil and forming beds are the final steps in soil preparation. Your soil will probably still contain lumps and debris, even after spading and tilling. Using a metal bow rake (the bow gives the rake springy, resilient action), break up any large clods, and remove stones and other materials. After one last leveling with either a metal bow rake or a level-head rake, you're ready to plant.

DOUBLE DIGGING

If your soil is extremely poor or has never been worked, double digging—digging down two spade depths into the soil and incorporating organic matter—will improve its condition. Double digging is hard work, but the improved soil will produce plants that make your efforts worthwhile.

Double digging has two purposes: (1) to amend the soil on the upper level, and (2) to break up the soil on the lower level so that roots can grow deeper. With double digging, you should be able to space plants closer than usual. This approach is a cornerstone of French intensive gardening, which calls for closely spaced plantings in richly amended beds (see pages 123–124).

The steps shown with the drawings at right explain how to double dig. Once you've done a bed, let it settle. After a few days, rake the soil to remove any large clods and work the soil into a fine, even texture.

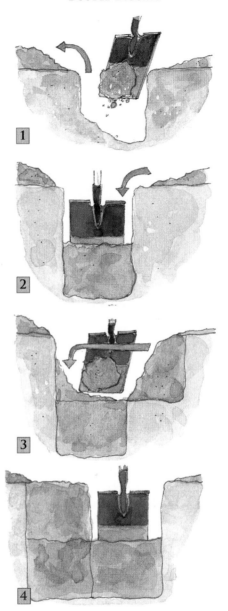

1 Dig trench for planting bed one spade deep. Set soil alongside trench (at left in drawing). Spread soil amendments on other side of trench (at right in drawing).

2 Dig one spade depth farther down in same trench, mixing some amendments with soil in lower level.

3 Dig second trench one spade deep alongside first one. Mix in soil amendments and move amended soil to first trench.

4 In second trench, dig one spade depth farther down. Mix in amendments. Continue process in adjacent third and subsequent trenches.

RAISED BEDS

Gardening in raised beds is one way to overcome the problem of poor soil or poor drainage. Rather than fighting vigorously to improve hard, infertile soil, you can start fresh with a light, rich soil mix in a raised, enclosed bed. As a bonus, you'll do less stooping as you water, weed, and cultivate, and the raised soil will drain better and tend to warm up faster in spring, resulting in earlier crops.

A good width for a raised bed is 3 to 4 feet (easy to reach across); the length can vary to fit your garden. Soil depth should be 12 to 18 inches. If you build several beds, be sure to leave room for a wheelbarrow to pass between them. The drawings at right illustrate simple raised beds, with helpful hints for better drainage. If your raised beds are made of wood, use decay-resistant woods such as redwood or cedar. Many gardeners prefer not to use new railroad ties or pressure-treated wood, because they contain toxic materials, although there is debate about whether the toxins affect vegetables.

First, till the existing topsoil a bit (see page 97). Then, fill the bed with a rich, light soil mix, such as equal parts peat moss, compost, and topsoil. As you begin to fill the bed, mix the new soil with the existing soil in the bottom of the bed.

Soak the bed before planting, so the soil will settle to 2 to 3 inches below the top of the bed. (If you wait until after planting to soak the soil, many plants will sink.)

Remember to replenish organic soil amendments each time you replant the bed (see "Soil amendments" on page 96).

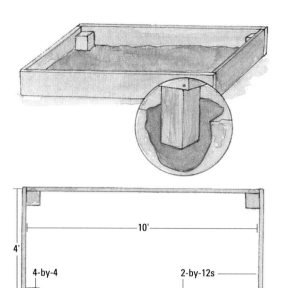

Large planter box makes good raised bed. Use decay-resistant wood or old railroad ties for construction. Anchor sides firmly.

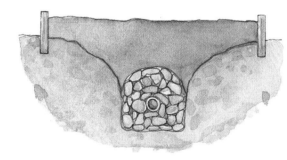

Poorly draining soil may require raised bed and drain tile. Perforated drain pipe (center circle), covered by rock, aids water runoff.

Old construction timbers make sturdy raised bed. Overlap ends for greater stability.

HOW TO MAKE COMPOST

A compost pile can turn waste materials from your garden and kitchen into a rich, organic soil amendment. Here are a few basic composting guidelines:

Construct a pile 4 to 6 feet high. This amount will hold the heat necessary to promote decomposition while allowing sufficient air to enter the pile and minimize odor; see the drawings on this page for ideas on constructing compost enclosures.

Spread a layer of plant debris (leaves, weeds, or grass clippings) 6 to 8 inches deep on the ground or in a bin. Follow with shallow layers (1 to 2 inches) of manure (or a few handfuls of nitrogen-rich fertilizer), topsoil, and kitchen scraps (except meat, fat, and bones). Continue adding layers, but don't put a lot of one material in one layer.

Chop or grind large materials such as big stems into small pieces; mix fine materials such as grass clippings with coarser pieces.

Keep the compost moist but not soggy; it should be about as wet as a squeezed-out sponge. During heavy rainfall, cover the pile with a plastic sheet or a tarpaulin.

Turn the pile at least every 3 to 4 weeks to discourage odor and flies and to help the compost decompose evenly.

Add small amounts of nitrogen—from sources such as fresh manure, blood meal, or commercial fertilizers—to the layers periodically if necessary, and water to keep the decomposition process going.

Compost is ready to use when it is very crumbly and the starting materials have decomposed beyond recognition—usually 1 to 3 months. Before using the compost, sift it through a coarse, 1-inch-mesh screen to remove large, undecomposed pieces. Put those in a new compost pile.

COMPOST RECEPTABLES

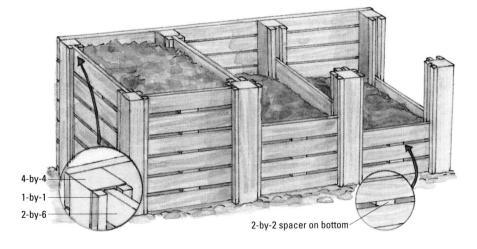

4-by-4
1-by-1
2-by-6

2-by-2 spacer on bottom

TOP: Simple compost receptacle is cylinder of welded wire. To turn composting material, lift up cylinder, move it to one side, fork material (to aerate it), and return material to cylinder.

MIDDLE: More complex compost bin is made of four wood frames covered with chicken wire. They are latched together at corners and can be unlatched to remove compost.

BOTTOM LEFT: Classic composting setup has three sections: left one holds new material, center one partially decomposed material, and right one finished compost. Fork material from bin to bin as composting progresses. Side boards are spaced for air penetration and slide out to make turning and removal of compost easy.

PLANTING

It's early spring, you have your vegetable seeds, and your soil is ready. To schedule your planting, consider two factors: the best method of planting and the best time.

Crops that are easy to germinate and don't require an early start can be sown outdoors directly in the ground. Crops that are difficult to sprout outdoors or that require a long growing season should be started indoors. Crops that are tricky for home gardeners to start can be purchased as transplants at nurseries. Our descriptions of individual vegetables and berries tell you the recommended method for planting.

To determine when to plant, check the last frost date of spring for your area (see the top map on page 8) and then refer to our individual plant descriptions.

STARTING SEEDS INDOORS

EQUIPMENT. You'll find the materials for starting seeds indoors at nurseries or garden centers, in seed catalogs, or right in your home. Seed starting kits include all the materials in one package. Here are the basics:

Sterilized potting soil

Milled sphagnum moss or vermiculite

Containers with drain holes (if your containers have been used before, disinfect them with a dilute solution of bleach)

Peat pots (2½ to 3 inches in diameter), peat pellets, growing cubes, or paper or plastic cups with drain holes (see drawing 1 at right).

Plastic bags

PLANTING STEPS. Sow your seeds in flats or trays, unless you are not sowing a large quantity; use peat pots or paper cups with drainage holes for just a few. The steps for planting the seeds are:

Fill the containers with soil mix, leveling and gently firming the soil to ½ inch from the top of the container.

Sow the seeds at the depth and spacing given on the seed packet or plant description.

For small seeds, cover the soil with a thin layer of moistened potting soil, sphagnum moss, or vermiculite.

Set the containers in an inch or two of water, and allow the water to move slowly upward until the soil surface is moist.

1 Peat pots, cubes, and pellets can be used to sow seeds indoors. Plant container and all when seedlings are big enough to move.

2 Shallow clay pot and foil tray with drain holes are starting chambers. Clear plastic keeps soil moist.

3 Separate seedlings are easy to transplant from egg carton sections or plastic or paper cups. Add drain holes.

4 To transplant seedlings from flat to individual containers, scoop them out with kitchen spoon, after they have at least second set of leaves.

Drain the containers, and place them in clear plastic bags. Either make small holes in the tops of the bags for ventilation or open the bags for 15 minutes each day.

Place the containers out of direct sunlight but where the temperature is 70° to 75°F/21° to 24°C. If the seeds you are starting require soil temperatures over 75°F/24°C, use a starting tray with an electric heating cable or a hotbed (see page 124) to provide the extra warmth needed for germination.

As soon as the seeds have sprouted, remove the plastic bags, and set the containers beside a sunny window or an artificial light source. If nights become very cold, move the containers away from the window glass. Keep the soil moist but not soggy.

If you have planted the seeds in a tray or flat, you can transplant the seedlings to individual containers after the second set of leaves appears. By giving each seedling room to develop its own roots freely, you save the plants considerable shock later when

SOWING SEEDS OUTDOORS

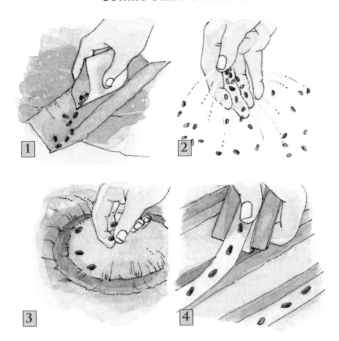

1 Use shallow furrows to sow seeds in rows. Make furrow as deep as seeds need, sow seeds evenly, cover with soil.

2 Broadcasting is used to sow wide bands of one vegetable such as lettuce or carrots. It takes a steady hand. Cover seeds with soil.

3 Hills—small clusters of seeds—are sowing method used for vining vegetables. Basin directs water to roots.

4 Seed tape spaces seeds proper distance apart. Lay tape in furrow, cover with soil. Tape soon decomposes.

you set them out in the garden. Be careful not to put the seedling deeper into the soil than it was before; this can kill it.

ARTIFICIAL LIGHT. If you can't provide a sunny location for transplants, try growing them under inexpensive light units, available in nurseries. As soon as the first sprout shows above the soil, light is needed for photosynthesis and growth. Once the seeds have germinated, they will grow into compact seedlings when temperatures are 60° to 65°F/16° to 18°C. Under special fluorescent "grow lights," place seedlings no more than 12 inches below the tubes, and then give them 12 to 16 hours of light daily. At greater distances from the light source, light intensity falls off drastically, and the seedlings become "leggy" (spindly).

"Grow lights" on adjustable stand help get seedlings started for earliest planting dates.

STARTING SEEDS OUTDOORS

Success in germinating seeds sown outdoors depends on four factors about the soil:

Soil condition. Soil should be loose and crumbly and raked fine (free of lumps or clods), so seeds can germinate easily. It should also be raked level, so water won't run off. It is a good idea to add a high-phosphate complete fertilizer at seeding time, to aid in root formation later.

Soil temperature. Seeds planted too early, when the soil is too cold for germination, may rot. The suggested planting times in the individual plant descriptions are designed to allow enough time for the soil to warm adequately.

Planting depth. Seeds planted too deep will not sprout. Examine the sidebar list in each plant description or the instructions on the seed packet for proper depth—usually about twice the thickness of the seed.

Soil moisture. The right amount of water keeps the soil moist but not soggy and prevents crusts from forming on the soil surface. Use a fine mist spray or perforated soaker (see page 104) to water, so seeds aren't washed away. For tiny seeds that are barely covered with soil, blanket the seed row with clear plastic sheeting or a floating row cover (see pages 106, 125) to keep moisture in. Allow ventilation, and remove the plastic sheeting as soon as the seeds sprout. For large vegetables, such as corn, squash, or tomatoes, which you may want to water by soaking, make furrows or basins before you plant (see drawings on page 105). Smaller vegetables, which can be watered by sprinkler, do not need basins or furrows.

KEEPING ROWS STRAIGHT

Lay board on soil surface, and plant or make furrow along its edge.

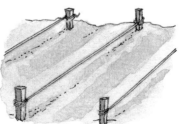

Stretch string between two stakes, and plant beneath it.

Seedlings started in a coldframe to get a jump on the season.

TRANSPLANTING SEEDLINGS

Seedlings started indoors or bought from a nursery are transplanted to the garden. Try to make their transition an easy one. Any sudden change in environment can cause a slowing or stunting of growth from which the plant may not fully recover.

For the best chance at success, start with healthy plants. If you are purchasing plants from a nursery, shop for plants that are compact and bushy (if they are branching plants), with leaves of a good green color and free of obvious insect damage. Roots should not be sticking out through the drain holes. Avoid plants that are spindly or leggy.

Plants that you have started indoors and some plants from the nursery have been raised in greenhouse conditions. To prevent undue stress to these tender seedlings, gradually accustom them to the outdoors. In this acclimation process, called "hardening off," you set the plants out in a shady place on a warm day and gradually extend the amount of time in the sun. Bring them indoors whenever cold or freezing temperatures are predicted. After several nights outdoors in their containers, plants should be ready.

WHAT'S A HILL?

"Hill" is a term that causes a lot of misunderstanding. In gardening, a "hill" refers to a grouping of seeds or plants in a cluster, not necessarily on a mound. A hill of squash or corn can consist of two or three plants growing together, level with the rest of the garden. Hills, or clusters, are usually contrasted with rows, in which plants are spaced equal distances apart in a line.

When transplanting seedlings to the garden, try to disturb the roots as little as possible. (Peat pots require no disturbance; you remove the lip to the soil level, and plant the entire pot.) Follow these steps for setting out purchased or home-grown plants:

Dig holes for receiving the plants, and fill the holes with water.

Water the seedlings thoroughly before setting them out.

Separate the root ball of each plant carefully from the larger mass of soil, preserving as much soil around the roots as possible, if the plants are not in individual pots. If a plant in an individual pot is rootbound, loosen the surface of the root ball with your fingers before planting.

Keep the roots moist until the young plants are planted.

Set out the plants so that the root mass of each is just slightly covered. Planting too deeply can slow or stop plant growth (tomatoes are an exception; see page 69). Cover each root ball with loose soil and gently firm it down; then water each plant.

Apply a high-phosphate starter solution, unless you added a high-phosphate fertilizer during soil preparation (see page 95).

Protect transplants from hot weather or frost and from pests (such as cutworms and snails) by using one of the protective devices illustrated at the top of page 103. Open plastic coverings during the day.

Floating row covers propped up to protect young pepper seedlings.

EASY WAYS TO PROTECT TRANSPLANTS

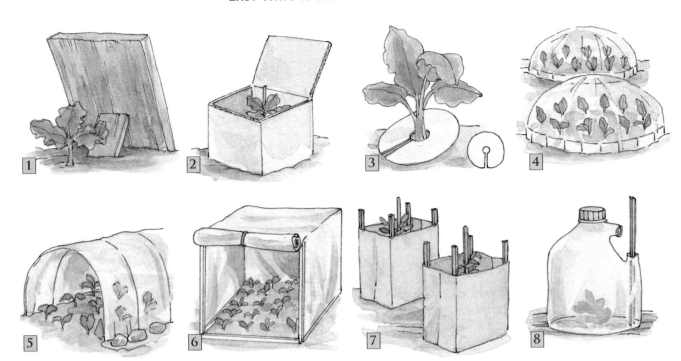

1 Piece of board or shingle shades seedling from hot sun. Prop up board immediately after setting out plant.

2 Cardboard box, upside down, keeps out cold, heat, bugs, birds. Cut out bottom on three sides to make lid. Be sure to remove box in morning.

3 Tarpaper or cardboard collar slips around stem of seedling to foil damage by cabbage root maggots and cutworms.

4 Ventilated paper or plastic caps over tender seedlings prevent late frost damage. Smaller versions cover just one plant.

5 Cloche to protect seedlings from cold is made of clear plastic sheeting over wire wickets. Rocks anchor it.

6 Plastic sheeting over wooden frame covers seedlings. Lower flap on cold nights for frost protection. Remove sheeting in morning.

7 Paper bags anchored by four stakes block wind, cold, heat. Plant will grow up center stake. Hole cut in bottom is just big enough for plant.

8 Plastic milk container with bottom cut out is held up by stake to protect seedlings from cold, wind, birds, insects.

SETS, ROOTS, AND CUTTINGS

Though most vegetables are started from seeds, some perennial vegetables are grown from sets (small-size bulbs or plants), roots (pieces of root from full-grown plants), or cuttings (pieces of a plant stem and leaves that have developed roots).

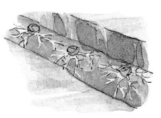

Roots, or divisions, are used to start perennial vegetables such as asparagus. Planting depth depends on crop.

Sets of small onion-family bulbs will grow full-size in one season. Plant sets in furrows ½ to 2 inches deep.

Cuttings can be made from tips of sweet potato sprouts. These cuttings have been rooted (see page 66) and now are being planted in mound.

WATERING

Food crops need a steady supply of water from planting until harvest. Giving plants too little water in their root zones will result first in wilting, then in stunted growth, and eventually, if not remedied, in death. Giving plants too much water may drown roots, encourage disease, and cause plants to stop growing and even die. Proper watering is something of an art—learned through experience.

HOW OFTEN TO WATER

How often you water depends on the kinds of crops you are growing, the age and size of the plants, the kind of soil you have, and the weather.

Different crops need different amounts of water. For example, shallow-rooted leafy crops require more than root crops.

Young vegetable seedlings with small, shallow roots that lie in the top layer of soil need to be watered frequently—sometimes two or three times a day—to keep their root zone moist. A mature grapevine with roots that extend deep into the soil may need deep watering only once a month if rainfall is not enough.

The proportion of clay, sand, silt, and organic matter in the planting soil also determines how often you have to water. Clay soils hold lots of water and release it slowly; sandy soils hold less water and release it quickly. Loam soils hold less water than clay and more than sand. Clay soils can be watered less often than loam soils, which, in turn, can be watered less often than sandy soils.

Cool, cloudy weather allows any soil to stay moist longer than does hot, dry weather. In some areas, rainfall during the growing season supplies all of the water needs of vegetables.

HOW MUCH TO WATER

Give your vegetables deep and infrequent waterings, rather than frequent shallow sprinklings. You need to apply enough water to penetrate the root zone of the plants. How deep a given amount of water will penetrate depends on the soil type. On the average, 1 inch of water applied at the surface will wet sandy soil 12 inches deep and clay soil 4 to 5 inches deep.

To determine how much water you have applied by sprinkling, set a coffee or soup can out in the garden, and measure the amount of water in the can after you've watered for a period. The only precise way to determine how deeply water has penetrated in your soil, however, is to dig down.

TOP: Drip irrigation soaks soil for individual 'White Polish' garlic plants. Useful where water is scarce, pressure low, or land sloping.

BOTTOM: Soaker hose delivers thin jets of water from pinprick-size holes. Good for slow soaking; no runoff.

METHODS OF WATERING

Several techniques for applying water are shown on these pages, but in principle they are variations of two approaches: soaking and sprinkling.

SOAKING. The slow soaking of water into the ground will wet the soil evenly to the depth you want.

Drip irrigation is one method of soaking the soil. Plastic tubing on the soil surface carries water to individual plants, and special emitters release the water slowly to each plant.

Drip systems require very little water pressure to deliver the water. By leaving the system on for a few hours, you can thoroughly moisten each plant's root zone. Drip irrigation is also very economical, because water is directed only to the soil that needs it. As a bonus, weeds are reduced.

Drip irrigation supplies are sold by agricultural supply stores, retail nurseries and garden supply centers, mail-order suppliers, and hardware stores.

Watering basins around plants are another method of soaking—often used with shrubby plants and large vegetables. Basins work in nearly any garden situation and soil, unlike furrows, which are most successful on level ground and with soil that is not very sandy. A basin is a circular doughnut-shaped depression in the soil surrounding a plant. Make your basins at least several inches wider than the plant width, and expand them as the plants grow.

Furrow watering works best where plants are no more than 3 to 4 inches in from the shoulder of the furrow, since lateral wetting of the soil doesn't go much beyond this. Dig the furrows before planting. Make them as much as 12 inches wide and 6 inches deep. Be sure they're as level as possible.

Send water into the furrows slowly so that soil won't wash away. Furrow watering is more effective in sandy soils if you divide long furrows into 6-foot segments. For less permeable soils, such as clay, you can increase the furrow length to 12 feet. To hold the water in a section of furrow until the soil is soaked, use a dam made of a board, a piece of metal, or a wide shovel placed upright across the furrow.

Occasionally you will need to do some furrow repair—dredging out the bottom or replacing soil that has eroded from the sides.

SPRINKLING. Using a good sprinkler that distributes water as evenly as possible is a time-saving way to water a garden, especially a large one. It's also a good way to leach excess salts from ridge and furrow plantings, and it is sometimes the only effective way to water where soils are very sandy. For best coverage, overlap areas of wetting by about a third.

Overhead sprinkling has a few disadvantages. Moisture on leaves may encourage diseases on some crops, especially in humid climates. Sprinkling also wastes water through evaporation, particularly in windy weather. The best times to use a sprinkler are in the morning (leaves will dry off during the day) and when the air is still.

BASINS AND FURROWS

Basins with sides 3 inches high hold water around large plants, such as tomatoes and peppers. On level ground link basins to make watering easier.

Furrows 3 to 6 inches deep help irrigate straight rows on level ground. Bubbler on hose end softens flow of water to prevent erosion. Good for crops that don't appreciate overhead watering. Works poorly in very sandy soils.

SPRINKLERS

1 Hose-end sprinkler delivers gentle "rain-fall." Area covered is determined by water pressure and spray pattern. Best way to water where soil is very sandy, but it can encourage foliage diseases.

2 Adjustable-height sprinkler "grows" as needed to keep foliage from blocking spray.

3 Watering can is handy for watering containers, patches of seedlings, or transplants and for applying liquid fertilizer.

4 Hand-watering with hose and sprinkler nozzle gives you control when watering seedbeds and transplants. You must be patient to water deeply.

Mulching

A mulch is any material spread or laid over soil to conserve moisture, help the growth of the desired plants, and suppress the growth of unwanted weeds. This definition covers the gamut from crushed rock, layered newspapers, and plastic sheeting to various organic materials such as grass clippings, straw, manure, leaves, and compost.

Mulching around your vegetables reduces evaporation, so the soil stays moist longer after each application of water; it keeps the soil temperature cooler and more stable during hot weather; and it suppresses the germination of weed seeds.

Several kinds of mulches provide a clean and fairly dry surface on which squash and melons, for example, may rest and ripen without risk of rotting from contact with damp soil.

In addition, organic mulches, as they decompose, keep the top few inches of soil loose and crumbly. Such a soil surface allows easy penetration of water and dissolved nutrients and encourages free growth of surface feeder roots. It also provides a looser foothold for any weeds that do sprout, so that weeding is easier.

Because organic mulches keep the soil beneath them cool, you should delay applying them until warm weather arrives. (Soil warmth is necessary to get most plants off to a good start.)

At least one kind of mulch, however—black plastic sheeting—helps warm the soil quickly in spring. After preparing the soil for planting, cover it with black plastic, and cut small holes where you want to sow seeds or set out plants. Black plastic is especially beneficial for growing warm-season crops where summers are cool or short. It also suppresses weed growth.

Apply a mulch so that it covers the soil completely but does not cover the bases of plants where they meet the soil (the plant crowns). Many plants will rot if kept too moist at their crowns.

TOP: Black plastic sheeting used as mulch helps warm soil, conserve moisture, and suppress weeds. Good for heat-loving plants such as melons.

MIDDLE: Clear white and red plastic sheeting works to warm soil, but it allows weeds to grow underneath.

BOTTOM: Straw is one widely available organic mulch.

STAKING VEGETABLES

Some vegetables benefit from support: climbing vegetables, such as pole beans and peas, and sprawling vegetables, such as tomatoes, cucumbers, and melons. Not only will you save space by tying or propping up these crops, but you'll also harvest more fruits—keeping fruits such as tomatoes and melons off the ground will avoid a common cause of rotting.

The best time to put up stakes, poles, trellises, and other supports for vegetables is at planting; because roots haven't yet formed, you needn't worry about disturbing them. Train or tie the plants as they grow.

Tepee of bamboo poles tied together at top supports beans planted beside poles.

Cylinder of welded wire and two stakes support tomato plant with minimum of tying. Reach through mesh to harvest.

Strings stretched over A-frame made of 2-by-2s are for beans, peas to climb.

Bamboo poles in ground, tied together at crosspole, will hold up row vegetables tied to them with cloth strips.

Sturdy frame leaning on wall makes trellis for cucumber or squash vines.

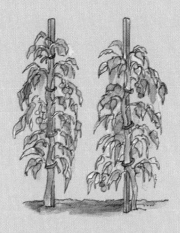

Tall wooden stakes hold up tomato plants. Use soft ties to fasten plant stems.

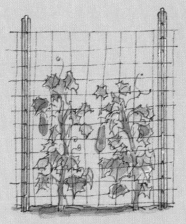

Broad-mesh plastic netting attached to hooks in metal fencing stakes can support cucumbers, squash, beans, peas.

FERTILIZING

Plants, like other living things, must have nourishment if they are to thrive. Soil contains the elements necessary for plant growth, but the supply gradually diminishes as plants use up available nutrients. Fertilizing your garden replenishes the nutrients.

ORGANIC OR INORGANIC?

Fertilizers can be grouped into two broad categories, organic and inorganic, depending on the source material of the nutrients. To a plant's roots, the important point is whether a nutrient is present at the period of critical need. The choice between organic and inorganic is a matter of personal preference, but the different ways they act will have a bearing on how and when you use either type.

Organic fertilizers, such as cottonseed meal, bonemeal, manure, fish emulsion, and blood meal, are derived from the remains of living organisms. Rather slow to decompose and give up their nutrients, organic fertilizers work over a long period, and some are not easily washed from the soil. You should work bonemeal, for instance, into the soil well before planting time.

Keep in mind that many organic fertilizers are high in just one of the three major nutrients (see "Nutrients in the soil" on pages 94–95) and low or lacking in the other two. (Some are chemically fortified to increase their nutrient content.)

Gardeners sometimes confuse organic amendments with organic fertilizers. Peat moss and compost are primarily soil amendments (see page 96), not fertilizers. Though they may contain small amounts of nutrients, they are best used to improve the structure (or tilth) of the soil.

Inorganic fertilizers—sometimes referred to as "chemical fertilizers"—are available in dry, liquid, and tablet form. With the exception of the slow- or timed-release kinds, the inorganic fertilizers are effective for a shorter time than organic ones. But, because their nutrients are usually released by dissolving rather than by bacterial action, the nutrients tend to be readily available to plants.

Inorganic fertilizers that contain all three major elements (see "Nutrients in the soil," pages 94–95) are called "complete fertilizers." The ratios of the nutrients may vary considerably (see "Reading fertilizer labels," on the next page). You can incorporate inorganic fertilizers into the soil as you prepare it for planting, and you can also apply them after crops are growing. In general, inorganic fertilizers are less expensive—pound for pound of actual nutrient—than organic ones.

WHEN AND HOW TO FERTILIZE

BEFORE PLANTING. Your first opportunity to apply fertilizer is when you prepare the soil for planting. Incorporate dry organic or complete inorganic fertilizer—especially phosphorus—into the soil as you dig or till it. This puts nutrients into the anticipated root zone of the crops you intend to grow. Phos-

Work complete fertilizer into soil with spading fork when you prepare beds for planting, to offer young plants nutrients they need for early growth push.

Apply water-soluble fertilizer mixture from watering can into basin around plant during growing season if crop requires side-dressing. This method is also effective for container plants.

Apply dry complete fertilizer as side-dressing during growing season, if needed, in band 4 to 6 inches from plants. Scratch fertilizer into soil lightly, then water thoroughly.

phorus doesn't readily penetrate into the soil from surface applications of fertilizer.

You can scatter fertilizer over bare ground by hand (as though you were flinging out birdseed) or you can use a mechanical spreader, which you may be able to rent from nurseries or garden equipment dealers. Scatter or spread the fertilizer as evenly as possible; then dig or till it into the soil. For general guidelines on amounts to use, see "How much to apply," below.

FOLLOW-UP FEEDING. For many vegetables, the fertilizer dug into the soil will provide sustenance for the entire growing season. But some crops are heavy feeders, needing supplemental boosts, particularly of nitrogen, during the growing season. (For more information, check the individual plant listings.) These additional applications, often referred to as "side-dressings," can be given in several ways.

If you use dry fertilizer, you can broadcast it over the soil surface (keep it off plant leaves), lightly scratch it into the soil, and water thoroughly. Or you might make a shallow trench 4 to 6 inches from the plants alongside the row (or in a ring around widely spaced plants such as melons and squash), scatter the fertilizer in the trench, cover it with soil, and water it thoroughly.

If yours is a small garden, you may prefer to mix a solution of water-soluble fertilizer and use a watering can to sprinkle it on the soil.

Perennial vegetables and the various berries—because they remain in place for many years—need to receive surface applications of fertilizer year after year. At the start of each growing season, use the scattering or spreading method outlined under "Before planting" on page 108; add a side-dressing only if suggested in the individual description for the plant.

HOW MUCH TO APPLY

Fertilizers packaged for home use generally specify the amount to be applied in terms of pounds per square feet of garden area. If, for example, directions specify 1 pound for each 100 square feet, you know that a 1-pound package will take care of a 10-by-10-foot plot, or a 5-by-20 foot one. Recommended amounts differ from one formulation to another; never assume that one recommended amount will hold for all fertilizers. Read the label or follow your soil test report, and then calculate your garden area.

GETTING MORE ADVICE ON FERTILIZING

The description of each vegetable mentions the crop's particular nutrient needs. Beyond that, your very best advice will come from the local Cooperative Extension Service, which is familiar with conditions in your specific area.

Fertilizer label shows percentages of major nutrients.

READING FERTILIZER LABELS

Nitrogen, phosphorus, and potassium occur in fertilizers in different amounts. The numbers on a fertilizer label refer to the percentage of these nutrients in the product: 5-10-10, for example, contains 5 percent nitrogen, 10 percent phosphorus (expressed as fertilizer phosphate or P_2O_6, and 10 percent potassium (expressed as fertilizer potash or K_2O). The rest of the mixture consists of various fillers and minerals. The order in which the elements are listed—nitrogen, phosphorus, and potassium—is always the same. Any fertilizer that contains all three primary elements is referred to as a complete fertilizer.

Your choice among fertilizers may seem bewildering at first, since formulas can vary so widely. Some are labeled "vegetable food" or are specifically recommended for food crops in general; these can be considered fairly safe choices. But if you want to be really thorough about the matter, and possibly save money in the long run, you'll have your soil tested (see page 96) to find out specifically what's needed and to protect the environment from excess fertilizer. Almost any crop will need supplemental nitrogen. But a test may disclose that phosphorus or potassium or both are plentiful enough in your soil so that there is no need for a supplement.

Weeding

Anyone who plants a garden sooner or later comes to grips with weeding. Removing weeds is a very important garden activity, because weeds compete with productive plants for water, food, and light.

Methods

Hand-pulling, hoeing, and cultivating are time-honored ways of ridding gardens of weeds. Soil solarization is a modern technique. Each method is suited to particular garden situations.

Pulling weeds by hand is the most time-consuming method. It is not too much of a chore if the weeds are few and widely spaced, and it is the safest way to remove small weeds growing close to your plants. A scratcher or trowel may help you hand-pull by loosening the soil around weeds a bit. You can dig out deep-rooted perennial weeds with a trowel, knife, or special weeding tool.

Hoeing works best on open patches of densely growing weeds. You get plenty of weeds with each hoe stroke, but you aren't working so close to crop plants that you risk harvesting them along with your weeds. Keep the hoe blade sharp. As you hoe, move forward, toward unhoed weeds. Cut horizontally to slice roots just below the surface. After hoeing, remove the chopped-down weeds and, if they haven't gone to seed, compost them.

Cultivation—plowing weeds under—works best in large gardens with plenty of space between rows. Whether you use a hand cultivator or a mechanical tiller, the goal of cultivation is to suppress weeds rather than to eliminate them totally. Weeds that are thoroughly plowed under will decay, but some will always regrow.

Soil solarization uses plastic sheeting and the sun to raise the soil temperature high enough to kill weed seeds (as well as many insect and disease organisms). It works best in areas with very hot, sunny summers, such as the U.S. Southwest. Just before the hottest time of the year (usually mid-July), and well before fall planting, till the soil, and remove the weeds. Water the soil deeply, then lay 1- to 4-mil clear plastic over it (or use two layers as shown in the drawing below), and anchor the edges with soil. Leave it in place for 4 to 6 weeks.

Here are some weeding tips:

Water the area first, regardless of which technique you use. Weeds will pull out more easily when soil is moist.

Pull or hoe weed seedlings as soon as you can. The smaller they are, the less they compete with crops and the more easily they come out.

Gather all pulled, hoed, and loose weeds, to keep them from taking root again. You can compost those that haven't gone to seed and that don't spread by underground rhizomes (as Bermuda grass does). Burn or discard the others.

Never let weeds mature and go to seed.

Solarize soil with plastic sheeting. You can use two sheets, one directly on soil, the other separated about 2 inches from the first by spacers, such as soda cans lying on their sides.

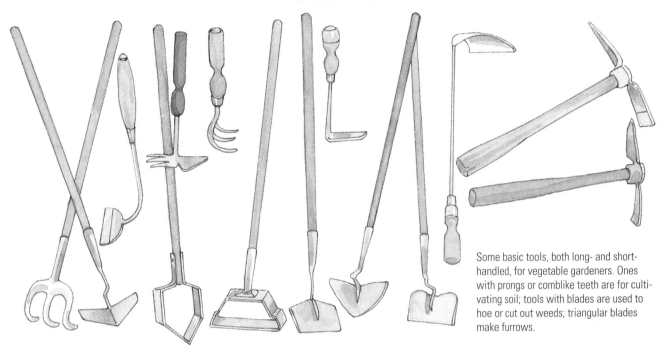

Some basic tools, both long- and short-handled, for vegetable gardeners. Ones with prongs or comblike teeth are for cultivating soil; tools with blades are used to hoe or cut out weeds; triangular blades make furrows.

CHEMICAL WEED CONTROLS

Herbicides—weed-killing chemical products—can be labor-saving aids to home gardeners if they are used with understanding and care. The critical point is to choose an herbicide that will remove the weeds without harming the crops you're growing. Those herbicides state on the label that they are safe to use on vegetables and berries. Be sure to choose only those, and *use them according to directions on the label.*

You can use pre-emergence herbicides (those that kill annual weeds as they sprout) among perennial crops such as asparagus, cane berries, and rhubarb. Don't use them in soil where you plan to grow from seeds.

If possible, avoid using herbicides that remain in the soil for a long time. A long-lived herbicide might be safe for the crop you plant in summer but harmful if it's still active when you plant a different crop in the same soil in autumn.

MULCHES TO CONTROL WEEDS

Weed seeds—like any seeds—need sunlight, warmth, and moisture to germinate and grow. Mulches help control weeds by depriving their seeds of necessary sunlight (see page 106).

Black plastic sheeting is one of the most effective mulches. Thick layers of organic material such as grass clippings and composted leaves also discourage the sprouting of weed seeds, and they keep the soil surface loose and moist, making it easier to pull out any weeds that do sprout.

INTENSIVE PLANTING

Another way to keep sunlight from soil is to blanket it with living plants. Planting some crops close together (carrots, beans, and strawberries, for example) results in a dense cover of leaves that denies both sunlight to weed seeds and growing room to weed seedlings. Close planting is discussed more fully under "French intensive gardening" on pages 123–124.

Intensively planted bed crowds out weeds and produces bountiful crops.

PESTS AND DISEASES

Because the joys of growing vegetables and berries can, from time to time, be interrupted by plant pests or diseases, you need to know how to recognize the most common problems and what remedies to use. Pests or diseases that are likely to visit particular vegetables and berries are mentioned in the individual plant descriptions. This section presents profiles of some troublemakers, along with appropriate controls.

If you see damage but you're uncertain about what is afflicting a particular crop, check with your Cooperative Extension Service. Here are some precautions you can take to offset or discourage crop damage.

Plant disease-resistant varieties if they are available. Hybrids have been developed that are resistant to the most troublesome vegetable diseases. Many tomato hybrids, for example, are resistant to both verticillium wilt and fusarium wilt.

Keep your garden clean. A number of insects and diseases overwinter or spend part of their life cycle on plant debris. Pulling up, shredding, and composting or discarding infected plant parts and spent plants, and tilling the soil, especially in fall, can slow the spread of many pests.

Provide the best possible growing conditions, to encourage healthy plant growth. A healthy plant is better able to resist pest and disease attacks.

Mix plants in an area. Large expanses of just one type of plant encourage large populations of any pest especially fond of that plant. A mixed planting of several kinds of vegetables and berries not only discourages large numbers of specific pests but also favors a larger number and greater assortment of insects that prey on the damaging ones. Rotate the locations of crops in your garden from year to year, to help prevent a buildup of pests in one spot.

Encourage natural controls. Toads, lizards, and many birds eat insects. Helpful predatory insects eat some plant-damaging ones. Ideally the balance of nature will keep plant damagers in check by natural controls. Chemical sprays generally wipe out the helpful insects along with the troublemakers, leaving the garden wide open for a new attack by pests.

Careful inspection detects insects, damage, and disease.

You can buy some beneficial insects (ladybugs, lacewings, trichogramma wasps) from mail-order sources. If you have a wide variety of pests for them to feed on, they may remain in and around your garden and cut down considerably on potential crop damage.

In any case, remember that predators won't appear—and imported ones won't stay—unless there is prey.

Be vigilant on a daily basis. While you're watering, weeding, and harvesting your crops, keep a watchful eye out for the first signs of damage. Hand-pick and dispatch the larger pests (snails, caterpillars, tomato hornworms). Try hosing off small pests, such as aphids, with a jet of water from the hose. Escalate to stronger measures only if your first efforts fail.

PEST CONTROL CHOICES

Slight damage to crops is not a signal to begin chemical warfare. It is just a notice to be on the alert and, if necessary, to take some first-step measures. Control measures other than chemical sprays can be effective in many cases. Packaged controls should be used only as last-resort procedures, when a specific pest or disease gets out of hand on a particular crop. In the charts on pages 114–118, the controls are grouped in order of preference: hand measures, cultural solutions, physical barriers, homemade sprays, biological controls, botanical sprays, and manufactured chemicals.

HAND MEASURES. The larger pests (such as snails, slugs, grasshoppers, and some beetles) are candidates for removal by hand. Pick them off the plant, and destroy them. Some of the smaller pests, such as aphids and mites, can be dislodged by a blast of water from the garden hose. The job is easiest if you select a hose nozzle that you can adjust to a hard spray or a pistol type of nozzle that gives strong jets of water. To control mites, you need to aim the water at leaf undersides.

PHYSICAL BARRIERS. You can often exclude pests from your vegetables. Floating row covers (see page 125), which are draped over plants, are very effective at excluding many insects, particularly flying insects that feed on plant foliage. Snails will not cross copper stripping. Small cardboard collars about 4 inches wide (paper cups with the bottoms torn out work perfectly) keep cutworms from reaching new seedlings or transplants.

HOMEMADE SPRAYS. Some gardeners use a spray of soap solution to destroy aphids, whiteflies, and other soft-bodied insects. Mix 2 to 3 tablespoons of nonconcentrated dish soap in 1 gallon of tepid water; spray it onto insects that infest plants. Several hours later, rinse the soap film off the plants you have sprayed.

Commercial insecticidal soaps can be used on a wide variety of food crops. They are less likely than homemade remedies to burn plants.

Other homemade sprays include solutions of ground-up hot peppers, crushed garlic, and ground-up insects.

BIOLOGICAL CONTROLS. Some bacterial cultures can kill insects without harming warm-blooded creatures. Several manufacturers offer products containing *Bacillus thuringiensis,* a species of bacteria that controls various caterpillars by destroying their digestive systems. One strain *(B. t. tenebrionis)* attacks the Colorado potato beetle.

Releasing beneficial insects, such as lacewings, predatory mites, and parasitic nematodes, which attack harmful ones, is another form of biological control.

BOTANICAL SPRAYS. Rotenone, pyrethrum, neem, and sabadilla, derived from natural substances, are toxic to insects but relatively safe to humans. Because they have little residual effect once sprayed on plants, you must apply these sprays directly to the pests in order to kill them. Botanical sprays control some of the common sucking and chewing insects, such as aphids, caterpillars, and whiteflies.

MANUFACTURED CHEMICALS. Three manufactured insecticides that are available to home gardeners are labeled for use on vegetables and berries: malathion, diazinon, and carbaryl. All are fairly broad-spectrum insecticides, killing helpful insects as well as undesirable ones. They are most effective against sucking insects, such as aphids, thrips, leafhoppers, and whiteflies. Carbaryl has the disadvantage that it also kills honeybees. Apply the chemicals strictly according to label directions.

Many sprays for vegetables contain a mixture of these chemicals. Always check the product label to be sure the pesticide is safe for edible crops. Never use any spray that isn't specifically labeled as safe for application to the crop you are growing. Be exact in following directions about the length of time you must wait between spraying and harvesting.

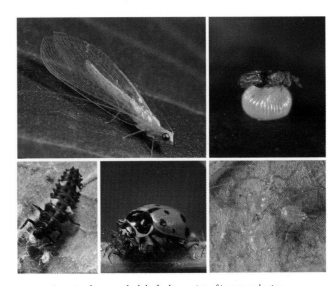

TOP LEFT: Lacewing larvae and adults feed on variety of insects and mites.

TOP RIGHT: Trichogramma wasp larvae develop within caterpillar eggs and eat their way out, destroying eggs. Adult wasps find new eggs to parasitize. Repeated releases are usually necessary to reduce caterpillar infestation.

BOTTOM LEFT AND MIDDLE: Ladybird beetle (ladybug) larvae and adults feed on aphids, mealybugs, small worms, spider mites, and similar soft-bodied insects. However, they migrate annually and tend to fly away once released. Release in evening to discourage flight.

BOTTOM RIGHT: Predator mites of various species feed on spider mites, and sometimes thrips, but do no damage to plants.

CROP-DAMAGING INSECTS

INSECT	DESCRIPTION	CONTROLS (IN ORDER OF PREFERENCE)
Aphids	Green, black, pink, or yellow sucking insects feed on young leaves, stems	Wait until beneficial insect populations build up and bring aphids under control. Hose off aphids with strong jet of water. Spray with insecticidal soap, pyrethrum, rotenone, malathion, or diazinon
Armyworms	Yellowish green to grayish green caterpillars are larvae of brownish gray moth. Feed in groups at night on young plants	Hand-pick. Eliminate grassy weeds, where infestations usually originate; till soil in autumn to expose larvae to birds and other predators. Try digging 6-in.-deep trench around vegetable garden or surrounding it with strip of aluminum foil; make side of trench near vegetable garden steeper, so worms in trench can't get to vegetables; then pick them at night. Release trichogramma wasps. Spray with *Bacillus thuringiensis*, malathion, or carbaryl
Asparagus beetles	Adults are about 1/4 in. long, shiny, blue black with yellow markings on wing covers. Larvae are about 1/2 in. long, green or dark gray. Adults feed on shoots when they come up in spring, lay eggs on shoots. Larvae eat shoots, leaves	Hand-pick adults. Cover young spears with floating row covers. Spray adults and larvae with rotenone or malathion
Borers	Raspberry cane borers attack raspberries and blackberries. Currant borers attack currants and gooseberries. Adults lay eggs in tips of canes or stems. Eggs hatch into larvae that bore down into canes and stems, killing them. Look for wilting tips of canes and stems	Cut off canes and stems 6 in. below dying tips, and discard or shred and compost them
Cabbage loopers	Greenish caterpillars, also called inchworms, feed on cabbages, related crops	Hand-pick adults and small white egg clusters. Use floating row covers. Release trichogramma wasps. Spray with *Bacillus thuringiensis*, rotenone, pyrethrum, or carbaryl
Cabbage root maggots	White larvae of flies eat roots; plants wilt or are stunted	Put tarpaper collars on soil around stems to prevent maggots from laying eggs; use floating row covers. Shred and compost or discard infected plants. Release parasitic nematodes. Dig diazinon into soil
Cabbageworms	Greenish caterpillars of white cabbage butterflies eat leaves and flowers of cole crops	Hand-pick adults and egg clusters. Use floating row covers. Release trichogramma wasps. Spray with *Bacillus thuringiensis*, rotenone, pyrethrum, or carbaryl

   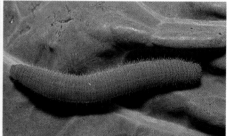

Asparagus beetle larva and adult   Yellow-striped armyworm moth larva on tomato   Cabbage looper

CROP-DAMAGING INSECTS

INSECT	DESCRIPTION	CONTROLS (IN ORDER OF PREFERENCE)
Colorado potato beetles	Yellow-and-black-striped beetles and red larvae eat leaves of potatoes, tomatoes, eggplant	Hand-pick adults and egg clusters. Shred and compost or discard all garden debris. Spray with *Bacillus thuringiensis tenebrionis*, rotenone, neem, pyrethrum, or carbaryl
Corn borers	Larvae of moths hatch from eggs laid on leaves of corn plants, tunnel into stalks both upward and downward. Larvae are 1 in. long, pink or brown, with rows of small dark brown spots. Look for signs of feeding first on leaves and tassels, then in leaf whorl (funnel) of plant. Tunneling may cause corn stalks to collapse	Shred and compost or discard corn debris in fall; plant resistant varieties (check with your local Cooperative Extension Service). Spread *Bacillus thuringiensis* baits around base of stalks; spray with diazinon or carbaryl
Corn earworms	Larvae of night-flying moths eat corn kernels under husks and eat green tomatoes. Most gardeners learn to live with earworms, simply cutting off damaged ends of ears, because control is difficult	Apply mineral oil (about 7 days after earworm silt appears) or carbaryl to corn silks. Inject parasitic nematodes into silks; release trichogramma wasps. Spray with *Bacillus thuringiensis*
Cucumber beetles	Oval-shaped beetles, greenish yellow with black spots or stripes, eat all parts of cucumbers, squashes, melons. Beetles also transmit bacterial wilt diseases	Shred and compost badly infested debris; plant resistant varieties. Use floating row covers. Release parasitic nematodes. Spray with pyrethrum, sabadilla, rotenone, malathion, or carbaryl
Cutworms	Moth larvae live in soil, feed on stems just above ground level or on lower leaves of seedlings	Hand-pick at night (or trap worms under boards and pick during day). Use protective collars around stems of young seedlings. Release parasitic nematodes. Spread cutworm bait. Spray with diazinon or carbaryl
Flea beetles	Tiny yellow, green, or black adults can jump like fleas. Adults chew holes in leaves of potatoes, radishes, eggplant, and Chinese cabbage; larvae feed on potato tubers and other roots	Remove and compost dead or damaged leaves and plants; till soil in fall. Use floating row covers to exclude adults. Use parasitic nematodes against larvae. Spray with rotenone, insecticidal soap, pyrethrum, sabadilla, or carbaryl
Grape berry moth larvae	Small green-to-purple larvae of first generation feed on flower buds and berries in early summer. Second-generation larvae tunnel directly into green berries and feed there	Shred and compost or discard leaf debris under vines in fall. Apply rotenone or diazinon (check with local Cooperative Extension Service for proper timing)

Corn earworm

Spotted cucumber beetle

Cutworm

CROP-DAMAGING INSECTS

INSECT	DESCRIPTION	CONTROLS (IN ORDER OF PREFERENCE)
Grasshoppers	Large but often well-camouflaged pests with big appetites eat crops during day	Hand-pick and destroy egg clusters (they look like rice) and adults during cool mornings when insects are sluggish. Plant under floating row covers. Spray adults with malathion or carbaryl
Harlequin bugs	Adults are black with reddish orange markings. Nymphs (immature insects) suck juices from leaves, can kill plants	Hand-pick. Shred and compost or discard plant debris and nearby weeds. Spray with insecticidal soap, sabadilla, pyrethrum, or carbaryl
Leafhoppers	Green or brown adults hop about, feed on undersides of leaves, cause stippling of leaf surface, spread leaf diseases. Beans are one favorite plant	Use row covers over seedlings. Spray with insecticidal soap, neem, pyrethrum, rotenone, malathion, or carbaryl
Leaf miners	Adults—various flies, moths, or beetles—lay eggs on vegetables, cane fruits, strawberries. Eggs hatch into larvae, or leaf miners, that bore into leaves, making tunnels as they feed. Tunneling makes leaves of beets, cabbage, spinach unattractive for food	Remove infested leaves if few in number. Plant under floating row covers. Sprays are not effective
Mexican bean beetles	Reddish yellow adult insects with black spots and yellow larvae feed on undersides of bean leaves, eating all but leaf veins	Hand-pick adults and yellow egg clusters on undersides of leaves. Shred and compost or discard garden debris in fall; plant resistant varieties. Plant under floating row covers. Spray with pyrethrum, rotenone, malathion, or carbaryl
Nematodes	Microscopic worms live in soil and feed chiefly on roots of plants. Some kinds cause plants to form root galls. All cause plants to be weaker, less productive. Most common in sandy soils	Use soil solarization; incorporate organic matter into soil; plant resistant varieties. Before planting, fumigate soil (check with local Cooperative Extension Service for appropriate products)
Rose chafers	Tan beetles eat leaves, flowers, fruit of cane berries, grapes, strawberries. Occur mostly east of Rockies	Hand-pick adults. Plant under floating row covers. Use parasitic nematodes to eat larvae. Spray with rotenone, pyrethrum, insecticidal soap, or carbaryl
Snails, slugs	Shelled and shell-less mollusks devour seedlings and leaves of many vegetables. Feed at night and on cloudy days	Hand-pick at night or trap under slightly raised boards during day. Enclose raised beds with copper strips (snails and slugs won't cross copper); leave small dishes of beer out in garden at night (mollusks will drown). Spread diatomaceous earth. Apply metaldehyde bait

Short-horned grasshopper

Mexican bean beetles

Snap bean root knots caused by nematode parasites

CROP-DAMAGING INSECTS

INSECT	DESCRIPTION	CONTROLS (IN ORDER OF PREFERENCE)
Spider mites	Tiny spiderlike creatures (you need magnifying lens to see them clearly) spin fine webs, suck juices on undersides of leaves	Keep plants well watered; shred and compost or discard badly infested plants. Blast leaves with water. Release predatory mites. Spray with insecticidal soap or sulfur
Squash bugs	Adults and nymphs feed on vines and fruit of squashes, pumpkins, gourds, melons	Hand-pick adults and brick red egg masses from undersides of leaves. Shred and compost or discard garden debris. Plant under floating row covers. Spray with sabadilla, rotenone, insecticidal soap, or carbaryl
Squash vine borers	Larvae of moths bore into vines near soil line, cause sudden wilting. Look for entry holes in vines and yellowish droppings	Slit open vines with knife, kill borers, and bury stems. Shred and compost or discard garden debris. Plant under floating row covers. Inject stems with parasitic nematodes
Strawberry root weevils	Larvae feed on roots; adults chew holes in leaves of strawberries, cane berries. Difficult to control	Shred and compost or discard garden debris. Release parasitic nematodes. Drench soil and spray leaves with carbaryl
Thrips	Almost microscopic insects leave small black pellet droppings. Feed on leaves—whitish streaks are first sign of damage. Common on onions and eggplant; also damage other crops	Spray off with strong jet of water from hose. Trap with yellow sticky traps. Spray with rotenone, neem, insecticidal soap, or malathion
Tomato hornworms	Large fleshy green caterpillars with black and white stripes devour leaves of plants and scar fruit	Hand-pick. Release trichogramma wasps. Spray with *Bacillus thuringiensis* or carbaryl
Whiteflies	Tiny, fluttery white insects cluster in great numbers on undersides of leaves of many plants, especially beans and tomatoes, fly about in clouds when plants are disturbed. Larvae and adults suck juices from leaves. Difficult to eradicate from garden or greenhouse	Trap with yellow sticky traps (yellow cards covered with petroleum jelly). Release *Encarsia formosa*, a predatory wasp that helps in greenhouse infestations. Spray leaves with strong jet of water, insecticidal soap, rotenone, neem, or malathion
Wireworms	Larvae of click beetles may damage root crops and roots of seedlings. Often found in soil where lawns were grown	Trap with bait crop of carrots. Dig diazinon into soil prior to planting

Slug

Tomato hornworm larva

Wireworm

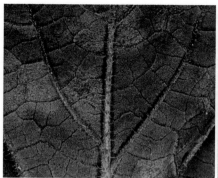
Downy mildew on cantaloupe leaf

Powdery mildew on cantaloupe leaf

Late blight damage to tomato

PLANT DISEASES

DISEASE	DESCRIPTION	CONTROLS (IN ORDER OF PREFERENCE)
Anthracnose (leaf spot)	Fungus disease causes small red-edged spots on leaves and stems of cane berries. Plants grow poorly, leaves may drop	Avoid overhead watering, which spreads fungus; prune out and discard or shred and compost old or badly infected canes. Spray with copper
Clubroot	Fungus disease causes roots to become swollen, twisted. Most common in acid soils. Stunts growth of plants. During hot days, plants wilt; eventually may wilt permanently	Avoid planting where cabbages and other cole crops were grown in last 3 years; apply lime to soil to raise pH to at least 7.2. Consult local Cooperative Extension Service about appropriate fungicides
Damping off	Various soil fungi cause disease in which seeds rot in soil or sprout and start to grow but then collapse. Most common in poorly drained or too-wet soils	Improve drainage; reduce watering; avoid planting seeds of warm-season crops when soil is still cold; use sterile potting soil if starting seeds indoors. Use soil solarization, Plant seeds that have been treated with fungicide to prevent decay
Downy mildew	Fungus disease causes oddly shaped brown spots on older leaves of melons, cucumbers, and watermelons. Leaves turn dry, curl up, and die. Look for outbreaks when weather is cool, damp	Plant disease-resistant varieties; don't plant in shade; avoid overhead watering or watering late in evening; let soil dry between waterings; increase air circulation; shred and compost or discard infected plant debris
Fusarium wilt	Disease is caused by fungus that can live in soil for many years. Infection goes through roots, up into water-carrying system of plant. Lower leaves on stem turn yellow and die; gradually whole stem dies	Plant disease-resistant varieties; avoid planting where disease has been problem before
Powdery mildew	Fungus thrives in humid weather, coating leaves and young stems with what appears to be gray powder. Poor air circulation, crowding of plants, shady locations all encourage growth of fungus	Improve air circulation; thin or separate crowded plants; plant in sunny location; shred and compost or discard infected plant parts. Spray or dust plants with sulfur (do not spray in hot weather; see sulfur label for temperature cautions)
Southern blight	Soilborne disease, common in southeastern United States, causes plants to rot at stem, wilt, turn yellow, and die. Control is difficult	Rotate crops; till soil in autumn; shred and compost or discard infected plants, root ball and all; avoid adding abundant organic matter to soil; use soil solarization
Verticillium wilt	Fungus that lives in soil for many years causes infection through roots up into water-carrying system of plant. Plants wilt in heat of day, may lose leaves, eventually die	Plant disease-resistant varieties; avoid planting in soil where disease has been problem before

ANIMAL PESTS

If your garden is likely to be bothered by birds, deer, rabbits, gophers, or moles, your best approach to crop security lies in understanding their habits and using preventive defenses.

BIRDS. The presence of birds in the garden should be no cause for alarm; many are helpful in pest control or at least are not harmful to your endeavors. But some birds are extraordinarily fond of berries and can tell—about a day before you can—that the fruit is ripe. Other birds may nibble on or devour tender seedlings.

In both cases the solution is netting of some sort, either wire or plastic. For berry protection, cover the plants with a broad-mesh plastic netting (½ to ¾ inch) several weeks before the fruit is due to ripen. Protect rows of vegetable seedlings or strawberries with a tent arrangement of wire or plastic mesh, closed at both ends, over the entire row, or with floating row covers (see page 125).

Rabbit

RABBITS. Rabbits can strip a garden overnight. The best preventive measure is fencing. A rabbit fence need be only 2 feet high. If it's made of wire, use a mesh small enough to keep rabbits from going through.

Rabbits are burrowers, so you also have to keep them from going under a fence and into the garden. One solution is to extend a wire mesh fence at least 6 inches underground. A rabbit can burrow beneath this, in time, however.

Another way to foil rabbits is to fold the bottom 12 inches of a wire mesh fence out away from the garden, making an L shape, and securely stake or weight the foot of the L to the ground; rabbits won't be able to burrow where the mesh covers the ground.

DEER. Deer, too, can demolish a garden in one visit, unless the plot is properly fenced. A 6-foot-high fence may suffice if the ground is level or slopes away from the garden on the outside of the fence. But a virtually foolproof deer fence should be 8 feet high.

If a fence that tall is out of the question, you may be able to take advantage of a deer's jumping limitations: it can leap high or wide but not both at once. Therefore, a 6-foot-high fence with a horizontal 3-foot piece across the top can keep deer out of a garden. Commercial electric fencing has been successful at discouraging deer in some areas and is relatively inexpensive. However, it must be installed before the vegetables are planted. Once deer get a taste of your crops, not even an electric fence will keep them away. The only other somewhat effective deer repellent is a large, barking dog.

Pocket gopher

GOPHERS AND MOLES. From tunnels beneath the soil, gophers feed on plant roots and bulbs. Signs of gopher sabotage include wilted plants that have no roots and mounds of fresh, finely pulverized soil.

Moles travel in shallow tunnels often so close to the surface that you can see the tunnels as raised ridges of soil. They also form soil mounds, but usually the soil is raised in a hump instead of the pulverized mound characteristic of gophers.

The greatest damage moles do is to disturb the soil while looking for grubs and earthworms. Not only does this uproot young plants and introduce air pockets in the soil, which then dry out roots, but it can also induce water to leave irrigation channels and follow mole tunnels instead.

An effective preventive measure is to protect the roots of your crops with chicken wire or hardware cloth. To keep out gophers, use a ½-inch mesh. If you plant in raised beds, wire mesh across the bottom will form a barrier. If you plant in the ground, you need to make individual mesh baskets for plant roots.

Various commercial traps are available for gophers and moles. Poison baits are also available for gophers.

Mole

Harvesting and Storage

The descriptions for individual vegetables and berries give general guidelines for harvesting each crop at its peak of tenderness and sweetness. But for many vegetables and berries, the most certain test of readiness is to pick and taste a few.

Picked too soon, vegetables and berries may lack not just size but also flavor. The resulting taste may be tart, bitter, or simply bland. If you wait too long, you may again sacrifice flavor and texture as well. The sugar of peas and corn turns to starch, beans become stringy, beets woody, and berries mushy, for example. Some vegetables will stop producing if their crop is not harvested regularly.

Homegrown vegetables and berries have the kind of flavor you can't buy in a store—especially when you get them to the table immediately after picking. If you have more than you can eat, though, you may want to store the surplus.

The objective of storage is to keep vegetables and berries from aging quickly. In storage, the process of aging uses the crop's stored food; the faster this stored food is used, the faster the crop's flavor and texture decline. As aging continues, the produce eventually rots.

The storage method appropriate to keep each vegetable or berry in prime shape is given in the sidebar list for that plant. The shortest-lived crops must be refrigerated and used promptly; others, stored correctly, can last for many months.

To enjoy vegetables and berries all year, preserve them by canning, freezing, or drying, as appropriate to the particular crop (see the sidebar lists for individual crops).

Cool and damp storage (32° to 40°F/0° to 4°C). Whether provided in a refrigerator or a root cellar, cool and damp conditions prolong the storage life of vegetables and berries that have a high moisture content and fairly thin skins through which moisture transpires. This type of storage slows the aging process in an atmosphere moist enough to prevent dehydration. Relative humidity of about 90 percent is satisfactory for most vegetables and berries in this category. The major point of difference is length of successful storage time. The extremes range from several days for some berries and tender vegetables to months for root crops.

For vegetables and berries with a short storage life, the vegetable crisper in the refrigerator provides a good environment; for best flavor, use them as soon as possible. Bumper crops that overflow the crisper should be canned, frozen, or dried—or given to a food bank—to keep them from going to waste.

Store the more long-lived vegetables in this category—the root crops, for example—in a root cellar or coldframe. In cold-winter areas, prepare crops for root cellaring before severe frosts hit. For root crops, such as carrots, beets, turnips, rutabagas, and parsnips, dig up the roots and remove the leaves. For heading crops, such as cabbage, brussels sprouts, and Chinese cabbage, dig up the plants—roots and all—when their foliage is dry; if it's wet when the plants are harvested they'll rot when piled up.

Knock the soil off the roots, and remove the outer leaves, but don't wash the vegetables. Make

ABOVE: Golden and 'Cylindra' beets need cool, damp storage.

TOP LEFT: Garlic bunches are left to cure in a dry, airy place.

a 6-inch layer of dry leaves or hay; lay the vegetables on it in a shallow layer. Mound a layer of hay 12 to 24 inches deep over the vegetables, and cover them with a plastic sheet held down with soil, to prevent the vegetables from freezing. Locate your root cellar under an overhang or in an area that's protected from extreme cold and heavy rains.

In a modern house, it's not easy to find a cool, damp room for storing vegetables. You can improvise a root cellar in a basement by insulating a room that stays cool. The insulation protects the area from frost on the outside and from furnace heat on the inside. Use a window for ventilation. The crops can be stored on shelves or in wooden crates or bins.

It's important to prevent the stored crops from withering. To maintain adequate humidity, use natural evaporation from bare earth, gravel, or sand; or sprinkle the floor occasionally with water.

If a basement isn't available, you can use a coldframe (see page 124) for fall storage of heading and rooting vegetables; place the vegetables on the ground, and then fill the frame with dry leaves for insulation. Or store vegetables in a trash can sunk into the ground, a method that works particularly well with root crops. Dig a hole deep enough so you can lower the can to within 3 to 4 inches of the rim. Use moist sand at the bottom of the can and between layers of vegetables to prevent them from drying out. For added insulation, place straw or leaf mulch over the can cover, and top the mulch with a sheet of plastic.

Cool and dry storage (35° to 50°F/2° to 10°C). Cool and dry conditions are needed to store the two most widely grown bulb crops: onions and garlic. If kept moist, they will continue to grow or quickly decay—or both.

These crops require an initial curing time at room temperature in a shady, dry spot—about 1½ weeks for garlic, up to 3 weeks for onions. Then they should be stored where it's cool, dry, and well ventilated.

In colder parts of the country, a basement or garage may offer ideal conditions. For good air circulation, either spread the bulbs out in shallow boxes or trays with slatted bottoms, or tie them up by the stubs of their dried tops, or put them in mesh bags or in old nylon stockings.

Warm and dry storage (55° to 60°F/13° to 16°C). Pumpkins, sweet potatoes, and hard-skinned winter squashes store well under warm and dry conditions. Right after harvest, cure these crops at a fairly high temperature (80° to 85°F/27° to 29°C) for about 10 days. Then place them in an upstairs storage room or a warm garage. Make sure the vegetables are not touching one another.

Whatever their size or color, onions keep well, given cool, dry storage.

TECHNIQUES FOR SPECIAL GARDEN SITUATIONS

Space, terrain, gardening methods, and climate can create conditions in a garden that require special techniques, described here.

CONTAINER GARDENS

Lack of space for a garden plot or lack of suitable soil need not deprive you of the pleasure of growing your own "farm-fresh" produce. Many vegetables, strawberries, and some shrubby berries can be grown productively in containers. You can have your own mini-farm on a patio, deck, or balcony. You can also use containers to overcome problems of poor garden soil, heavy root competition, or shade.

For success in container gardening, you need to consider the location and size of the container, the soil mixture in the container, and the watering and fertilizing needs of the plants.

LOCATION. Nearly all vegetables and most berries require full sunlight. Crops will grow faster and produce more in full sun than in partial shade. Plants grown for their fruits, such as tomatoes, squashes, and strawberries, need at least 6 to 8 hours of sunlight. If all you have is a partly shaded site, you can still get a harvest of root and leaf crops. Using the descriptions of individual crops, match your choices to the location of your containers.

PLANT SIZE. Many vegetables are available in dwarf varieties or varieties that have more restrained growth than usual. These are ideal for growing in containers. 'Pixie' tomatoes, finger or round carrots, and bush types of beans, cucumbers, melons, and squash are examples of small versions of normally big plants.

CONTAINER CHOICE. Nearly anything that will hold soil and let water drain from it can be used as a container. The most important consideration is that the container offer enough room for the roots of the crop you plan to grow. You can raise a fine stand of chives in an 8-inch clay pot, but a squash plant in the same container will fail resoundingly. Most crops need soil that is at least 12 inches deep, and bigger is definitely better.

Large wooden boxes, wooden barrels, pressed pulp tubs, and large (1 foot in diameter or greater) clay and plastic pots will hold enough soil for all but the largest vegetables. Remember that the smaller a container is, the faster it will dry out and the more it will be subject to changes in temperature.

Lettuces, tomatoes, peppers, and herbs can be harvested from pot to salad bowl in this bright container garden.

Hanging containers—in which you might plant tomatoes, for example—can dry out rapidly because they are so thoroughly exposed to sunlight and wind. Since they become quite heavy when filled with mature plants, be sure to use sturdy hooks and wire or chain for suspending them.

SOIL MIXTURE. Container soil must provide free penetration of water and air, but ideally it should retain moisture as well. A liberal quantity of organic matter in the soil mixture helps.

Gardeners who make their own compost (see page 99) may find that compost alone will work well as a container soil. Nurseries and garden centers carry potting soil mixes—usually containing some combination of peat moss or other organic material and sand, perlite, or vermiculite; these can be used right from the sack. They are lightweight and sterile, but they dry out quickly and often do not contain nutrients. If you prefer, you can mix your own container soil. A satisfactory mixture consists of two parts good garden soil (not clay soil), one part sand, and one part peat moss, ground bark, or similar organic material.

WATERING AND FERTILIZING. Soil in a container dries out more rapidly than a comparable volume of soil in the ground. A container is exposed on the sides as well as the top to the drying effects of sun and wind and often is exposed on the bottom and sides to reflected heat from a paved surface. Clay or terra-cotta pots lose moisture from their sides and need to be watered even more frequently. Therefore, you have to be watchful about watering your container vegetables and berries.

At first, when plants are small and the weather is moderate, you may need to water only every 2 to 3 days. In the heat of summer and when plants are mature, daily watering may be needed. Apply enough water each time so that water runs out the container's drain holes.

To maintain steady growth, container vegetables need a steady nutrient supply. One method is to use a controlled-release fertilizer, which provides small amounts of nutrients every time you water. Another method is to use a granular vegetable fertilizer in the amount and frequency recommended on the label of the product. Some gardeners prefer soluble fertilizers, applying them every 1 to 2 weeks when they water.

For a list of vegetables and berries that do particularly well in containers, turn to page 15.

HILLSIDE GARDENS

Sloping land isn't a complete obstacle to the growing of vegetables and berries, but it does present several challenges that must be met so the plants will have the conditions they need for best production. Applying water is the number one hillside challenge. You want to have well-watered plants without water runoff and soil erosion.

TERRACES. On a gentle slope, you can run planting rows across the slope, following the land's contour lines. Each row becomes, in effect, a natural miniature terrace.

Convert hillside land for vegetable growing by building level terraces.

On moderate to steep slopes, however, you need to construct terraces—a steplike series of level planting areas. The soil for each is kept level and in place by a retaining wall, ideally of decay-resistant wood (see drawing on page 122), concrete block, brick, or stone.

Any solid retaining wall needs drainage holes at its base about every 2 feet to allow excess water to escape from the terrace. Otherwise, water may build up in the soil and buckle or break down the retaining wall.

When you remove soil to make the terraces, set it aside so you can return it to fill and level the planting beds behind the retaining walls.

BOTTOMLESS BOXES. A somewhat less ambitious solution to the challenge of hillside gardening is to make some bottomless boxes and set them into the hillside so that the soil within them can be made level and watered easily. Each box can be made large enough to accommodate several vegetable plants. Make small bottomless boxes (about 1½ feet square), or buy large-diameter, shallow flue tiles. Set them into the slope to provide individual "containers."

FRENCH INTENSIVE GARDENS

Growing vegetables by the French intensive method requires more hand labor than other methods, but the production per square foot of soil is greater. Some gardeners believe that the vegetable quality is also superior.

There are three elements that, in combination, distinguish the French intensive system from all others: (1) very thorough soil preparation, incorporating all nutrients before planting; (2) preparation of beds rather than rows, each bed mounded up above normal grade to form a body of soil that warms quickly, drains well, and takes in air easily; and (3) close planting.

At almost all stages of growth, leaves of the crops completely shade the soil, reducing moisture loss and preventing extreme fluctuations in soil temperature. In other words, the plants act as a living mulch. Fast, steady growth produces tender, full-flavored vegetables.

PREPARING THE SOIL. First, divide your planting area into beds running north to south. Beds for plants that need vertical support—beans, peas, cucumbers, tomatoes—should be only 1½ feet wide. Beds for other vegetables can be wider, but keep them narrow enough for easy reaching (3 to 5 feet across).

Double dig the soil (see page 97), incorporating organic matter and sand to make a planting mix that's approximately one-third organic matter, one-third sand, and one-third original garden soil. Leave the surface rough for 2 to 5 days to air out. Then break up the clods, and work the surface into a smooth, mounded profile (high in the middle, sloping down at all four sides). Set aside enough soil to cover your seeds.

Apply a complete fertilizer or organic source of nutrients (see pages 108–109). Dig the material into the top 6 inches of the bed; then rake the soil into a smooth mound.

SOWING SEEDS. You have to sow some kinds of vegetables directly into their bed because they don't transplant well. Sow seeds of bush beans, dwarf peas, and various root crops, for example, at about the same distance apart as recommended for row sowing, but scatter them over the entire bed (be sure to cover the corners and edges). Just barely cover the seeds with the soil you set aside.

Sowing crops such as beets, bush beans, dwarf peas, and spinach is simple because their seeds are large enough for you to see how thickly they are sown. Fine-seeded crops, such as carrots and turnips, are trickier. (Some gardeners mix these seeds into sand or fine soil and then sow the mixture.)

FRENCH INTENSIVE PLANTING

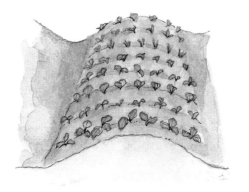

For French intensive gardening, double dig and amend soil before planting. Then contour soil into mound that is highest in center of bed and tapers down at all four edges. Water soil, let settle, then plant.

Plant crops close together to reap greater crop productivity, stifle weeds, and form living mulch—conserving moisture and regulating soil temperature. To allow growing room, thin plants repeatedly as they mature.

You can plant root crops such as carrots closer than is usual for other types of crops because you begin harvesting them when they are fingerling size. Thin the crop so that the remaining plants can mature to normal size.

Don't broadcast chard seeds; instead plant them in furrows on top of the bed, leaving a 1-foot space between the furrows. When the seedlings are about 2 inches tall, thin them to about 3 inches apart.

Some plants grow so tall or large that solid coverage of a wide mound isn't practical. You can still grow such plants in double-dug mounds, but you plant them in the usual way—clusters (hills) of seeds for melons and squash, and rows for climbing peas, pole beans, corn, cucumbers, potatoes, and tomatoes, spaced in normal fashion.

SETTING OUT TRANSPLANTS. In the French intensive method, spacing between plants is important. Setting out young plants gives you much more control over spacing than sowing does. The goal is to space the plants so their outer leaves will touch as they approach mature size.

PROTECTIVE DEVICES

Gardeners use protective techniques to get a jump on planting, to extend the growing season in areas where it's short, to produce garden-fresh crops all year in some areas, and to avoid the hazards of unpredictable weather.

COLDFRAMES. A coldframe is a low-profile structure that has a slanting, transparent roof. Its purpose is to provide a protected area for starting seedlings, rooting cuttings, and hardening off young plants in early spring and late autumn, when the temperature is uncertain. It works by capturing solar heat during the day and holding some of it through the night.

Construction can be as simple or elaborate as you choose. The sides are usually made of decay-resistant wood or concrete blocks; the roof can be made of glass, fiberglass, acrylic plastic, or clear plastic sheeting. (Old window sashes are the traditional coldframe roof.) There is no standard size.

Since the coldframe is designed to be heated by the sun, put it in a sunny location, and slant the roof toward the south. If cold north winds prevail during the months you will use your coldframe, choose a location protected on the north side by a wall or hedge.

Cover the floor of the coldframe with a 3- to 6-inch layer of sand, which will let water drain away quickly from the plants. If you want to start seeds directly in the coldframe soil rather than in individual containers, spread a 3-inch layer of potting mix on top of the sand, and sow the seeds in the mix.

A coldframe will give some protection against freezing, but you'd be wise to play it safe and cover the frame with a tarpaulin, a piece of old carpeting, or a sheet of styrene foam when the

Greenhouse is aid to raising vegetables that need warmth or longer season.

temperature is expected to drop below 32°F/0°C. On warm days, prop open the roof.

HOTBEDS. A hotbed is merely a coldframe with special electric heating cables buried in the floor or some other source of heat. It's useful for germinating seeds early and quickly. You can sow seeds directly in the soil above the heating cables and actually raise crops of cold-season vegetables when outdoor temperatures would prohibit this.

To set up a hotbed, first spread a 2-inch-deep layer of sand on the floor of your coldframe. Then loop the special heating cable back and forth over the sand (don't overlap the loops), and cover the cable with a ½-inch wire mesh. If you're going to put containers in the hotbed, add a 2-inch layer of sand on top of the mesh. If you intend to plant directly in the hotbed, spread about 4 inches of potting soil, instead of the sand, over the mesh.

GREENHOUSES. The word "greenhouse" suggests a profusion of tropical plants or exotic orchids and a steamy atmosphere. But the purpose of a greenhouse is simply to provide a more favorable environment for plants that won't survive outdoors during a particular season.

Tomatoes are a favorite greenhouse crop. They do best in a warm greenhouse, where you maintain the temperatures they need for good growth and fruit set. Generally these are in the 55° to 70°F/13° to 21°C range at night and up to 85°F/29°C during the day. Cucumbers and peppers also are good choices for a warm greenhouse.

If you have a cool greenhouse (night temperatures from 40° to 55°F/4° to 13°C and daytime highs of 70° to 75°F/21° to 24°C), you might try cool-season crops such as lettuce, broccoli, and carrots. During the winter these vegetables will need full sunlight. For summer production in hot-weather regions, they will need some shading and good ventilation.

Most greenhouse gardeners grow plants in containers (see pages 121–122) or raised beds (see page 98). If you use containers, you can place crops where they will receive the right amount of sunlight or shade.

For vining crops—cucumbers and tomatoes, for example—you can make the most of available space by training the plants on stakes or on the greenhouse roof supports. Because greenhouse space is usually at a premium, choose smaller vegetables or dwarf varieties to reap greater rewards for the amount of space occupied.

Vegetables that need pollination of their flowers to produce a crop may need some assistance, because greenhouses lack the natural outdoor pollinators: wind and insects. You can ensure pollination in three ways: use a camel's hair brush to transfer pollen from one flower to another; gently shake or tap the plant to release pollen into the air; or run a fan to simulate a natural breeze.

FLOATING ROW COVERS. Row covers, made of various permeable materials similar to fabric, are one of the most useful tools for extending vegetable harvest seasons—both to get a jump on the growing season and to extend it into the chill of autumn. Sold in rolls, the covers are designed to be laid over vegetables either at planting time or toward the season's end, where they serve as miniature greenhouses—trapping heat, warming the soil, boosting plant growth, and protecting plants from frost. Extremely light in weight, the various materials transmit 80 to 95 percent of sunlight and let both water and air pass through. The edges are secured to seal out pests (although any already on the plants may proliferate).

Lay the material over a row of plants 1 to 3 feet wide, and secure the edges by burying them with soil or placing 2-by-4s on them. The covers need to float on top of the plants without restricting them or distorting their growth.

Most gardeners who use covers put them over plants for 4 to 6 weeks in early spring. As the weather turns warm, they take the covers off. When air temperatures climb above 80°F/27°C, temperatures under the covers can be 30°F/16°C warmer. But in areas where frosts can occur anytime during the growing season, gardeners cover their plants on dangerous nights and days, then remove the covers on warm days. For plants that require assistance in pollination, such as cucumbers and melons, row covers also need to be removed to allow insects to reach the blooms. In cool-summer climates, row covers can be used to protect warm-season vegetables, particularly melons, that normally wouldn't receive enough heat to mature. At the end of the growing season, row covers can, for example, allow the last crop of tomatoes, which would otherwise remain green, to ripen.

Because all the materials used to make row covers are permeable, rainfall and sprinkling will water the covered plants. Young plants will be somewhat weighed down after sprinkling but will pop back once the material dries. The simplest watering system to use with row covers, however, is drip irrigation (see page 104).

OTHER SEASON EXTENDERS. Vegetable seed catalogs include many other useful devices to extend the growing season and provide frost protection: clear plastic cloches held above rows of plants with small hoops, and various plastic or paper caps known as hotcaps. There is also a product designed especially for tomatoes: small, hollow plastic cylinders are connected to form a cap shaped like a tepee, which is placed over a tomato plant; when the cylinders are filled with water, the device traps a great deal of heat, boosting growth and providing frost protection.

You can make your own simple transplant protectors by cutting the bottoms off clear plastic gallon jugs.

TOP: Simple coldframe gets vegetable plants off to early start by holding warmth.

MIDDLE: Special plastic hotcaps for tomato plants consist of water-filled cylinders that trap heat.

BOTTOM: Floating row covers protect plants from frost, trap heat, warm soil, and keep pests out. Made of lightweight material, they are easily put on and taken off.

BUYING FROM MAIL-ORDER NURSERIES

The racks of seed packets and stocks of young plants at your local nursery or garden center may give you a sufficient selection to provide the crop garden you need, but you're missing a lot of fun if you don't send for a few mail-order catalogs.

The big seed companies publish catalogs that contain many more offerings than the average nursery stocks. Catalogs generally feature the latest hybrids. Some companies also

sell old-fashioned varieties or those that are hard to find—not because they are inferior (quite the contrary) but because the crops don't ship well to produce markets or are not as widely adapted or disease-resistant as modern commercial varieties.

Some catalogs feature color photographs; others offer only lists. A few companies, though they sell quality seeds, print their offerings on not-very-glamorous newsprint. Many companies request a small fee for their catalog, which often is applied as a credit if you purchase their seeds.

Catalogs are ready for mailing well in advance of planting season, and you should order your seeds or plants early for best availability. Plants of perennial vegetables and the various berries are sent through the mails at their appropriate planting time. They arrive with their roots encased in moisture-retaining material.

Here are a few of the major sources of mail-order vegetables and berries, to get you started. Many others, some with interesting specialties, are worth exploring. Addresses and phone numbers are subject to change.

GENERALISTS

W. ATLEE BURPEE COMPANY
300 Park Avenue
Warminster, PA 18974
(800) 888-1447;
fax (800) 487-5530
http://garden.burpee.com
Vegetable and berry seeds; tools.

FERRY-MORSE SEEDS
Box 488
Fulton, KY 42041-0488
(800) 283-3400
advasee@apex.net
Good selection of vegetable and herb seeds; informative catalog with good plant descriptions.

HENRY FIELD SEED & NURSERY COMPANY
415 North Burnett
Shenandoah, IA 51602
(605) 665-9391; fax (605) 665-2601
Selection of wide variety of vegetable and berry seeds.

GURNEY'S SEED & NURSERY
110 Capital Street
Yankton, SD 57079
customer service (605) 665-1671;
orders (605) 665-1930; fax (605) 665-9718
Full range of vegetable and berry plants and seeds.

PARK SEED COMPANY
1 Parkton Avenue
Greenwood, SC 29647
(800) 845-3369; fax (800) 275-9941
Seeds, plants, and sets for nearly 2,000 vegetables and flowers.

STOKES SEEDS, INC.
Box 548
Buffalo, NY 14240
(716) 695-6980;
fax (888) 834-3334
Herbs and vegetables, including Asian varieties.

VEGETABLE AND HERB SPECIALISTS

THE COOK'S GARDEN
Box 535
Londonderry, VT 05148
(800) 457-9703; fax (800) 457-9705
Herb and vegetable seeds for serious kitchen gardeners; peppers, lettuces, broccoli; some selections from France and Italy.

DEGIORGI SEED COMPANY
6011 N Street
Omaha, NE 68117-1634
(800) 858-2580; fax (402) 731-8475
Herbs and vegetables.

JOHNNY'S SELECTED SEEDS
310 Foss Hill Road
Albion, ME 04910
(207) 437-4301; fax (800) 437-4290
homegarden@johnnyseeds.com
Unusual corn, bean, squash varieties; heirloom tomatoes; other vegetables.

RONNIGER'S SEED POTATOES
P.O. Box 307
Ellensburg, WA 98926
(800) 846-6178; fax (509) 925-9238
Large selection of seed potatoes, described by color, flavor, disease resistance, and keeping qualities; also Jerusalem artichokes, garlic, onions, shallots.

SHEPHERD'S GARDEN SEEDS
30 Irene Street
Torrington, CT 06790
(860) 482-3638; fax (860) 482-0532
http://www.shepherdseeds.com
Herbs such as scented basils; greens such as roquette (arugula) and French dandelion greens; hot peppers; sunflowers; other vegetables; flowers for attracting beneficial insects; catalog includes recipes.

TOMATO GROWERS SUPPLY COMPANY
Box 2237
Fort Myers, FL 33902
(941) 768-1119
Seeds for more than 250 tomato varieties, from beefsteaks to cherry tomatoes.

VERMONT BEAN SEED COMPANY
Garden Lane
Fair Haven, VT 05743-0250
(802) 663-0217; fax (888) 500-7333
Numerous varieties of beans, cabbages, melons, corn, gourds, greens, tomatoes, other vegetables; herbs.

HEIRLOOM AND UNHYBRIDIZED SEED SPECIALISTS

NATIVE SEEDS/SEARCH
3509 North Campbell Avenue
Box 325
Tucson, AZ 85719
(520) 622-5561; fax (520) 622-5591
jhhosofaz@aol.com
http://desert.net/seeds/home.htm
Nonprofit seed conservation organization working to preserve traditional crops of Southwest and northern Mexico and their wild relatives; seeds of tepary beans, hot peppers, gourds, corn, herbs, unusual squashes, pumpkins (including 'Hopi', 'Acoma'), tomatillos.

SEEDS OF CHANGE
Box 15700
Santa Fe, NM 87506-5700
(888) 762-7333;
fax (888) 329-4762
http://www.seedsofchange.com
Many rare heirloom and traditional native vegetables; sizable collections of beans, corn, sunflowers, tomatoes; unique selection of culinary herbs.

INDEX

Boldface numbers *refer to the primary vegetable and berry descriptions.*

Acid soil, 95, 96
Alkaline soil, 95, 96
Amaranth, 15, **18**
American grapes, 80–81, 82, 84
Artichokes, 13, 15, **18–19**, 28, 42
Arugula. *See* Roquette
Asian vegetables, 15, **19–21**
Asparagus, 9, 15, **22**, 103, 111, 114
Asparagus bean, 21

Basil, 39
Batavian endive, 37
Beans, 9, 11, 12, 15, 19, 21, **23–25**, 107, 116, 117, 120, 121, 123, 124
Beets, 15, **25**, 116, 120, 122, 123
Belgian endive, 31, 37
Berries, 73–91. *See also specific berries*
Birds, 119
Bitter melon, 21
Blackberries, 15, **74–76**, 114
Black-eyed peas, 61
Black plastic sheeting, 106, 111
Blanching, 22, 28, 30, 44
Blueberries, **76–77**
Bok choy, 20
Boysenberries, 74
Broadleaf mustard, 19
Broccoli, 10, 15, 19, 20, **26**, 27, 124
Broccoli raab, 26
Brussels sprouts, 15, **26–27**, 120
Bush beans, 11, 12, 23, 24, 121, 123

Cabbage, 10, 11, 15, 20, **27–28**, 114, 115, 116, 120
Cane pruning, 84
Cantaloupe, 48, 118
Cardoon, 15, **28**
Carrots, 10–11, 12, 13, 15, **28–29**, 120, 121, 123–124
Catalogs, 126–127
Cauliflower, 10, 15, 26, 27, **30**
Celeriac, 15, **30**
Celery, 15, 28, **30**
Celtuce, 15, 45, 47
Chayote, 15, **31**
Chervil, 39
Chicory, 15, **31**
Chinese broccoli, 20
Chinese cabbage, 20, 115, 120
Chinese chives (Chinese leeks), 39
Chinese mustard greens, 19
Chinese okra, 21
Chinese parsley, 19, 39–40
Chinese spinach. *See* Amaranth
Ching soy sum. *See* Chinese cabbage
Chives, 39, 67
Chop suey potato, **43**
Choy sum. *See* Chinese cabbage
Cilantro, 39–40
Clay soil, 5, 94, 104
Climate, 5, 6, 7–8
Cloches, 103, 125
Coldframes, 7, 120, 121, 124, 125
Cold-winter areas, 7–8
Collards, 15, 27, **32**
Community gardens, 17
Compost, 96, 99, 108, 122
Container gardening, 13, 15, 29, 36, 45, 47, 56, 67, 70, 91, 121–122
Continuous-harvest gardens, 10–11
Cool-season plants, 6, 10, 11, 14, 15, 124
Coriander, 19, 39–40

Corn, 9, 10, 12, 13, 15, 17, **32–34**, 101, 102, 115, 120, 124
Cowpeas, 21, 61
Cress, 15, **35**, 48, 59
Crowder peas, 61
Cucumbers, 15, 21, **35–36**, 107, 115, 118, 121, 123, 124, 125
Cultivating, 110, 111
Currants, **78–79**, 114
Cuttings, 66, 103, 124

Dai gai choy, 19
Daikon, 21
Decorative plants, 13, 15, 27, 43, 67
Deer, 119
Dewberries, 74
Dill, 40
Diseases, 93, 112, 118
Doong gwah, 20
Double-cropping, 10, 11, 12
Double digging, 12, 96, 97
Dow gauk, 21
Drip irrigation, 9, 12, 104–105

Eggplant, 15, **37**, 115, 117
Endive, 15, 31, **37**
Escarole, 37
European grapes, 80, 81, 82, 83–84

Fast-maturing crops, 15
Fava beans, 23, 25
Fertilizing, 94–95, 96, 108–109, 122
Field peas. *See* Southern peas
Floating row covers, 101, 125
Floricanes, 75, 85
Foo gwah, 21
French endive, 31, 37
French intensive gardening, 12, 14, 15, 97, 111, 123–124
Furrow irrigation, 105
Fuzzy melon, 20–21

Gai choy, 19
Gai lohn, 20
Garden layout, 9–15
Garden plans, 5–15
Garlic, 15, **38**, 39, 51, 121
Gooseberries, **79–80**, 114
Gophers, 119
Gourds, 15, 21, **38**, 117
Gow choy, 39
Grapes, 15, **80–84**, 115
Green beans, 23–24
Greenhouses, 7, 36, 124–125
Green manure, 96
Green onions, 11, 12, 13, 15, 49, 50

Hanging containers, 91, 122
Harvesting, 10–11, 13, 120–121
Heirloom vegetables, 70, 127
Herbicides, 111
Herbs, 13, 15, 19, **39–41**, 67, 122
Hills, 89, 102, 124
Hillside gardening, 5, 6, 9, 122–123
Hin choy. *See* Amaranth
Hoeing, 110, 111
Horseradish, 15, **42**, 59
Horticultural beans, 24
Hotbeds, 7
Hotcaps, 103, 125
Hot peppers, 54, 55

Insects, 13, 93, 112–119, 125
Intercropping, 10, 11, 12, 29
Irrigation, 9, 12, 93, 104–105, 122

Japanese radish, 21
Jerusalem artichokes, 15, **42**
Jicama, 15, **43**

Kale, 15, **43**
Kohlrabi, 15, 27, **44**

Landscapes, 13, 27, 33, 43, 66, 67
Leeks, 15, 19, 39, **44**
Lettuce, 10, 11, 12, 13, 15, **45–47**, 122, 124
Lima beans, 23, 24
Lodging, 51
Loganberries, 74
Luffa, 21

Mail-order catalogs, 126–127
Malabar spinach, 15, 63
Mango squash. *See* Chayote
Manure, 96
Marjoram, 41
Matted rows, 89
Melons, 12, 15, 20–21, **47–48**, 71, 107, 109, 115, 117, 118, 121, 124, 125
Melon squash, 65
Mild-winter areas, 6
Mint, 40
Mirliton. *See* Chayote
Moh gwah, 20–21
Moles, 119
Mounds, 89, 102, 124
Mulching, 93, 106, 111
Muscadine grapes, 80, 81, 82, 83–84
Muskmelon, 48
Mustard greens, 15, 19, **48**

New Zealand spinach, 15, 62–63
Nitrogen, 94, 109
Nutrients, 94–95, 108–109

Okra, 15, 21, **49**
Olallieberries, 74
Onions, 11, 12, 13, 15, **49–51**, 103, 117, 121
Oregano, 40
Organic gardens, 65, 108
Oseille. *See* Sorrel
Oyster plant. *See* Salsify

Parsley, 13, 19, 40, 67
Parsnips, 15, **52**, 120
Peanuts, 15, **52**
Peas, 10, 15, 21, **53**, 61–62, 107, 120, 123, 124
Peat moss, 96, 108
Pepper grass, 35
Peppers, 15, **54–55**, 124
Perennials, 9, 13, 22, 39, 40, 41, 58, 73, 103, 109, 111, 126
Pests, 13, 93, 112–119, 125
pH, 95, 96
Phosphorus, 94, 95, 108–109
Planning gardens, 5–15
Planting, 10–11, 100–103
Plant selection, 12, 15, 17, 73
Plastic sheeting, 101, 103, 106, 110, 111, 124
Pole beans, 9, 23, 24, 107, 124
Potassium, 94, 95, 109
Potatoes, 15, **55–56**, 115, 124
Preserving, 120
Primocanes, 75, 85
Prolific producers, 15
Protection, 5, 7, 102–103, 124–125
Pruning, 73, 75–76, 77, 78, 80, 82–84, 86–87
Pumpkins, 15, **57**, 117, 121

Rabbits, 119
Radicchio, **31**
Radishes, 11, 12, 15, 21, 29, **57–58**, 115
Raised beds, 12, 98
Raking, 97
Raspberries, 10, 15, **85–87**, 114
Rhubarb, 13, 15, **58**, 111
Rocket. *See* Roquette
Romano beans, 23
Root crops, 15, 104, 120, 121, 123, 124
Roots, for planting, 103
Roquette, 15, **59**
Rosemary, 40
Rutabagas, 15, **59**, 120

Sage, 40–41
Salsify, 15, **60**
Savoy cabbage, 27
Scallions, 11, 12, 13, 15, 49, 50
Schav. *See* Sorrel
Seed catalogs, 126–127
Seeds, 100–101, 123, 124, 126–127
See gwah, 21
Sets, 50, 103
Shallots, 15, **60**
Site selection, 5, 73, 88
Size of garden, 5
Slips, 66
Small-space gardens, 12, 91
Snap beans, 23–24
Snow peas, 53
Soaking, 104–105
Soil, 5, 12, 94–99, 101, 104, 106, 122, 123
Soil amendments, 12, 94, 95, 96
Soil pH, 95, 96
Soil structure, 94
Soil testing, 5, 94, 96, 109
Sorrel, 15, **61**
Southern peas, 15, 21, **61–62**
Soybeans, 23, 25
Spaced matted rows, 89–90
Spading, 97
Spaghetti squash, 65
Spinach, 11, 12, 15, 18, 21, **62–63**, 116, 122, 123
Sponge gourd, 21
Sprays, for pests, 113
Sprinkling, 9, 105
Sprouts, 15, 26–27, **63**
Spur pruning, 83–84
Squash, 1, 10, 12, 13, 15, 20–21, 31, **64–65**, 101, 102, 107, 109, 115, 116, 117, 121, 124
Staking, 12, 107, 125
Storage, 120–121
Strawberries, 15, 73, **88–91**, 116, 117, 121
Succession planting, 10–11
Sugar peas, 53
Summer savory, 41
Summer squash, 21, 64–65
Sun chokes. *See* Jerusalem artichokes
Sunflowers, 15, **66**
Sweet marjoram, 41
Sweet peppers, 54–55
Sweet potatoes, 15, **66**, 103, 121
Swiss chard, 13, 15, **67**, 124

Tampala. *See* Amaranth
Tarpaper collars, 103
Tarragon, 41
Terracing, 122–123
Thyme, 41
Tilling, 97
Tomatillos, 15, **67**
Tomatoes, 10, 11, 15, **68–70**, 95, 101, 107, 114, 115, 117, 118, 121, 122, 123, 124, 125
Transplanting, 102
Trellises, 12, 20, 21, 75–76, 82–83, 86–87, 107
Turnips, 15, **71**, 120, 123

Vegetable pear. *See* Chayote
Vines, 13, 15, 20, 31, 35–36, 107

Warm-season plants, 6, 10, 11, 14, 15, 125
Watercress, 35, 48
Watering, 9, 12, 93, 104–105, 122
Watermelon, 15, 48, **71**, 118
Weeding, 93, 110–111
Winter melon, 20
Winter savory, 41
Winter squash, 20, 64, 65, 121

Yao choy. *See* Chinese cabbage
Yard-long beans, 21
Youngberries, 74

Zucchini, 13